P9-BVH-106

NUMBER 626

THE ENGLISH EXPERIENCE

ITS RECORD IN EARLY PRINTED BOOKS
PUBLISHED IN FACSIMILE

MATTHEW SUTCLIFFE

ECCLESIASTICALL DISCIPLINE

LONDON, 1590

DA CAPO PRESS
THEATRVM ORBIS TERRARVM LTD.
AMSTERDAM 1973 NEW YORK

The publishers acknowledge their gratitude to the Curators of the Bodleian Library, Oxford for their permission to reproduce the Library's copy, Shelfmark: G.Pamph.1327 (1)

S.T.C.No. 23471

Collation: A-Z^4, Aa-Gg^4, Hh^2

Published in 1973 by

Theatrum Orbis Terrarum Ltd.,
O.Z. Voorburgwal 85, Amsterdam

&

Da Capo Press Inc.
- a subsidiary of Plenum Publishing Corporation
277 West 17th Street, New York N.Y. 1011

Printed in the Netherlands

ISBN 90 221 0626 8

Library of Congress Catalog Card Number:
73-7082

A TREATISE OF ECCLESIASTICALL DISCIPLINE:

Wherein that confused forme of gouernment, which certeine vnder false pretence, and title of reformation, and true discipline, do striue to bring into the Church of England, is examined and confuted:

By MATTH. SVTCLIFFE.

I. TIMOTH. I.

Τὸ δὲ τέλος τῆς παραγγελίας ἐστὶν ἀγάπη ἐκ καθαρᾶς καρδίας, καὶ συνειδήσεως ἀγαθῆς, καὶ πίστεως ἀνυποκρίτου, ὧν τινὲς ἀστοχήσαντες ἐξετράπησαν εἰς ματαιολογίαν.

The end of the commandement (which is the summe of discipline) is loue with sinceritie of heart, sound conscience, and faith vnfeined: which some missing, are turned aside into vaine brabling about words.

GREG. NAZ. *in orat. in* Basilij *laudem.*

Facilius benè instituta dissoluuntur, quàm dissoluta restituuntur.

Good orders are easily dissolued, but being once dissolued, are hardly restored.

AT LONDON
Printed by GEORGE BISHOP and RALPH NEWBERIE.
Anno 1590.

TO THE RIGHT HONOVRABLE THE EARLE OF BATHE, HIS VERIE GOOD LORD.

Number there be, (my good Lord) which considering the beginnings, continuance, and bitter pursuit of the quarrell about discipline, do of good zeale lament the pitifull effects of our disagreement: others there are, that of idle conceit fall into woonderment at the causes. But as long as either the one doe nothing but lament, and the other (as men amazed) gape and woonder: neither the causes nor effects are remooued. For as in distresse of weather, and danger of wracke, matters are not remedied nor setled by vaine lamentations, and idle woonderment, but by prudent counsell, and setting hands to the tacle: so in the danger of wracke of this our Church, occasioned not onely by the disagreement of the pilots and sailers, but also of the passengers themselues; neither colde complaints nor vaine admiration can serue, but good and godly counsell, and diligent labour in discouering and remoouing the causes of our contentions and troubles. Wherein, that I may not onely (as idle lookers on) giue aduise, but with example helpe to satisfie those that are discontent, and ioyne with those that seeke to remooue contention and contentious persons, that will not be satisfied: although not best able, yet as willing as the best, I haue first (after long silence of others) entred the lists. I know, not without danger: but God that hath giuen me courage not to feare either their force or their practises, I trust, will giue

 me

me meanes to eſcape them,if I cannot auoid them.

Of all theſe contentions and quarrels there is but one iſſue,which I will tender vnto the aduerſe parties : If the diſcipline which they extoll and commend vnto vs, be (as they ſay) commanded by Chriſt, let them neuer trouble themſelues further,but ſhew that onely,and it ſhalbe receiued : for ſcarſe doeth he deſerue the name of a Chriſtian, that will refuſe or denie the lawes and commandements of Chriſt. Let them therefore leaue their declamations and exclamations againſt the gouernment, let them alſo leaue their models and libels, for they are to no purpoſe, and do but holde men in ſuſpence, that doe continually looke for proofe out of Gods word, of their promiſed and future diſcipline : but on the other ſide, if their presbyteries and the parts of their presbyteries, and their presbyteriall gouernment, their conferences, and their ſynods, and the ſoueraigntie of the people, and their deuiſes of doctors, elders, deacons, & widowes, together with diuers nouelties and quirks in the Paſtors office, be nothing but a maſſe of diſtempered fancies,proceeding from melancholike braines, and blowen out with mightie words without authoritie of Gods word, or antiquitie, as I truſt, I haue ſhewed in this diſcourſe, and with the grace of God ſhall alwayes be able to mainteine : then I would deſire them to ſettle themſelues, and to bragge no more of their glorious diſcipline. for beſide that it is deſtitute of authoritie, the ſame is moſt confuſed, abſurd, imperfect, yea, almoſt vaine and ridiculous . at the firſt it was deuiſed by men ignorant of ſtate and gouernment, now it is mainteined by men deuoyd of iudgement.

Thoſe that are in authoritie,when they ſee theſe things, (I doubt not) will be more bolde and carefull to mainteine religion, lawes and orders, without which no ſtate can be mainteined : and to correct the ſtubburne and diſobedient,

ent, whoſe diſobedience and contumacie hath hitherto paſſed vnder a maske of zeale & conſcience. Priuate men, they will (I truſt) be wiſe with ſobrietie, or be aduiſed better, if they taſte the puniſhment of preſumptuous curioſitie: for it is not tolerable that ſubiects ſhould rule their gouernours, nor offenders iudge of lawes, nor iudges be put to anſwere the parties. Yet this hath bene hitherto the caſe of the Church of England. euery modellor and libellor taketh on him to preſcribe lawes, tranſgreſſours of eccleſiaſticall orders are admitted to plead that the lawes are leud and corrupt, and that the Parliament, yea and Prince was not wiſe that made them. Eccleſiaſticall gouernours, they are, as it were, called foorth to anſwere, whether the lawes they practiſe be good or no: and who muſt ſit iudge in the cauſe? forſooth Hicke, Hob, and Clim of Clough, yea, and Margaret and Ioan too: for they forſooth now do prate apace of diſcipline, and giue vs out their cenſures. Let it be as beſt may be for them, yet muſt the conſiſtorie conſiſting for the moſt part of merchants, artificers, yea and husbandmen, decide all theſe controuerſies. Which things when I haue ſhewed to haue bene taken vp without authoritie or commandement, and vrged without all reaſon; they muſt be very obſtinate, that will continue in theſe diſorders, and very negligent, that will ſuffer ſuch a ſcandall, ſo preiudiciall to all law and gouernment.

Some will percaſe finde fault, that I handle theſe men too raſhly, being lambs of Chriſtes flocke, and weake brethren eaſily ſcandalized: but the matter is eaſily anſwered. for if they be ſo weake and brittle as they pretend, why are they not onely ſtill contending, but like cunning leaders, alwayes commanding & preſcribing? if they be brethren, why are they continually railing and wrangling with their brethren? if they be lambs, where learned they to barke & bite? theſe be no properties of brethren or of lambs.

 Wherefore,

Wherefore, ſeeing they haue declamed at full, and degorged all their malice againſt our gouernment, they muſt haue patience to heare what we haue to ſay againſt their presbyteries and all their platformes. If it greeue them to ſee their myſteries diſcouered, and their plats diſgraced, let them impute it to themſelues: for ſeeing they haue begun this luſtie courſe, they muſt be content to receiue our modeſt anſwere, and (as the Poet ſaith) to haue their deuiſes retorted. Yet may I not compare with *Th. Cartw.* who for biting and for gybing hath ſcarſe his ſecond: and had he, yet would not I be the man.

Eurip. ὑμεῖς δ' ἔχητ' ὅμοια τοῖς βουλεύμασι.

If it be lawfull for them to deny the princes ſupreme authoritie in eccleſiaſticall cauſes, and to reuel at lawes and gouernment, I truſt my ſpeech for the princes authoritie & lawfull gouernment, againſt the incrochments of new lordings of the conſiſtory, may haue fauourable audience. Their ſpeaks that are as one ſaith (τῆς ἰλιάδος μακρότεροι) longer then the diſcourſe of the Troian warres, and more fabulous and vaine then the tales of the Troians proweſſe, haue notwithſtanding bene heard: my diſcourſe ſhall not be long, but ſo true that all the diſciplinarian faction ſhall not diſprooue it: and therfore I truſt it ſhall obteine fauour to be read. The ſame I haue made bolde to preſent to your Lordſhip, and vnder your name to the view of all that luſt to read it: for I inuite none, nor refuſe any reader. And this I doe, not to draw your Lordſhip into theſe quarrels, vnto whom I owe all ſeruice, & deſire of God all increaſe of loue and honour, but to ſubmit my ſelfe to your honors iudgement, or any indifferent perſons doome, for the matters therein conteined and diſcourſed. As your Lordſhip is a true Chriſtian, nouſled in religion euen from the cradle: ſo I doubt not, but you will for your part take vpon you the cauſe of religion wounded, and diſgraced by theſe ciuill, and almoſt domeſticall warres, which committeth,

and

and casteth her selfe into the armes of all well affected Christians, desiring to be relieued, and that this matter of controuersie may be ended by conference, disputation or writing, or any meanes. As your Lordships noble house hath alwayes woonne honour in seruice of their prince: so it will be a most honourable seruice for you, to vpholde the prerogatiue and maiestie of so gracious a Prince, oppugned and troden vnder foot by the new desired presbyteries. The cause of lawes, orders, learning, and reward, commeth also now in question: for if that, which the presbyterie shall deeme to be according to Gods word, must passe for law, what hope of law and order? if the vnlearned husbandman and artificer be iudge and disposer of the rewards of learning, let euery man leaue the Vniuersitie and Schooles, and betake himselfe to the plough, or some good occupation, that he may learne to be an elder rather then a scholar. But of this there followeth a larger discourse hereafter, and therefore this may now suffice. Vouchsafe my good Lord, to accept this simple present, as witnesse of a gratefull minde: it should haue bene better, if my power had bene to my will: but this is all that present occasion could affoord. God which hath indued you with a noble minde to doe your countrey honour, grant you opportunitie and meanes to shew the same, to the honour of God especially, and next to the benefit of this Church & Common wealth. *London the 1. of Ianuary, this present yeere* 1590.

Your Lordships most bounden,

MATTH. SVTCLIFFE.

To all those into whose hands and vnder whose *censures this Treatise may come,* Matth. Sutcliffe wisheth the increase of Gods Spirit without parcialitie in iudgement, and zeale in godly knowledge, from our Sauiour Christ Iesus.

He pretence of trueth and reformation (good Reader) being a matter so plausible, and the defence of errour and superstition being so odious; it is not to be marueiled if the weake & vnstable which are caried about with euery blast of false doctrine, be mooued with the clamorous pursuite of such as pretend nothing but the abolishing of errours, and establishment of true discipline, either to allowe of the presbyteriall *gouernement which certaine commend for true and reformed, or to dislike the orders of our Church, which with open mouth and great heate of words the same giue out to be superstitious, false, and disordered. Of which cause, although many bitter aduersaries of our state, and open fauourers of the aduerse partie are sprung vp: yet are they nothing so dangerous, as those that hate vs without cause, for some secret purpose, which they keepe to themselues, and yet not so closely but that others feele it. The Church hath yet some small remainder of those large indowments, which the bountifull princes of this land, and some well disposed subiectes bestowed on the Church for the honour of God, and maintenance of learning, and the Ministerie. Vnto this portion (I feare me) we haue too many importunate sutors, and may say of the goods of the Church, as* Euclio *said of his pot of golde, that they haue many enemies, if we may call them enemies of the Church goods, that are so much enamored of them.*

Plaut. in Aul. Næ tu, olla, multos inimicos habes.

Those that haue consumed their owne goods and deuoured the late landes of Abbeyes, their stomackes are nowe so eager, that they can digest not only tythes, but also glebe and Parish Churches.

For

For as Rauens doe followe great armies for praye, and as certaine sory Hindes, and Ragazzoes that come along with the baggage of the Campe, and follow the warres not for any deuotion to fight, but rather for hope and desire to spoyle those, which the souldiers shall haue slaine : so diuers there are in our Church musteerd in the rolle of reformers, which notwithstanding haue as much religion as their mules, and onely desire and seeke, when the Church by contention and faction is layde downe flat, to gather vp the spoyles. Others there are that hope that the goods of the church shall come to the Consistorie, and led with wanne hope dreame therof many golden dreames. These make accompt to be chosen Elders of their Churches, and to haue the disposition & sharing out of euery mans portion : the remainder, if nothing els, they hope shalbe deuided among themselues, and many farmes and tenements in conceite they appoynt to their friendes.

Some there be, that haue passed away their annuities and tenements, whose onely hope is that which others haue, hauing nothing themselues. These must either haue a partition, or els some portion, or place in the Church, if it be but some Deacons roume: for they are good for nothing in the common wealth, therefore doth it stand them vpon to haue some innouation, if so be they can thrust themselues into the Church.

There is also another sort, I cannot tell what title to giue them, but they take vpon them vnder the name of Ministers, to rayle against all that withstand their fancies; which wandring vp and downe without calling, or certaine stay of liuing, meane to take that from others, which by honest meanes they haue not themselues. I meane not T. Cartw. *for he is too stout hearted to wander any more, or to gather crummes vnder other mens tables: and like a wise fellowe, hath purchased more in persecution, then any minister in England in so short space in his greatest prosperitie: yet if to his Hospitall, and other purchase hee could adde some hundred pound pension, I thinke hee will finde no text against it, and therefore they say hee is still vnderhand thundring out the praiſes of his diſcipline.*

And ſome there be alſo of the Miniſterie, which now tempo-rize, and make faire weather, but ſticke not couertly to preferre the newe diſcipline : men moſt vnworthie of their places, which vnkindely bite their mother that nurſeth them : and fooliſh, that like Lycurgus *(of whom Poets fable) doe hewe their owne legges which do ſupport them, & ſpeake againſt that which maintaineth them. Theſe, although they talke much of equalitie, yet hope to bee choſen Preſidents of the Conſiſtorie : ſo violent a thing is ambition, that although they liue nowe well, yet will they hazard all to haue part in the gouernement : they diſdaine to bee gouerned by others. Theſe although among equals none is chiefe, yet by their owne proper diſpenſation, they will needes be taken for principall men.*

Terent. Se omnium primos haberi volunt.

Adde hereunto the ſtirring mindes of men Malecontent, *which howſoeuer they fare, thinke their preſent condition moſt burdenſome, ſo they may ſee an innouation and change, they care not whether Church or common wealth be changed: but oft times it falleth out, that ſuch men change for the worſe, and verifie that prouerbe that ſaith, In changes ſeldom comes the better. Generally it is imputed to our nation that we loue ſtrange vanities, and that as the common ſaying is, we lothe our familiars, and ſet our mindes on ſtrangers and vncouth nouelties: and therefore no maruell if partly through couetouſnes, partly through pouerty, partly through ambition, and deſire of innouation, there be many that not content with the preſent ſtate, deſire the newe* Preſbyteries*: but being aſhamed of the cauſes that drawe them into this faction, with one voyce they profeſſe that they deſire reformation, and the eſtabliſhment of Chriſts diſcipline, and hypocritically they ſeeme to ſigh for Chriſts kingdome: for ſo they intitle that new gouernment. So that their arguments anſwered whereby they would prooue their diſcipline to haue her originall from Chriſt, and his Apoſtles, their leaders cannot chuſe but confeſſe, that they are falſe Apoſtles, and vainely pretend the name of Chriſt, being ſtirred vp by Satan, to hinder*

ἐρῶμεν ἀλλοτρίων παρορῶμεν συγγενεῖς.

hinder the course of Christs Gospel: their followers cannot chuse but be ashamed of such leaders, and their owne practises.

I haue therefore chosen that argument, which conteineth the whole differēce, & undertaken to shew the vanitie of their brags, and that the whole substāce of their discipline (as they call it) wherin they differ from vs, is a meere humane deuise, neither instituted by Christ, nor practised by his Apostles, nor approued in the ancient Church of Christ: nay further, that the same is preiudiciall to the state, to her Maiesties gouernment, and the liberties of her subiects: in summe, that it is a masse of indigested deuises, and full of confusion and disorder. And therefore I conclude, that they haue profanely abused the worde of God, to the commendation of their owne deuises, & that wickedly they haue intitled it The discipline of Christ, The eternal counsel of God, A part of the Gospel, & the word of God, A marke of the true Church, & impiously haue called it The tabernacle of God, The Temple of the Lord, The beautie of Zion, & whatsoeuer their vntemperat affection suggested to their mindes, and that falsly they haue torne, racked & abused the Scriptures to serue their violent humors.

The Argument of the whole discourse.

Which if I make so manifest that the indifferent reader shall confesse it, and the obstinate and most factious dare not publikely defend their Presbyterial *nouelties; I trust thou wilt acknowledge how much thou hast bene abused with vaine words and hypocriticall gloses, and bee more warie howe thou giuest credite to faire protestations, and detest those that make reformation a cloke for their greedie spoyles: those that are in authoritie will be more bolde, and (I trust) watchful to represse the malice of seditious and vagrant perturbors of the Church, and vaine ianglors of matters which they vnderstand not. As for the Ministerie & learned sort, I wonder what reason they haue to fauour those that seeke the ouerthrow of the Ministerie and decay of the Vniuersities, as examples of other places where this goodly reformation is receiued, might teach thē, if they were not either blind & deuoid of iudgement, or wilfully bent to haue their cōceited church gouernment.*

But may ſome ſay, If the caſe bee thus cleare, howe are matters growen to this extremitie? the anſwere is ſhort: that where men hope for profite, they are hardly induced by reaſon againſt their cõmoditie: this contention was good for ſome. Againe, while good men deteſted contention, they thought it ſufficient to defend their owne orders, and ſo were vnwilling to diſgrace others: and becauſe they acknowledged the godly labours of Caluin, *and them of* Geneua *in matters of faith, they woulde not ſtriue againſt ſome of their errours in poynts of gouernement: but ſeeing the importunitie of them that both by their autoritie, and practiſes oppugne our gouernment and diſgrace it: wee haue bene inforced to lay open their infirmities alſo, ſo that all men may ſee they be but men, and in matter of gouernmẽt not comparable to antiquity. Seeking the very fountaines of this controuerſie, we found the weakeneſſe of their cauſe, which I doubt not but I haue layd open, ſo that thou mayeſt ſee it alſo.*

Beza in his Epiſtles to diuers of our countreymen.

Wherein that thou mayeſt the better conceiue my meaning, and vnderſtand the controuerſie, this I would haue thee to remember. The frame of their building the diſciplinarians lay as it were vpon fiue pillars: that is, Doctors, Paſtors, Elders, Deacons, and Widowes: yet doe they not giue the gouernment, but to the Conſiſtory conſiſting (they ſay) of the Doctors, Paſtors, Elders & (as ſome ſay) Deacons. In diuers caſes matters are referred to conferences conſiſting of Conſiſtories within a precinct, and ſometimes to Synodes, which they make prouinciall & nationall. in al matters of weight, they require the conſent of the people. This deuiſe (I ſay) hath no grounde of Gods worde, nor approbation of antiquitie. the very groundworke of their building is faultie: the Doctor as they vnderſtand him, is by thẽ newly framed, his aucthoritie is vſurped: their maner of electing and depoſing the Paſtor is newe: the equalitie and embaſing of Paſtors is no where commanded: pluralitie of Paſtors in one Church is ſtrange: Elders are officers of a newe erection, and haue nothing to ſhewe for all their office: The office of Deacons by them is profaned: widowes are not obſerued in the

The ſumme and ſubſtance of that diſcipline which is confuted in this booke *Diſcipl. ſacra.*

churches

churches of France nor Scotland: The consistorie & whole practise of it is without institution of Christ or approbation of Scriptures. which may be said also of their maner of conferences & Synodes. As for the supremacie of the people, it is not only vsurped without commission, but also absurd and deuoyd of reason. In summe, their whole discipline is taken vp without authoritie of Scripture, and, which is also to be considered, it is a confused and imperfect proceeding, preiudiciall to Princes authoritie, which by Scriptures is due vnto them, and not to be compared in any respect with the gouernment by Bishops, which haue both better autoritie of Scripture, and most assured testimonie of all antiquitie. This is that which in this discourse I haue auouched, and I trust, haue proued. And in this order which I haue here set downe. It had bene I confesse a better course to begin with those that haue chief autoritie, and to descend to inferiour partes and persons: but their confused proceeding hath caried me out of the way, to followe wayward men in their owne footesteppes.

If thou pardon me this fault, the rest I hope shall better satisfie thy expectation. Wherefore crauing onely indifferencie, and that iudgement which vpright Iudges neuer denie, that sentence may be framed according to proofes: I commit this treatise to thy view, and thy selfe to the protection of the Almightie: and for the rest, I referre the curing of the greefes of our Church to Christ Iesus the soueraigne Physition, that hath purged it and redeemed it with his blood.

Yours in all Christian and hearty affection,
MATTH. SVTCLIFFE.

A TREATISE OF ECCLESIASTICALL Discipline, against such as falsly *pretend the reformation of our* Church-gouernment.

CHAP. I.

Wherein three reasons are alleged against the generall frame of their discipline: First, that they haue neither truely described it nor diuided it, as is prooued by their seuerall treatises, and the descriptions and partitions therein conteined. Secondly, that they are not yet agreed about the fundamentall points of their discipline: but one saith one thing, another another thing, and therefore ought not, nor cannot be heard, nor satisfied in their demands, nor haue reason to complaine of repulse, seeing they know not what, nor how much to aske. Thirdly, that they fondly pretend their discipline to be of God, seeing neither the fathers euer knew it, nor themselues euer found it in the word of God. Afterward, the signification and description of discipline is deliuered, and the state of the question betwixt them and vs, set downe.

T may percase seeme strange, that in so many Treatises framed about discipline, so few haue gone about to tell vs the diuers significations of the word, and to describe that forme of discipline which they would haue, and to assigne the parts of it; none haue done it sufficiently, especially the word being taken so diuersly, and the matter being so generall, and the parts of it so intricate and perplexed. Was it, thinke you, that they might conuey away matters in the darke: and that whatsoeuer in generall is spoken of discipline, they might ascribe to their maner of discipline? The first errour therefore I obserue in their formes is this, that debating of discipline, they haue obserued no Logicall, nor orderly discipline in their discourses. *Caluin* handling the argument of the Churches discipline, doth not so much, as in a word, shew what it is: his diuision of Ecclesiasticall discipline, is very pitifull: Either (saith he) it is common to all the Church, or proper to the Clergy or Ministerie. Againe, That which is common consisteth in admonitions, excommunication, fasting, solemne prayers, and other exercises. The discipline of the Clergie consisteth in certeine canons made of purpose,

Instit.lib.4.c.12.

That *Caluin*, *Beza*, *Daniau* and others haue handled the argument of discipline confusedly.

purpose to conteine them within the compasse of their duetie: in which diuisions these faults are notorious.

First he diuideth things confounded, and in talking of discipline of maners, he according to the rules of Popery (from which he would seeme to depart so farre) singleth the discipline of the Ministery from the rest of the Church: as if the discipline of the Ministers there set downe by him, as that they should not dice, riot, dance lasciuiously, were not common to other Christians.

Secondly, in setting downe the parts of discipline common to all the Church, he maketh those exercises to be parts of Church discipline, which are vsed by those that are not of the Church: as admonition, which is a ciuill matter: and fasting & prayer vsed by Pagans.

Thirdly, he doth make his presbyterie and synods subiect to admonition and excommunication of others, in saying that all the Church is subiect to the common discipline.

Fourthly, he maketh no difference betwixt those which rule, and those that are subiect: for the discipline (saith he) is common.

Fiftly, his diuision is most defectiue: for he omitteth the discipline obserued, in making lawes and orders, in election and deposing of officers, in deciding of controuersies, which are principall parts of discipline.

Sixtly, very absurdly he distinguisheth iurisdiction and the power of the Church from discipline, which without them is nothing: which is as much, as if he should separate a man from a liuing creature, and make *genus & speciem* members of one diuision.

Lastly, prayer and fasting, and exercises of humilitie, being the dueties of all Christians seuerally, are not fitly made parts of discipline of the whole Church ioyntly: and admonitions that are priuate, are leudly made part of the Church censures that are publike, and with publike authoritie executed.

Instit. lib. 4. c. 1. d. 1. The same man talking of the Church, doth vnskilfully diuide the gouernment, orders, power, and sacraments of the Church: for in diuisions it is absurd that one member should be conteined vnder another, as in this, gouernment vnder power (for what lawfull gouernment can be without lawfull power and authoritie) and orders vnder gouernment. And very inconuenient it is, that things of diuerse natures should be mingled, as matters of right (which is a qualitie) with substances, matters of order with sacraments. And absurd it is to separate sacraments from the word, as it were seales from the writing. This is sufficient to admonish thee that nothing can be

more

more confused then *Caluins* Treatise of discipline, and the gouernment of the Church.

Beza doth neither define nor diuide the discipline of the Church, for any thing that euer I could reade, no not in all those questions which he handleth of discipline, and the gouernment of the Church. He talketh of the power and authoritie of the Church, but the description thereof is but one part of discipline, and respecteth onely the gouernours: the duetie of the rest of the Church, and of the whole body he omitteth. In his Treatise against *Erastus*, he telleth vs that discipline is a certeine order, but what, he sheweth not: he mistaketh generall councels for the whole body of the Church: for in generall councels there is not the whole body, but the whole company of the gouernours of the Church represented. He vnskilfully diuideth the members of the Church (I need not to admonish him, how vnproperly he calleth the functions of the Church members) into those that preach the word, and those that distribute the goods of the Church, and those that are gouernours of discipline, and magistrates that administer both ciuill iustice, and procure the peace of the Church: for if this diuision were good, then were ministers of the word not to deale in discipline; for parts and members of one diuision may not be confounded. Now that the magistrate should be an officer of the Church, the disciplinarians cannot abide: sure it is not tolerable, that he is put the last among the officers of the Church. Further, it is absurd that he placeth the office of the presbytery in iurisdiction onely, seeing admonitions, elections, and decision of doctrine, and consultations, and commandements, and execution of excommunication, and making of orders, cannot be comprised vnder iurisdiction; which notwithstanding are the principall parts of the office of presbyteries, as they say. Fasting is likewise without cause put vnder the title of iurisdiction, and matrimoniall causes without title discussed by the presbyteries: all which disorders shew, that this discipline which they striue for, is a matter confused, and farre out of order.

Conf. c. 5. num. 10. *Conf. c. 5.* *Ibidem.* The magistrate put last among those that deale in Church-gouernment.

Daneau hath discoursed more particularly of discipline then the former; yet neither to the satisfaction of those that desire to learne, nor to the contentment of our disciplinarian faction. For the first it may appeare, in that he distinguisheth the Church from the persons whereof it consisteth, as if it were a Platonicall *Idæa*: and the power of the Church from the persons and doctrine: he deuideth the power of the Church into authoritie of making lawes, and iurisdiction: by which diuision, consultations, matters of elections and deposing of

Dan. Isag. part. 3. c. 1.

Ministers, admonitions, solemne prayers and fasts which *Caluin* compriseth vnder Discipline, are left without the power of the Church, vnlesse we will haue, contrary to logicke rules, things deuided to comprehend more then the partes into which they are deuided. The second is manifest, in that contrary to our platformers, hee deuideth the censures of the Church into excommunication and deposition, then which nothing can bee more blunt nor strange: for by this meanes, admonition shoulde not bee comprised vnder the censures, and the cōmon sort shoulde be lesse subiect to censures then officers, for deposition is of those only that beare office, and the magistrates which depose Ministers at *Geneua*, shoulde haue the power of the keyes, which they will not grant: & in some that should be accōpted censure, which ancient writers neuer so called nor so vsed. Both his definitions and deuisions also are most contrary to the course of our disciplinarians. He vseth the word *Discipline* in a spirituall signification, for some part of the power, or policie of the Church: that which they call discipline, he calleth policie of the Church: the discourse of the persons of whom the Church standeth, and their functions, hee doth not comprehend either vnder his Church policie or discipline, farre contrary to our platformers, which make the diuision of officers the ground of their discipline. Discipline hee defineth to be the iustice of mens reason, they make it an order appoynted by God: hee maketh it to consist in things externall and indifferent, they make their discipline spirituall, and to touch the conscience: he maketh it changeable, they make it vnchangeable, and constant, as is the word of God, then which nothing can be more repugnant and contrary.

Dan. Isag. par. 3.

Ordon de Gen.

Isag. par 3. c. 58.

ibidem. c. 28

ib. c. 28.

The substance both *Beza* and and our plotters make vnchangeable.

Tho. Cartw. caried away with heate of contention, forgot to tell vs what that discipline is, and what it comprehendeth, for which hee striueth. contrary to his master *Daneau*, hee affirmeth that it is an order left by God, and calleth it Christes discipline, and the word of God, yet neuer knew he any such matter, nor can tell where to finde it: let him yet if he can, tell vs whether it consist in lawes written, or cabalistical tradition, or customs as *Daneau* holdeth, or in apostolical examples, or equitie of the ceremoniall lawe, or in his replies, or in any such other frappling discourse concerning the officers of the Church and their offices, as the learned discourse woulde insinuate, and what the same differeth from the doctrine of faith and the morall law: whether it be publike or priuat: externall, or internall: changeable, or vnchangeable: and to conclude, whether the decrees of the Church may bee called the discipline of Christ, as the Canons

2. reply. pref.

Ordon. de Gen.

of

of *Geneua* affirme, and *Caluin* denieth not. If he declare this vnto vs directly without stammering, or doubting: then I will beleeue that he knoweth the nature and partes of discipline: otherwise, all the world will condemne him for a wrangler, that would haue he knoweth not what.

Those that made the admonition to the Parliament, they vnderstood not the matter in question, nor their master *Caluin*: they define nothing: their diuisions are but slender: they make but two partes of discipline, Admonition & Excōmunication, & like carnall fellowes, forgot prayer & fasting, which their master *Caluin* placed among the partes of discipline. It is sufficient for them, that they broched vs first these contentions, and were the Patriarkes of *Brownistes* and *Disciplinarians*: vnlesse they had broached treason and rebellion, they could not haue done more harme.

He that made the discourse of Ecclesiasticall discipline commended by *T.Cartw.* purposing aswell to reforme his fellowes methode, as the Church gouernment, like a clerkely bacheler he taketh on him to define and deuide his discipline: but when he seeth that their opinions of discipline are so extrauagant, and farre different, that they can not bee brought within the compasse, either of good definition, or diuision: it may be, it will repent him of his rash boldenesse. Ecclesiasticall discipline (saith he) is the policie of the Church of Christ, ordeined and appoynted of God for the good administration and gouernment of the same. If I demaund of him in what place this pollicie was ordeined, whether in mount Sinah or at Ierusalem, hee cannot tell: nay, hee knoweth not in what place the same is to bee found. For bold though he be, he will not say (I thinke) that all his Ecclesiasticall discipline is to be found in the old or new Testament. If I aske him at what time this pollicie was ordeined, he wil be mute, vnlesse he care not what he answereth. This definition is defectiue: by the same, the morall law, which indeede is true discipline of maners, is omitted: for the same was not published for the Church onely, but for all men: it was further published for reformation of mens maners singly considered by themselues, not as they were conioyned in the fellowship of the Church. Secondly, all Ecclesiasticall canons made in Synodes by this definition, are excluded from discipline: for they were not made by God, but by holy men, yet obserued for order sake. Thirdly, the *Presbyterial* constitutions & ordinances of *Geneua* doe here receiue their doome, that they belong not to the discipline of the Church: for I trust they will admit some difference betwixt *Eccl.discipl.*

 the

the decrees of God and their Consistorie, and not as do the *Papistes*, challenge to themselues the continuall guidance of Gods holy Spirit so inseparably, that whatsoeuer the Cōsistorie decreeth, must be taken as proceeding from the Holy Ghost. Fourthly, the dueties of priuate persons singly considered by themselues, are here kept without the compasse of discipline: for the policie of the Church which is a societie, differeth from the gouernment of singuler persons. Fiftly, the rules of discipline set downe by himselfe, by *T. Cartw.* and their followers, are falsly termed discipline, forasmuch as they are the vaine conceites of wayward men, and not the orders appoynted by God. Sixtly, he sheweth not by whom this discipline should be executed and maintained. Seuenthly, he declareth not the nature of it, to wit, whether it bee internall, or externall, mutable or immutable, nor howe it differeth from the morall lawe, or howe it may be discerned from temporarie lawes. Lastly, where the man pretendeth to cōmend vnto vs a forme of discipline which we want in the church of England, this description maketh nothing against the orders established already, which we doubt not to prooue to bee more consonant to the ordinance of Christ, then their confused platformes.

The same discription is the ouerthrow of their synodes, conferences, mute Elders, Doctors, profane Deacons, yea of their synodicall and presbyteriall constitutions, which all sauour of the slimie inuention of distempred braynes, and not of God. The same further ouerthroweth the substance of their discipline, and the famous distinction of officers & offices which the Counterpoyson and learned discourse take to be the marrow of their discipline: for they are not in the compasse of this definition, which should conteine the very substance of matters: nay, it placeth the substance in lawes, not in officers and their actions.

The same description is contrary to trueth and all ancient practise of the Church. all antiquitie, yea Christ Iesus the ancient of dayes giueth libertie to the Church to make lawes in externall matters for order and decencie, and diuers orders vsed in the Apostolike Churches, are nowe ceased; as washing of feete, christning with dipping vnder the water, greeting with kissing, loue feastes, communitie of possessions, absteining from blood, and diuers other; and these inconueniences followe that description. First, nothing may be added or altered if Christ had appoynted a certaine forme of discipline. Secondly, all those that did not vse that order, shoulde bee damned without repentance. Thirdly, those Churches that refuse Christs ordinance,

Matth. 16.
1. Cor. 14.

dinance, are not the Churches of God. For his sheepe heare his voice: therefore *Cartwr.* had neede to hold hard against *Browne.* Fourthly, then should the externall discipline binde the conscience. Fiftly, then should not the morall lawe be perfect. Sixtly, then should Christ be a lawgiuer, which soundeth harshly in Christian eares. Seuenthly, the constitutions of the Church shoulde bee equall to the morall lawe, forasmuch as both alike are supposed to come directly from God.

Besides all other faultes this description hath, it standeth vpon a meere tautologie or repetition of words: for to say that the policie of the Church is appoynted for the gouernement of the Church, is nothing els but this, that the gouernment (for that is πολιτεία) of the church is for the gouernment of the church, which is an absurd kinde of dallying or rather babling, and sheweth that hee that is as curious and well sighted as *Lynx* in the faultes of others, was as blinde and blunt as a Plough Coultre in his owne cause.

To recompence the faultes of his description, the same man bringeth forth a worse diuision of discipline: for as it is false & defectiue in some things, so it is redundant in others. Discipline (saith he) hath two parts: the first belonging to them that beare office in the church, the second respecting the duties of priuate men, making vp the rest of the body of the Church: as if their discipline comprehended the duetie of euery priuate person, which is the argument of the morall law. The discipline of the Church concerneth the whole societie, (as himselfe saide better before) and is publike, and respecteth not priuate and secret dueties of particulars, but as they are publike persons: and very absurd it were, that husbandes and wiues, parents and children, masters and seruants, should learne their dueties out of the lawes of discipline, and not rather out of the lawes of God and the Realme.

The same diuision is redundant: first for that it compriseth the morall law, which is the only rule of mens liues, and the direction of priuate mens actions, and is without the compasse of the discipline of the Church in question. Secondly, the dueties of priuate men both internall of the minde, and meere ciuill, which are without the reach of Ecclesiasticall discipline, are notwithstanding shuffled vp in this diuision.

Many respects make the same diuision defectiue: and first, for that it compriseth onely the dueties of persons, and not the ordering of things, as of the goods of the Church, the places of prayer, and ſuch like. Neither doth hee touch the determination of matters or proceeding in making of orders, hearing cauſes, executing the cenſures of the Church, and many matters more. Of which, as the autors of theſe ſtirres are ignorant, ſo their plats and models are ignorantly and abſurdly defectiue . neither excepting the circumſtance of the perſon, doe they determine almoſt any circumſtances or ſet downe orders for times and places, ſo that both this diuiſion and their plats are infinitly imperfect. Secondly, it comprehendeth not the dueties belonging to the whole Church, which Eccleſiaſticall diſcipline ſhould principally reſpect, but onely certeine duties belonging to ſeuerall perſons. Thirdly, it diſtinguiſheth not the dueties of perſons that are of the Church, from thoſe dueties that are required of them as they are members of the Commonwealth, or maſters of families. Laſtly, as both definition and diuiſion are defectiue, ſo the authors of thẽ diſloyall, that paſſe by the magiſtrate in deepe ſilence, whoſe power notwithſtanding is ſouereigne, and (as *Beza* himſelfe confeſſeth) architectonicall. Wherefore ſeeing they aske they know not what, and would haue they cannot tell how much; let them not be angry with vs for ſending them backe to ſeeke wherefore they came: and ſo much the rather, for that they differ not onely about the deſcription and parts of diſcipline, but alſo about the principall grounds and pillars thereof, which are ſo contrary, that like *Cadmus* his brood that ſproong of ſerpents teeth, one of them deſtroyeth an other. They of *Geneua* haue but one conſiſtory in ſeuenteene pariſhes: according to which cuſtome *Daneau* contenteth himſelfe with a conſiſtory in euery city . *T. C.* and his followers holde that a conſiſtory muſt be placed in euery pariſh: ſome content themſelues with presbyteries: they of the admonition giue all power to their elderſhips: others adde conferences and ſynods as neceſſarie offices. The admonitors of the Parliament, and their champion *T. C.* ſometime made their elderſhips to conſiſt of paſtours, elders, and deacons: now vpon more mature aduiſe, they haue added doctours, & quite excluded deacons from the feaſt: ſome make doctours a neceſſarie part of the Church: others holde them not neceſſarie, nor vſe them. our platformers make widowes neceſſary members of the Church; yet they of other Churches thinke not their gouernment to be deformed, although they want them.

[Margin: The Diſciplinarians not agreed about principall matters.]

[Margin: *Iſag. part. 3.*]

[Margin: *Sac. diſc.*]

[Margin: *Fint. ſer. contryp.*]

Th. Cartw. once would haue the people to chuſe their Miniſter, and gaue out great words that Chriſt died to purchaſe that liberty to the people: they of the Admonition likewiſe fauoured the peoples

gouernment:

gouernment : now *Th. Cartw.* hath changed haire, and telleth vs, that it is sufficient if the people do consent after election; nay that it is sufficient if the people dissent not; which is now the practise of *Geneua.* Our platformers holde, excommunication to be a substantiall poynt of discipline : they of *Geneua* practise none but suspension from the sacraments. Some holde imposition of hands, and fasting at the election of the minister, to be materiall : others thinke otherwise, and so practise it. To prosecute all the contrarieties of their discipline, requireth more time, and a more speciall treatise. Of these that haue already bene specified, and that which shall more particularly be set downe in this discourse; this conclusion followeth, that seeing truth is one, that this their discipline, consisting of so contrary pieces, cannot sauor of truth.

Bez. aduers. Erast. in pref.

The same is further euident by the weakenesse of their proofes brought for confirmation of their chiefe positions. They holde that the substance of their discipline is described in the word of God ; yet when it commeth to hammering, they cannot finde their presbyteries, nor their maner of conferences and synods : they haue beene long searching about their mute elders, and yet haue found nothing. Where those elders euer tooke vpon them to excommunicate, to pronounce iudgement , to set orders , or to handle any part of Church-gouernment, they shall neuer be able to shew. In the word of God, they haue no confirmation : the ancient fathers neuer knew any such men or maner of discipline : nay, they neither vsed that forme of excommunication, nor election, nor determination of controuersies that is now vsed among those that pretend correction of all gouernment. neither is there any proofe for the same out of Scriptures, nor out of fathers. Wherefore, vnlesse they seeke better, and agree better, they are like to receiue but colde enterteinment for their frozen deuises newly forged.

The weaknes of the disciplinarians cause declared, for that yet they haue not foũd their discipline in Scripture or fathers.

This as I haue shewed in generall, I shall (God willing) make good in the particular positions and grounds of their new discipline. Wherein that I may proceed more orderly, I will declare first, what this word *Discipline* signifieth, and how diuersly it is taken. Secondly, what is meant in this controuersie by Ecclesiasticall discipline. And lastly, what is the state of the question, concerning discipline, betweene the disciplinarians and vs.

Discipline, as it is a word borowed of the Latine tongue, so with vs as with them, it signifieth diuersly. Generally it signifieth whatsoeuer is learned : and as doctrine in a generall signification is taken for

Discipline, what it signifieth.

whatsoeuer is taught; so discipline in a generall acception is made to signifie whatsoeuer is learned : so in Latine *Disciplina viuendi, &c.* and *Disciplina morum,* signifieth a common course of ciuility & maners, learned by practise, or otherwise : and *Vetus disciplina,* is that
Cic.de orat.1. which we call the olde guise. *Disciplina militaris,* is the knowledge
academ.1. of armes. *Græcorum artes & disciplinæ,* are by vs interpreted, the arts and learning of the Greeks. Sometime *Disciplinæ* are taken for sects,
Cic.2. de natur. or singular opinions : as where *Tullie* saith, *Tres trium disciplinarum*
deorum. *principes conuenistis* : You three, which are the principall patrons of three seuerall sects of Philosophie, are heere met together. and the
Pet.Gal.lib.1. Talmudists digressing from the law, call their writings *Talmud,* that is, *Discipline,* or as in Latine, *Disciplinatio.* In which signification the new platformers doe very naturally brooke the name of *Discipline,* which digressing from the word, haue torne this Church into diuers
De patientia. sects. Sometime *Discipline* is taken in euill part: so *Tertullian* vseth it, where he hath *Disciplina Marcyonis,* that is, Marcyons heresie: and *Tullie* termeth the Epicureans sect, *Disciplina Epicuri.* And thus is it commonly taken of those that speake Latine.

Besides that is common and general, vse hath brought it to a more speciall signification, to signifie correction, and chastisement, which as it should seeme to beginne with Christian writers, so it hath bene
Sap.3. much by them so vsed : *Disciplinam qui abijcit infelix est,* that is, vnhappie is he that refuseth correction saith the olde interpreter, and in
Epist.11.l.1. *Ierem. 2. Noluerunt accipere disciplinam.* In which sense *Cyprian* doth call the Censures of the church *disciplinam:* as where he saith *obseruatione disciplinæ præcepta diuina teneamus* : in obseruation of discipline,
De bono discip. let vs hold the lawes of God. *Augustine* doth vse it in both the significations. This obserued, let vs now declare, what is meant by Ecclesiasticall discipline. As discipline is taken either generally or specially, so Ecclesiasticall discipline is taken either generally, for the whole forme of the gouernment of the Church, whether it bee according to lawe onely, or custome onely, or both ioyntly: or specially for Ec-
De habitu virg. clesiasticall corrections vsed in the Church. for doctrine is it vsed by *Cyprian,* where he caleth the Gospel *Apostolicam et euangelicam disciplinam lib.2.ep.3.* and ioyneth discipline and Christian faith together as two wordes of one thing: and for correction, where he calleth the censures *Deificam et Ecclesiasticam disciplinam,* the diuine & Ecclesiasticall discipline

But Ecclesiasticall discipline which we speake of, is neither taken according to the generall, nor speciall vse of other authors : but for

Ecclesiasticall

Ecclesiasticall orders concerning persons, matters, and proceedings of the Church, and the parts thereof. Of these orders the aduersarie woulde haue those that concerne the substance of discipline to be appoynted by God, and to be alwayes firme and immutable, and to bee executed by the Eldership. The substance of discipline they call the orders concerning the appoyntment of their Doctors, Pastors, Elders, Deacons, widowes, presbyteryes, conferences, synodes, and autoritie of the people, together with their autoritie and function: nowe of late I heare in their holy discipline (as they terme it,) they make some part before accompted substance, circumstance. *Beza de Presb.*

We say that so much as Christ hath appoynted to be obserued, as that there be Pastors to teach, & a certaine gouernment, and such like discipline is diligently to be kept: where he hath left it free, there the gouernours of the Church, that is Christian princes and bishops may set orders and see the same executed: and the orders appoynted by Christ & Canons, and customs of the Church we call Ecclesiasticall discipline: and this we accompt to be changeable, so farre forth as is not by Christ commanded to be kept.

Concerning circumstances of time and place, they grant that the gouernours of the Church may set order. We say the distinction of substance and circumstance is absurd, & that some circumstance cannot bee changed, and that some thing they call substance, may bee changed, as shall further appeare in this discourse.

What is not in controuersie.

So that the controuersie is not about the morall lawe, nor such orders as Christ enioyned to be kept, nor of the doctrine of the Gospel, nor the word of God, whether it be to be kept or no: these things, although called in a generall signification discipline, we confesse cannot be changed: but the same is nothing concerning this question; which is, by what persons the Church shall be gouerned, and what externall orders are to bee obserued. This is then the question: first, whether Christ hath prescribed such a forme of gouernment for the Church, that in substance (as they call it) nothing is to be added, diminished, or altered: they affirme it, we denie it. Secondly, whether that fourme which they prescribe, which hath in euery Parish or precinct a presbyterie of Doctors, Pastors, Elders, & Deacons, at least of Pastors & Elders: & of diuers Presbyteries, Conferences & Synodes, with that power which they assigne to thẽ, & hath beside the presbyteries to gouerne, doctors to teach, pastors to exhort, elders to admonish, Deacons to distribute, & widowes to attend the sicke: whether (I say) this fourme be prescribed in the word: they say it is: we denie

The state of the question declared.

that it can bee proued. Thirdly, whether the Magistrate, and vnder him the Bishoppes haue lawfull power in the gouernement of the Church: they say no: we offer to proue it.

We say therefore, that the discipline of the Church is an externall order prescribed partly by the worde, partly by the Christian Magistrate, or by the chiefe Ministers of the church, (where the Magistrate fauoureth not Religion) according to the rules of Gods word: for the gouernment of the whole Church, and euery member thereof, in respect they are of the Church: that maners may be reformed, and the peace of the Church maintained, and God glorified, and order and decencie procured.

Discipline prescribeth orders either for the whole assemblie of the Church, or the ministers of the church, about which the greatest part of the controuersie standeth: or priuat persons as they are members of the church, about which we make no contention: or for the goods of the church and maintenance of the ministerie, and other necessities of church: or for the proceeding in all matters of church gouernment, as setting lawes or orders, iudiciall cognition, censures, elections of officers, and such like causes. Wherein because the models of disciplne say litle to the purpose, we challenge them for defectiue, and imperfect: and because they haue no testimonie of the word of God, nor of antiquitie, we refuse them for want of autoritie: and because they be full of iniustice, and voyde of iudgement, and were compiled by men presumptuous in opinion, and ignorant of gouernment, we say they are to be banished out of this state and common wealth.

These things as we haue in general termes affirmed, so now (God willing) we meane to auow & make good by discourse of particulars. generall propositions comprehend much, but particular proofes enforce more. First therefore wee will begin to examine those poyntes which are in controuersie, concerning the parish doctor & his office. Some of them doe make him the first man in the list of Church officers, and therfore by right he may challenge the first place: al of them doe make him a distinct person from the pastor: concerning his office, they hold that it consisteth in bare teaching, without applicatiō. of late time he hath obteined such fauour, that he is become a principall part of the Consistory & Synode: some are of conceit that he is a necessarie member of the church, and ought to be in euery congregation. Which things although they seeme very fine and sauorie in the platformers conceit, yet are they strange and improbable when they come to scanning, as may appeare in the treatise insuing.

Of

Of the Parish Doctor, and his office.

CHAP. 2. SECT. 1.

Wherein is declared, that the Doctor is not a degree aboue or before the Pastor: First, for that the Scriptures make them one office, and ioyne teaching and feeding in one person, which is an interpretation likewise receiued by the fathers. Secondly, being supposed that Doctors and Pastors are diuers, yet the Scriptures preferre Pastors, so doe the fathers. Thirdly, most of the disciplinarians preferre Pastor before Doctor, as indued with more giftes, and more necessarily required then Doctor.

SO long as the troublers of the Church had any calling in the ministerie, they made small accompt of Doctors; and so farre were they from preferring doctors before pastors, that they of the admonition place them among those callings which in their wise censures they condemne as vnlawfull: and *Th. Cartw.* maketh a very base accompt of doctors in his first reply. But nowe that by order they are thrust out as Schismaticall perturbers of the Church, and range about as false apostles to winne men to their faction: they haue deuised this office of doctors, to excuse their vagrant and ranging ministerie. they see nowe that there is but two waies for them to winde out: for eyther they must be *Euangelistes* extraordinarily raised vp of God to restore religion, which for modesty sake the blush to take vpon them: or els they must be an order of doctors, which they now giue out to be an ordinarie officer of the Church: or els (which is most true) they must confesse they runne where no man sent them, and intrude themselues without calling, and range the Countrey without warrant or passe-port. But they should haue considered if they bee doctors, that they ought to haue an ordinarie calling: as we say, from the gouernours of the Church: as themselues say, by election of the Presbyteries, consent of the people, and imposition of hands: and that in a Church ordered, there can none enter the ministerie without ordinarie calling by the gouernours of this Church. They may remember that by the canons of the Church of France, such are called runners or roguers, and condemned for Scihsmatickes.

Admonition to the Parliament.

First replie.

How Doctor came first into credite.

Discipline *de Fraunce. tit. Coureurs*

All this notwithstanding, our platformers doe not only take themselues for doctors, but preferre doctors before pastors. because they take vpon themselues the name of doctors, they will needes perch aboue pastors: so cunning is ambition, that what it disalloweth and detesteth in others, it maketh them to accompt most lawfull in themselues. herein (I say) they haue done wrong, and taken a course contrary to the word, to antiquitie, and their owne rules.

The office of bishops & ministers hath autoritie & confirmation from God: the office of Doctor, barely teaching, is a deuise of man: for as touching the Doctors mencioned *1.Cor.12.* and *Ephe.4.* they are nothing but Bishops and teaching Elders, and sauour not of the nature of the new Doctor. The Apostle *Paul* and other Bishops and fellow helpers of the Apostles are called doctors in a generall signification: this proper Doctor is no where found: nay, the Apostle setling the Churches of *Asia* & *Crete* by the ministerie of *Timothie* and *Titus*, and setting downe the office of Bishops & Deacons, doth not so much as mention any such doctor, as they would haue. Wherfore no reason, that a newe vpstart should take the place of the ancient order of Pastors, that comming in by humane errour, this being estblished by God. The fathers make doctor & pastor both one: *Policarpus* is called by *Euseb.ecl.hist.lib.4.* διδάσκαλος καὶ ἐπίσκοπος, that is, doctor & bishop, & *Iohn* the Apostle is called ἱερεὺς καὶ διδάσκαλος, that is, priest & doctor. and that is the opinion of *Ierom* and *Augustin*, vpon the fourth to the *Ephesians.* But were the facultie of doctors or teachers distinguished frõ that of pastors, & were it granted that some are doctors, which are not pastors: yet what reasõ haue the disciplinarians to prefer doctors, seeing the holy Ghost preferreth pastors before doctors: and seeing pastors were appointed, where no mention is made of doctors? The office of Bishops & ministers is requisit in the Church: for by their voyce the sheepe is gathered into Christs folde, by their gouernement the flocke is kept in order: that doctor is required, they cannot proue. Let them therefore giue ouer these idle fancies, and while they striue for dainties and nouelties, let them not lose things required of necessitie: which they may percase doe, if they put their doctor before the pastor, the doctor being in no other Church but ours thought necessarie to be placed in euery congregation.

Act.13.

Ephe.4.
Act.14.
Tit.1.

The Apostles so long as they liued, ruled the Church of God: they had the same committed to them by the head shepherd Christ Iesus: when they were remoued, who succeeded them in the gouernment? whether the Apostles successors, or some others come wee knowe not from whence? sure, seeing bishoppes and ministers, that led the Church, succeeded the Apostles in their charge, as *Cyprian* and all antiquitie acknowledgeth: it is absurd to attribute the autoritie and preeminence to others, that haue neither right of succession, nor other iust claime of the place. If the parish doctor succeede any, he succeedeth the doctors of the great synagogue: but let him take heede, if he lay holde on this claime, that like the *Rabbins* of the *Iewes*, he preferre not the traditions of discipline before the word of God.

Cypr.ep.9. lib.1.

All

All antiquity giueth testimony to pastours. *Tertullian* acknowledged no other for presidents and gouernours: these are the presidents or rulers of the Church, of which *Iustine Martyr* speaketh of. But what need other testimony, when the Apostle, *Hebr.13.* calleth pastours ἡγουμένους, or leaders, when these doctours for gouernment are neither authorised of Scriptures nor ancient fathers? Those doctours which they then had, are of another sort: *Origen,* and those that taught before him in the schoole of *Alexandria,* were schoole doctours, not parish doctours: they had no imposition of hands, or degree in the ministerie, but onely had allowance of the bishop, to whom they were subiect. Beside these schoole doctours, let the platformers, if they can, shew me in all antiquitie, but one parish doctor, which was neither bishop, priest, nor deacon; and if they can not, let them be ashamed of the weaknesse of their cause, and their foolish vantery. *De cor milit. & apol.* *Apol. ad Antonium 2.*

The precedence of the doctour before the pastour, is not allowed by the greatest of that side, from whence our men borow their inuentions. *Caluin* placeth doctours a degree vnder pastours. *Beza* placeth the doctours gouernment in schooles: and though sometimes he can be content that he shall haue a voyce in the consistory, yet doth he make him come behinde pastours. *Iunius* maketh him president of schooles, not of the parish. The Canons of French discipline make the ministers or pastours presidents of the consistory, hauing litle regard to the doctours. Yea, *T.Cartw.* and he that made the booke of *Ecclesiasticall discipline,* doth prefer pastours in degree and necessity before doctours. The Admonition leaueth them out of the consistory. The same is contrary to the rules of their discipline, which prefer those that haue most, and most excellent gifts, and yet will haue the doctour, whose gift they place in teaching before pastour, whome they indue with teaching, exhortation, and gouernment. And thus doth ambition & desire of preheminence cary them blindfolde vpon walles and stumbling blocks, which themselues placed in their owne way. But what should we contend longer, which of the pastour or doctour should be greatest, seeing Christ was gouernour of the Church, not as he was called doctor, in which respect he onely taught; but in respect he was a pastour and a king? I would proceed further, but it is not consonant for those that stand vpon the equality of ministers so much, and vrge the place, *It shall not be so with you,* against the degree of bishops, to fight and brable about the preheminence of the doctour, any longer. *Instit.4.* *Iun.eccles.* *Eccl. discip.* *Luke 22.* ὑμεῖς δ' οὐχ οὕτως.

Of the Doctour, and his office.

CHAP. 2. SECT. 2.

In this section is prooued that doctours mentioned in Scriptures, are not seuerall officers of the Church, nor specially distinct from pastours. First, for that doctours and pastours are ioyned, as distinct officers are disioyned. Eph.4. *Secondly, for that the function of doctors falleth wholly into the office of pastors. Thirdly, for that it were burthensome and superfluous to haue a doctor in euery parish, beside a pastor. Fourthly, for that both are vnderstood vnder the word Teachers,* 1.Cor.12. *Fiftly, for that the same man may be a doctor and a pastor, and so was in the Apostolike churches. Sixtly, for that the place,* Rom.12, *doth diuersly make against the difference of doctors and pastors. Seuenthly, all antiquitie was ignorant of this difference, and the late writers that are indifferent, disallow it. Lastly, the reasons alleged to the contrary, as that* Paul, Barnabas, *and* Apollos, *and* Origen, *are called doctors, prooue no such doctors as they would haue.*

IT is a more important question, whether doctor in Scriptures be a seuerall officer distinct from pastor. More important I call it, not in respect of the profit, for it is a contention about words; but in respect of the patrons of this opinion, whose authority without plaine reason, I doe not contemne. *Caluin* and *Beza*, and the whole crew of disciplinarians doe holde that doctor is an officer of the Church, distinct from the pastor. but for that I see no reason out of the Scripture, why they should so thinke, & see all antiquity holde against them: they must pardon me, if I folow antiquity, whose gray haires, and experience in matters of gouernment, made them venerable; rather then yoong men, that seeme to seeke admiration by their strange nouelties; especially so many reasons leading me to holde with them, and refuse these mens new deuises.

Doctours and pastours conioyned. *Ephe*.4.

The apostle hauing separated apostles, prophets, and euangelists by a note of distinction, ioyneth pastours and doctours, by a word or note, that coupleth together; of which I frame this reason against them: If the apostle had meant to make pastors & doctors so different as apostles and prophets, then would he haue vsed the same note of distinction, and not haue changed the phrase: and contrariwise, not vsing the note of distinction, and changing the phrase, it is manifest that he doth not so distinguish them. but that he doth there vse a note of distinction, speaking of apostles, prophets and euangelists, and not betweene pastours and doctours; the words declare manifestly, ἔδωκε τοὺς μὲν ἀποστόλους, τοὺς δὲ προφήτας, τοὺς δὲ εὐαγγελιστάς, τοὺς δὲ ποιμένας καὶ διδασκάλους. that is, he gaue some apostles, some prophets, some euangelists, some pastours, and teachers. if he had meant to make pastours and doctors distinct, then the phrase of speech would not haue bene altered, and

τοὺς

τοὺς δὲ διδασκάλους put for καὶ διδασκάλους. *Cartwright* answereth that it is an elegancie of speech: but we acknowledge him for no teacher of Grammer, much lesse of elegancies. the elegancie and necessitie of the matter (if any such had bene meant) required the other formes. Where he answereth further, that pastours and doctours are not coupled in signification, but are couples of Christes liberalitie, he (good man) taketh that for granted, which is in controuersie; for we deny that they are couples of officers: and maketh a speake to no purpose: for we deny not that the words are diuers and signifie diuers respects; but this signification of diuers respects in one person, doth not make two officers. To the argument grounded on the change of the apostles phrase, and leauing out the article of distinction, he saith nothing, though wide he seeme to gape: a scholar of his saith that pastors and doctors are distinguished, as male and female: *Galat. 3. 28.* but the phrase is diuers. there it is a negatiue, in *Eph. 4.* affirmatiue.

Againe, if pastors and doctors were diuers officers as they suppose, 2
then should they haue diuers functions and offices, and not the one incroch vpon the others office; which is a matter by them not onely affirmed, but much stood vpon, & proued out of the apostles words, *Rom. 12.* but the doctor hath no diuers function frõ the pastor. for as the doctors office is in teaching, so is the pastors. of the pastor it is required that he be διδακτικὸς, which they giue to the doctor; they both teach. and nothing hath the doctor which truely agreeth not to the pastor: and therefore it is absurd to make the doctor a distinct person from the pastour. That which they reply of bare teaching, in his proper place shall haue his full answere.

Rom. 12.

One function of pastor and doctor.

Besides, it would be a superfluous burthen, where the pastor ought 3
and can doe both offices, to charge the parish with the maintenance of a doctour, which is not lightly to be esteemed, where the parish is poore. As for teaching and catechising, which is the doctours grant made vnto him by their assignment; it is a speciall part of the pastors duty Let them therfore chuse whether they will make doctor & pastor one and the same office, or els make doctors superfluous where there is a pastor; which would be both a superfluous charge, & a deformity to the Church. *T. C.* reiecteth this reason, drawen from charge: yet neither ought meanes of maintenance be neglected; nor can the obiection of superfluitie be answered.

Now where they argue from the diuersitie of names and titles, to
make them diuers offices, I will thus turne that argument backe vpon 4
them.

One word cō-prehendeth paſtour and doctour. 1.*Cor*.12.

them. If diuerſity of names and titles make diuers offices, as they beare vs in hand, and would prooue out of the place before alleged, *Eph.4.* where teachers and paſtours are ſeparated in name; and out of *Rom. 12.* where teaching and exhorting is diſtinguiſhed, that is, by the Diſciplinarian grammer, doctours and paſtours: then will it fall out that biſhops, elders, rulers, ſhould make diuers officers, and apoſtles ſhould be diuers from Chriſtes twelue diſciples, becauſe the names are diuers. Againe, if diuers names and titles make diuers officers, then muſt the ſame names and titles make them the ſame: and ſo much the rather, for that, *1.Cor.12.* the word and name of doctors doth comprehend paſtours or biſhops. for it is abſurd to ſay that the Holy ghoſt, making an enumeration of the officers of the Church, ſhould leaue out the moſt ordinary and neceſſary function of paſtors, which was to continue in the Church, diuers of the other ceaſing. And therefore, if by doctours in that place, as *Caluin* himſelfe granteth, paſtours be vnderſtood, let them ſhew by what rule of diſcipline, doctours and paſtours be diuers officers; ſeeing rules of reaſon teach vs, that members of one diuiſion may not be confounded.

5 Againe, if doctour be a diuers officer from apoſtles and paſtours, then can not the ſame perſon be an apoſtle and a doctour, or a paſtor
Rom. 1. & a doctor at one time. But *S.Paul*, who was an apoſtle from his firſt
Act.13. calling, and *Barnabas*, who was his fellow helper, was alſo a doctor,
Euſeb. eccl. hiſt. as themſelues confeſſe. *Euſebius* calleth *Polycarpus* a biſhop and a doctour: and one *Theodoret* is called paſtour and doctour, *Conc.Calc. Act. 8.* Likewiſe, *Caluin* in his time, and *Beza*, were both paſtours & doctours in the Church of *Geneua* at one time, as euery one know-
De polit.Iudaic. in epiſt. ad B. eth. *Bertram* giueth both titles to *Beza*, whome he calleth paſtour and doctour; which were an abſurd and ſtrange confuſion of members, if as they ſay, doctour and paſtour be two diſtinct members of the Church. Thus thoſe that make ſuch an outcry againſt two benefices, can ſwallow ſecretly two offices, and confound the Church, and maime it, if *Penrie*, the fooliſh prophet of Wales, ſay true in his booke called *Martin.*

6 Moreouer, if the diuers faculties of teaching and exhorting, make

Diuers faculties make not diuers perſons or officers.

diuers officers, becauſe they are diſtinguiſhed, *Rom. 12.* then by the ſame reaſon, the faculty of miniſtring and faculty of propheſying, mentioned in the ſame place, ſhall make diuers officers diſtinct from paſtours, for they are by like reaſon diſtinguiſhed; and praying, preaching and adminiſtring the ſacraments would make diuers ſorts and formes of paſtours. Likewiſe, where in that chapter the apoſtle ſeparateth

parateth ἀποστυγοῦντας τὸ πονηρὸν καὶ κολλωμένους τῷ ἀγαθῷ, and ἐλεῶντας: that is, those that hate euill, and cleaue to that which is good, and shew mercy; there will fall out a diuers office of those that cleaue to good, from those that hate that which is euill; and those that shew mercy, will prooue diuers from the rest: for all these things are in like order and maner distinguished.

The very ground of this distinction doth make against the diuer- 7
sity of pastours and doctours: for if the doctour may not exhort, be- *Rom.*12.
cause that is distinguished from teaching, then may not the pastour teach, neither may he gouerne, for that he that exhorteth, is distinguished from him that teacheth, and ruleth: for these things are all alike distinguished by the apostle; then which nothing can be more absurd, nor direct against their platformes of discipline.

And if pastour were so distinct from doctour as from apostles, 8
which they affirme, and it followeth of the place; in case doctours be diuers from pastours; then as well may the pastour meddle with the apostles office as with teaching, which they giue to the doctours; which is no small inconuenience in their platformes.

Lastly, all ancient writers are not onely ignorant of this newe 9
forme of doctours, but expresly make pastours and doctours, men- *Vide* B.
tioned *Ephes.* 4. one office, and ioyneth them in one person. *Chryso-*
stome and *Augustine* both consent in this opinion. *Ierome* affirmeth *In Eph.* 4.
doctours and pastours be one. *Eusebius* calleth *Polycarpus* both bi- *Eccl. hist.*
shop of *Smyrna* and an apostolicall doctour and a godly prophet. *lib.*4.*c.*14.

No father euer spoke of other doctour then the ministers of the word (schoole doctours onely except) which are of another sort and fashion. I would see what he is, that contemning such an harmonie and consent of Fathers, dare bring in a forme of doctours neuer spoken of by them, or knowen. The Talmudists had doctours in their *Philo. lib.*3.*de*
Synagogues, but they had no other pastours. Of late writers, *Bullin-* *vit. Mos.*
ger saith, that the words *Pastour* and *Doctour* are confounded. *Mus-* *In Eph.*4.
culus affirmeth Pastours and Doctours to be all one, which are also
called (saith he) elders and bishops. *Peter Martyr*, though abused *In* 1.*Sam.c.*19.
by authority of some men, he fauoureth the distinction of pastours *v.*23.
and doctours; yet giuing exhortation and consolation to doctours, he taketh away the ground of the distinction, without which it can not stand. *Caluin* and *Beza*, although they taught first this distinction, yet obserued it not in their practise: and therefore seeing they said one thing, did another, and deposed for their owne state very partially, we may take iust exception against their witnesse.

The reasons which *Cartwright*, and others bring, to make vp this breach, are too slender and weake to stoppe the course of trueth. Where they allege that *Barnabas* and *Apollos* are called doctours, they waste wordes; for such doctours were *Timothie, Titus, Luke, Marke, Syluanus*, and others : but they were not the speciall doctours they seeke, which barely taught, or that were ordinarily chosen, as I thinke themselues will confesse, when they haue better weyed the matter. The places, *Eph.4.* and *Rom. 12.* haue beene answered, and rebated vpon them. That *Rom. 12.* maketh nothing to purpose, the apostle distinguisheth not pastour from doctour, as they surmise, but διδάσκοντα καὶ παρακαλοῦντα, that is, him that teacheth and exhorteth. neither doe we deny but the faculties or actions of teaching and exhorting in some respects differ. So praying differeth from preaching, and preaching from administring the sacraments. These we grant to be diuers actions, but we deny that they make diuers persons, or are to be placed in diuers persons. The words are plaine : for he distinguisheth not the doctor from him that exhorteth; but teaching from exhorting, which gifts may concur in one person, as well as simplicity, & diligence, and doctrine meet friendly in the pastour. The strange Philosophy of the platformers (for so it is to be called, rather then Diuinitie) about the members of a body mentioned *Rom. 12.* shall be discussed other where. The difference of members *vers. 4.* is not to be stretched to teaching, exhorting, ruling, distributing, as the platformers force it : for it agreeth not, and the words ἔχοντες δὲ doe shew that the apostle passeth to another purpose. That *Caluin* and *Beza* drawe the same so farre, and expound teaching, and exhorting, and ruling at pleasure; it is litle to be esteemed, seeing the text refuseth to follow, and all ancient interpretors cary the words to another meaning.

The last reason that *Cartwright* vseth to prooue the difference pretended, betwixt doctour and pastour, *viz.* that many are fit to teach which are not fit to exhort, which being placed in the arierward, should haue some force, is weake and nothing woorth : for howsoeuer he beleeue thinges fitting his purpose (for desire, they say, is credulous) yet I can not conceiue how a man should be fit to teach, that can not exhort; and a strange doctour he must be, that is able to teach, and hath not the wit, nor the skill to exhort them to beleue that he teacheth. If he had not forgot his principles of Rhetorike, he might haue remembred that men are not taught without exhortation. But be it, some were, like the platformers, carued out of wood, that

Ad Heren.

that can not apply that they reade, and speake onely *Caluins* and *Bezaes* commentaries : yet what is that to prooue doctors and pastors diuers? Some preachers haue not vtterance, some want audacitie, some haue knowledge of tongues, some want them; yet do not either the faculty or want of these things make a difference of pastors: so that *Th. Cartwr.* hath said somewhat of men, litle of the matter. Those offices that are required in the pastour, are with more dexterity executed of some then others; yet doe they not make so many diuers kindes of pastours. euery piece of wood is not fit for all purposes, nor euery pastour fit for gouernment : yet they will haue all pastours to gouerne like men that will make boltes of euery piece of wood. Will they also make so many diuers sorts of pastours, as there are diuers giftes required in them, which they are not able to performe, all alike? If they doe, we will better consider of *Cartwrights* reason.

But what need we further answere that which hath scarce any apparance of doubt? They themselues make doctours rulers of schooles. *Iunius* calleth them, *Scholasticæ administrationis curatores*, that is, gouernours of schooles, and reckoneth those that teach profane arts and tongues, among doctours : so that by his rule *Lucian* teaching Rhetorike, might be a member of the Church being a doctour, which some make principall members of the Church. *Beza* placeth doctours in schooles. They of *Geneua* distinguish betwixt the gouernment of the Church and the schooles. What good a doctour may doe, teaching arts among the rudesbies of his parish, I can not see, vnlesse he can teach a sowe to dance, or an asse to harpe, which percase they hope to compasse by some miracle of reformation. In Cathedrall Churches there is a lecture read: but how it differeth from a sermon, they must be subtile if they can shew. This lecturer, I know, differeth little from pastours, for I know none of them, but they are pastours. wherefore vnlesse they stand better to it, then hitherto they haue done, they are like to lose a pillar of their new discipline, called the Newe Parish Doctour.

Eccle. lib. 2. c. 5.

Confess.

Ordon. de Geneu.

Of Doctours, and their office.

Chap. 2. Sect. 3.

The Doctours office is declared to consist in exhortation, and not onely in bare teaching. First, for that doctors and pastors, Eph.4. *are all one. Secondly, for that the apostle ioyneth exhortation and doctrine in one person.* 1.Tim.4. *Thirdly, Paul, Barnabas, and Appollos, supposed to be doctors, are declared to haue vsed exhortation. Fourthly, doctours of schooles were not barred from exhortation, as both the labours of* Origen *and other late doctours shew euidently. Fiftly, olde & late writers testifie against bare teaching of doctors. Sixtly, they are no more debarred frô exhorting, then pastors from teaching. Seuenthly, the ancient prophets & Iewish rabbins exhorted. Lastly, the place of* Rom.12. *is extorted from them.*

Doctors (as before I haue in part touched) either are generally taken for all teachers, and that both in Scriptures, or
*Act.*13. ancient writers, in which signification *Paul* the apostle is called a doctor, and commonly the doctor of the Gentils, and *Barnabas* and *Apollos* were called doctors, because they ioyned with the apostles in teaching and declaring the Gospel: and bishops
*Eph.*4. and elders are called pastours and doctours, for that they teach the
1.*Cor.*12. word of God, and so the ancient fathers vpon the fourth to the *E-*
Chrysost. *phesians* vse it: and in common speech the godly fathers and writers
August. are called doctours of the Church: Or els doctors are expounded to
Ierome. signifie those that teach, or haue degree in schooles, of which sort was *Origen*; and before him *Pantenus*; and now, are those that teach or take degree in schooles. Take the word either in the generall signification, or in the speciall, yet will it fall out, that the doctour exhorted sometimes, and not onely taught.

Of the apostles, bishops, and pastors, there is no question, but that they exhorted. The apostle ioyneth exhortation and doctrine toge-
Πρόσεχε τῇ ἀναγνώσει, τῇ παρακλήσει, καὶ διδασκαλίᾳ. 1.*Tim.*4. ther, where he exhorteth *Timothie* to attend or continue in reading, exhortation and doctrine. Of pastours it is likewise manifest by their owne confession, and by this also, that the same persons were pastors and doctors as hath bene shewed.

The apostle *S. Paul,* when they suppose that he was a doctour of
*Act.*9. their new creation, vsed both exhortation and application: it is said that he taught in such sort, that all that heard him were amazed: which how it can be done without application or exhortation, I report me to some new reason, shortly to be coyned. That he moued affections, which is the sequell of exhortation and application, the words of the text declare, where the fretting of the Iewes and their conspiracie against him is noted.

In *Barnabas* it is yet more euident, the text hath in expresse termes that he did exhort, καὶ παρεκάλει πάντας τῇ προθέσει τῆς καρδίας προσμένειν τῷ κυρίῳ, that

is,

is, he exhorted them all with purpose of heart to cleaue to the Lord: in which speech there are euident markes of affectionate words and perswasions vsed by *Barnabas*, which name if it doe signifie the sonne of consolation as *S.Luke* interpreteth the same, euill shoulde hee deserue it, if he did neither comfort, exhort, nor apply, but onley barely teach. *Act.4.36.*

Of *Apollos* the Scriptures giue testimonie that he was an eloquent man, & mightie in the Scriptures, & that he proued with great vehemency that Iesus was the Christ: but meane scholers can tel, that there is small eloquence in teaching the first rudiments and principles of any science, and that the ende of eloquence is to perswade, and to mooue. which if the disciplinarians can doe without exhortation or application, they must sure doe it by miracle, or like the loadestone by some secret naturall qualitie. Further, if the Scriptures bee not for refutation onely, but for exhortation also, and many other purposes: and if also they profite not without application no more then if *Tho. Cartw.* should haue a sore finger, and keepe the plaster in his sachell: then must it follow that *Apollos* eyther was mightie but in some part and vse of Scripture, & that he taught to small purpose & profit of his hearers, or that with his teaching, he ioyned application, & exhortation which the wordes (*with great vehemencie*) doe also declare. For obseruing decencie, vehemencie cannot be vsed in short conclusions, nor in deliuerie of generall rules, but in forcible and earnest perswasion or exhortation. Moreouer, as the Apostle taketh planting to himselfe: so he giueth watring to *Apollos*, which requireth some more labour, affection and perswasion, then is vsuall in bare and ordinarie teaching. And if as ancient writers affirme, *Apollos* succeeded *Paul* in the ministerie at *Corinth*, or as a certaine doctor affirmeth, baptized, which he proueth in that he watred: then must he do the office of the pastor, not onely of doctor, at the least he must passe the boundes of bare teaching. *Act.18.* *1.Cor.1.*

Let vs descend to speake of the doctors of schooles, and we shall further perceiue, that it is a strange deuise to tie them to bare teaching, without exhortation and application. *Origens* lectures whom the disciplinarians transforme into a bare teaching doctor, were full of exhortations and applications. The man is by the iudgement of all learned, most eloquent: I appeale to *Th.Cartw.* himselfe, whether being doctor, or, that I displease him not, professor of Diuinitie, he did not often slippe aside into exhortation; and whether hee thinke it the part of a doctor, to leaue the place he handleth, without making vſe of his doctrine:or whether the doctors of *Geneua*, as they would limit others, doe keepe within compaſſe themſelues.

As the office of doctors, ſo the preciſe limitation of his labours to bare teaching, is a thing not heard of nor founde in ancient Eccleſiaſticall writers. Let them turne ouer *Chryſoſtome, Auguſtine, Ierom* and the reſt, and ſee if they can finde this limitation of offices, in any of
1.*Cor*.12. their writings. *Theodoret*, vpon the word *Doctores*, giueth vnto Doctors morall exhortation. What man then is ſo abſurd, as to heare the iarring of the diſciplinarians prating of their newe doctor, againſt generall conſent and harmonie of the ancient fathers, eſpecially ſeeing moſt of the newe writers yeelde their voyce to the fathers? *Peter*
In 1.*Sam*.19.23 *Martyr* furniſheth doctors as hath bene ſaide with gifts to teach, to exhort, to comfort. *Bullinger*, as he maketh paſtor and doctor all one,
In Act.13.1. ſo he nameth doctrine and exhortation in one man: yea, *Caluin* ſometime forgetting this nicety of bare teaching, giueth exhortation and teaching to doctors, whome hee ioyneth in ſignification with prophets. To conclude this diſtinction, as it hath bin ſhewed to be contrary to ſcripture, practiſe, and antiquitie: ſo it is voyde of ſence and reaſon. For what man can teach without perſwaſion, exhortation, and application? and ſeeing ſo much profite commeth of exhortation after the trueth is knowen, who will debarre the Church of this profite, or forbid a teacher to profite his audititorie?

Moreouer, ſeeing the doctor is no otherwiſe reſtreined to teaching, & kept from exhortation, then the paſtor reſtreined to exhortation & kept frō teaching (this ſuppoſed, that by him that teacheth, a doctor, and by him that exhorteth, a paſtor is vnderſtoode, which is but a weake dreame of diſcipline) either the office of paſtor is to be reſtrained to exhortation and kept from teaching, which they may not yeelde (for the Apoſtle requireth that he be διδακτικός) or els the doctors office to be inlarged to exhortation, which muſt needes follow. For the Apoſtle limitteth exhortation to him that exhorteth, as teaching to him that teacheth, both alike, and by like reaſon.

Laſtly, if the doctors of the Church of the Chriſtians repreſent either the ancient Prophets or the *Leuiticall* Doctors vnder the law, or the Sinagogical *Rabbins* which to build vp the doctors office as a corner of the Conſiſtorie, the diſciplinarians are readie to affirme: then
* *Ioſeph. adu.* as the Prophets taught and applied the lawe with continuall and
Appion. lib.2. moſt effectuall exhortations, as appeareth not by one place, but by
et Philo. lib.3. the whole tenour of their Prophecies: and as the Doctors that ſate
de vit. Moſ. in *Moſes* chayre, and the * *Rabbins* of the *Iewes* taught and exhorted,

in

in so much as the *Iewes* demaunded of *Saint Paul* if hee had any wordes of exhortation: so these newe Doctors, whether they succeede the Prophets, or sitte in the chaire of the Leuiticall or Synagogicall doctors, they are to teach and to exhort, or else they lose the glorie of their succession. But this is their plea for their doctors, that they succeede the Prophets and Leuiticall Doctors, and therefore they had neede to beware that their Doctor passe not his boundes of bare teaching, especially the gouernours of Synagogues, supplying the place of Pastor and Doctor.

The onely reason they haue to support the Doctors limitation in teaching (which they had neede to holde stiffly, lest they lose a principall part of their reformation) is their simple collection and argument grounded vpon the similitude drawne from the members of a bodie which the Apostle vseth *Rom.12.* to prooue the sobrietie that ought to be in the members of Christ. They leauing the termes which the Apostle vseth, frame other termes, and conceiue that diuersitie of giftes are compared to the diuersitie of actions of the members of mans body. Against which the text doth manifestly repugne: for not the actions, but the members of Christ and the partes of a naturall body are compared together: and actions in the sentences following the similitude, are nor limitted but distributed without limitation. After the comparison ended *verse 5.* the *Apostle* passeth forward to speake of diuers giftes, as appeareth by the note of transition δὲ. in ἔχοντες δὲ χαρίσματα that is, hauing moreouer graces, which hath relation and dependance of the wordes ὡς ὁ Θεὸς ἐμέρισε μέτρον πίστεως, and tendeth to perswade euery man to measure himselfe according to the graces giuen him: and not of the wordes: all haue not one action.

This then we answere to their obiection, that their reason drawne from a similitnde holdeth not, for that they passe the termes of Scripture. Secondly, that it maketh against their platformes interpreted as they would haue it: for if the Apostle woulde not haue Dostors to meddle with exhortation, for that euery one is to keepe himselfe to his gift; then may not the Pastors by like reason meddle with teaching, nor ruling, nor distributing, which is contrary to the *Analogie* of Scriptures.

But I stand all too long arguing against that, which for that it is contrary to Diuine and humahe authoritie, is reiected of all that haue any sparke of iudgement, and knowledge. Now therefore, let vs passe to talke of the Doctors gouernment.

Of the Parish Doctor and his office.

CHAP. 2 SECT. 4.

The course of this Section by diuers reasons carieth away the gouernment of Parish Doctors in Church affaires: First, for that they haue no title nor commission for gouernement. Secondly, no giftes sounding that way. Thirdly, for that they are supposed to succeede the Leuites and Prophets of the Iewes, which by vertue of their office had no gouernment. Fourthly, for that gouernment will hinder their schoole teaching. Fiftly, for that gouernment of the Church was committed to the Apostles and their successors. Sixtly, for that there is no practise of Doctors gouernment in Scriptures or Ecclesiasticall stories to be found. Seuenthly, the auctors of this opinion are not agreed vpon the Doctors gouernment themselues. Lastly, for that neither the name of Elder is giuen to Doctor, neither hath hee any likenesse or resemblance to the Leuiticall or Talmudicall Doctors.

NExt to the office of naked and bare teaching, commeth the doctors large office in gouernment of the Church to be scanned. Let not the doctor be offended with me, though I denigrate his dignitie. The course of this matter doth leade me thither. As for *T.Cartw.* he neede not be offended: for though hee loose the office of doctor, yet can he liue by his owne purchase.

The platformers giue vnto the doctor great dignitie: they place him with the first in the Consistorie: they adorne him with Consistoriall robes: they giue vnto him together with the rest of the Eldership, power to command, decree, set order, chuse, iudge, and vse the censures: by what authoritie, we cannot learne. And therefore we except against these newe intruders, and say that they are no competent Iudges.

1 For no man ought to take vpon him the gouernment of the Church, but those that haue authoritie and a lawfull calling, as had *Aaron* and other Priests, Prophets, and Ministers of God: but this doctor hath neither authoritie from God nor man, nor calling, nor warrant to gouerne, he cannot so much as shewe his title, much lesse his authoritie: if any man say otherwise, let him shewe where the doctor hath power to commaund, to iudge and excommunicate: if he cannot, let vs heare no more of an officer without warrant or commission.

This is a common hole of the disciplinarians.

2 The rules of discipline which say that no man is sent vpon a message without sufficient giftes, debarre the doctor from the gouernement of the Church: for hee hath nothing but the gift of teaching. wisedome, diligence and ruling are giuen to others. Wherefore, vnlesse he can shewe a better record of his office, as mariners are wont, we must call for a new man to the Helme of Church gouernment.

3 If

3 If the Doctors succeede the Leuites, then are they not to command. For the Leuites office was to minister by the lawes of the first ordination of Leuites: but that the disciplinarians do hold, and therefore vniustly thrust their doctors into the gouernment of the church. If the Leuites were iudges, it was not by vertue of their office, but by speciall commission from the Prince.

4 And so much the rather wee refuse the gouernment of parish doctors, for that they call them from a necessarie charge of teaching, and arguing in Schooles, wherein they are most exercised, and haue most skill, to vndertake an vnnecessarie burden no where imposed vpon them, and which for want of skill & experience, they are most vnfit to welde: especially if they bee so hastie and passionate, as the *Rabbins* of discipline, that challenge the name of Doctors.

5 The commission of our Sauiour graunted to his Apostles and to their successors the godly bishops and pastors, might teach doctors to be wise with sobrietie, and not to inuade that which belongeth to others. To them our Sauiour graunted the keyes of gouernment, and committed the flocke to be fedde. they are called rulers and gouernours of the Church: and others beside the Christian magistrate, and them, we knowe none: they are called ἡγούμενοι rulers. *Heb. 13.* Of these doctors there is not so much as any mention, and therefore they cannot without transgressing Christes order, and doing wrong to the Apostles and their successours, meddle with that belongeth to others.

6 The gouernment of doctors hath no example nor rule to warrant it in Scriptures. Let the aduerse party produce one place where any one doctor hath prescribed orders, excōmunicated, or proceeded iudicially against any person if they can. of the masters of Synagogues there is some suspicion, that they did excommunicate. the *Talmudists* report that *Rabbi Iehosuas* excommunicated *Iesus* of *Nazaret*: but *Petr. Gal.* what is this to doctors that seeke autoritie from the word rather then *lib. 1. c. 7.* the fantasticall traditions of the *Iewes*?

7 The same is condemned of all antiquitie, admit *Origen, Pantenus*, and *Clement* were such doctors as they conceiue; yet Ecclesiasticall stories say they gouerned not, but were gouerned by the bishops. Search all antiquitie, they shall not finde either any doctors gouernement, or other gouernment then by the Prince and by Bishops. These haue the presidentship giuen by *Iustin Martyr*, who calleth them προεστῶτες, and *Tertullian* that calleth them Presidents: these were they that in Synodes decided controuersies, and set orders, in which there is not the least steppe, or appearance of doctorall gouernment.

F 8 Lastly

8 Lastly, the platformers are in this poynt forsaken of their owne friends. *Doctores* (saith *Caluin*) *Nec disciplinæ nec sacramentorũ administrationi, nec monitionibus nec exhortationibus præsunt.&c. Pastorale munus hæc omnia in se continet.* Doctors haue not to deale in discipline, administration of sacraments, admonitions or exhortations &c. But the office of pastors comprehendeth all these things. *Zanchius* that graue father & learned diuine, although otherwise caried away with the receiued opinion of late writers in the matter of discipline, yet in this matter speaketh against them, *Hi* (saith he speaking of doctors) *tantũ docebant, illi verò (vz pastores) sacramenta etiã administrabant et disciplinæ præerant.* the doctors (saith he) taught only: pastors, they administred the Sacraments, and had the administration of discipline: neither doth he disallowe the fathers gouernement by bishops, and the orders wee haue in our Church. *Iunius* doth circumscribe the doctor, within the compasse of scholes, and therefore entitleth him *Scholasticum Doctorem. Beza* although he thrust doctors in the croud among Elders, yet doe I not finde where he maketh, much lesse proueth them necessarie parts of the consistorie, as do the disciplinarians, men of famous name. The practise of Churches notwithstanding is quite against them: they of *Geneua* haue no doctors of Diuinitie but pastors, the regents of scholes come not into the Consistorie. In the French Churches the doctors haue no credite. the Scottish Churches leaue thẽ out of ẏ rolle of the consist. & so did *T.C.* once, though now euery day he waxe wiser then other, & change his opiniõs. his masters of the Admonition raile doctors out of their consistorial robes, & few there be that fauour them saue certaine vagrant ministers, which vnlesse they hide themselues vnder this title, are like generally to bee condemned, as intruders into the ministerie, & perturbers of the state.

Instit. lib. 4. c. 3.

Zanch. conf.

Ecclesi. lib. 2. c. 5.

Adu. Erast.

To hide the nakednesse of the doctor, they make him, notwithstanding his maiestie and greatnesse, to creepe into two pore holes, the first found out by *Daneau*, though with small iudgement, the other by one of our Church plotters directed, as it seemeth, thither by *Beza*, or found out as they were raking in the *Iewes* Talmud. *Daneau* considering, & as it were lamenting the nakednes of their down-feathered doctor newly hatched, giueth vnto him the garments that belong to bishops & pastors to cloth him, Bishops, Elders, Pastors & doctors, (saith he) are names cõfounded, & interchanged in scriptures: & therfore what belõgeth to any one, belõgth vnto al & euery of thẽ seuerally. but what if his *antecedent* were denied? sure then is he at the end of his matter: for he proueth nothing: he will not confesse I trow,

Isag. part. 3.

that

that all elders are bishops: if he doe, away must the profane elders, which are not ministers of the word, bee packing. and although pastors and doctors be diuers names of one person in scriptures, yet doth it not followe that the doctor which they woulde haue, is the doctor spoken of in the scriptures, or that their parish doctor is called elder. Nowe, seeing neither *Antecedent* is true nor consequent good, the reason is starke nought. for Apostles are called ministers, bishops, and pastors, and contrariwise, some bishops are in a generall signification called Apostles: yet doe I not suppose that *Daneau* will grant that whatsoeuer belongeth to the Apostles, is common to pastors or bishops: the communitie of names is no argument of the communication of properties of things. there is an instrument of musicke called a harpe: the Hatters they call a certaine instrument they haue, a Harpe likewise: yet is that a melodious instrument, this a iarring and absurd implement. and therefore were it graunted, that bishops and doctours were sometimes spoken of one person: yet vnlesse the office be one, which they denie, the name shall not helpe the doctor so, but that if he vndertake the gouernment of the Church, hee may be remoued with a writ of *Nouel disseisin.*

Certaine of our disciplinarians placing small hope in the other argument, deriue the doctors authoritie from the *Iewish* presbyterie, and Leuiticall doctors: which argument consisteth of many pieces. Answere to *Br.* sland.

First, they take as graunted, that Christ translated the Consistorie or Sanedrin from the *Iewes* into his Church, at least they desire it to be graunted *tanquam* αἴτημα γεωμετρικόν: which if it be denyed, they can goe no further, vnlesse it be to them of *Geneua* to complaine that wee admit not their fancies. Secondly, they desire vs to beleeue that the same Consistorie is to be placed in euery congregation. Thirdly, they must presuppose that it was not cracked, nor dissolued in the remoouing of it, but that it came into the church with all his partes. Fourthly, they desire vs to beleeue that the Presbyterie of the *Iewes* had doctors likewise. Fiftly, that they had the same authoritie that is giuen to these doctors. Sixtly, that the same is translated to the doctors which they haue. It is long to set downe the rest of their desires. by this you may easily coniecture what a frame we are like to haue, whẽ the partes are so weake & so euill glued together: all which are answered with one worde, that these thinges are very handsome to bee conceiued, but incredible & impossible to be proued, as they shall see when they list to trie. They only attempt to proue that the *Iewes* had doctors of the lawe: the rest they dispaire of, and therefore wisely neuer goe about it: well, let vs see their skill in proouing.

As a ground of Geometrie.

The Iewish *sanedrin* maketh nothing for Doctors gouernment.

Deut.31.26. *Moses* (say they) speaking to the *Leuites* saith, Take ye this booke of the Lawe, and put it into the side of the Arke, &c. that it may bee there for a witnes against you, *ergo* the Leuitical doctors were of the Iewish Presbyterie, and handled matters of Church gouernment, which is a miserable and pitifull kinde of consequence, not to be answered in one word. for not so much as teaching is in this place prooued to belong to the Leuites. for they are commaunded to put vp, not to open the booke, and the booke is layd vp for a record, and not layde open for instruction: of gouernement there is no
Deut.33.10. mention. againe *Moses* saith, that they shall teach *Iacob* the iudgements of God, and *Israel* his lawe, and shall put incense before the presence of God: which belong to the priestes, whose office it was to burne incense, and not to the rest of the Leuites. of the Leuiticall doctors, beside priestes, and of their gouernment there is here no mention. These and such like places forced by the disciplinarians against their meaning, doe rather conuince them of forging and facing, then prooue the matter in question.

This therefore is euident, that as many reasons make against the gouernment of doctors: so there is neither autoritie of Scripture, nor fathers to couer them. Now let vs see what reason they haue to place doctors in euery congregation.

Of the Parish Doctor, and his office.

CHAP. 2 SECT. 5.

Wherein is shewed that Doctors are not necessarily to be placed in euery congregation, by reasons drawen first from the noueltie of the office. Secondly from the examples of Barnabas *and* Apollo, Origen *&* Pantenus. *Thirdly, from the practise of the Apostolike & ancient Church. Fourthly, from the customes of late Churches. Fiftly, from the charge and impossibilitie. Lastly, for that* T. Cartw. *reasons prooue nothing to the contrary. In the same section, the imperfection of their platformes concerning the Doctor is prooued, for that diuers matters of great weight are neither resolued nor thought of, which must needes breede both question and trouble in the gouernment.*

That they are not necessarie for euery congregation, doth necessarily followe of the former conclusions: for if there were no such Doctor as they surmise, nor had any commission of gouernement such as they giue vnto him; what shoulde wee doe with an office that was neuer, and encrocheth vpon gouernours that euer haue bene? what shoulde he doe in any parish?

My

My firſt reaſon therefore againſt the placing of doctours in euery 1
pariſh, is this, That he is a new creature, riſing (as *Venus* did out of the
ſea) of the froth of mens fancies: for the doctours of the primitiue
Church were of another ſort; and the doctours of ſchooles are for
ſchooles, not for villages.

And were the doctour ſuch as *Apollos* or *Barnabas*; yet can not the 2
example of either of theſe helpe them to prooue that doctors ſhould
be in euery congregation, but the contrary rather: for of ſuch as theſe
were, few were in any Congregation, and theſe were not tied to any
one place. *Apollos* was of the citie of *Alexandria*: he taught before *Act.*18.
he came to *Epheſus*: for he was δυνατὸς ἐν ταῖς γραφαῖς before he came thither. Mightie in
he taught at *Epheſus*: he taught afterward in *Achaia*, and laſtly, at *Co-* Scriptures.
rinth, the head citie of that countrie. I thinke our diſciplinarians will
not allow their doctours to roue at ſo many marks, nor go from their
churches at pleaſure, as did *Apollos* from *Epheſus*. If then (as they
ſay) doctours be bound to their churches, the example of *Apollos*
helpeth them nothing. Of *Barnabas* the acts do giue teſtimony, that
he was companion with *Paul* in moſt of his iourneyes: which doth
ouerthrow the reſtreint of doctours to pariſhes, this being ſuppoſed
that *Barnabas* was a doctour.

Such doctours as was *Origen*, *Pantenus*, and their fellowes, were 3
ſingular to the Church of *Alexandria*, and ſuch churches as had
ſchooles. *Euſebius* doth ſhew that theſe doctours were not reputed *Eccl. hiſt.*
any degree of the miniſtery. Such are our doctours of the Diuinitie *lib.6.*
ſchoole in the Vniuerſities, which ſort of doctours it is ridiculous to
place in euery pariſh.

If this had bene the inſtitution of Chriſt, then would the apoſtle 4
haue placed doctours in euery pariſh, as he placed elders in euery citie. But looke the whole hiſtory of the firſt Church, there appeareth *Epiſt.ad Tim.*1.
no notice of doctours; where the Apoſtle preſcribeth, as it were, a *& ad Tit.*
ſtate of the miniſtery, and orders for the Church, very exactly, he
doth not ſo much as mention doctors, other then biſhops & paſtors.

In the time of the ancient Fathers, we reade of no miniſters of the 5
Church, but biſhops, prieſts, deacons, and inferiour clerks: what *Can. Apoſt.*
an errour had it bene, if doctours had bene gouernours, to haue omit- *Conc.Nic.*
ted them? and how incredible is it, that there ſhould not be found in *Tertul.de*
any one pariſh, ſuch an officer as they ſuppoſe to haue bene in euery *baptiſ.*
Church?

Nay, how abſurd is it, ſeeing the Scriptures know no doctours but 6
paſtours, as it is euident *1.Cor.12.* to deuiſe an other kinde of doctor,

and to place him without warrant in euery parish? If there were do-ctors beside pastors, let them name them, & shew who they shuld be. At *Philippi* there were none; for there were onely bishops & deacons: if they say doctours were saluted by the name of bishops, there is no reason for it. Men do not salute *Richard* by the name of *Thomas*, nor when a man doth name a man, doth he vnderstand a beast. In the church of *Antioch* the doctors were apostles & bishops. In the churches of *Asia* and *Crete*, and those named in the Acts of the apostles, there were no parish doctors: where were they then? forsooth in *Platoes* Commonwealth, or *Mores vtopia* gouerning the Church there.

Phil.1.

7 But if their doctours be so necessary in euery parish, as they conceiue, how chance they haue none in the French Churches, saue in great cities, and so few in Scotland and the Low countries? if the doctor be a member of the Church (as they beleeue) why are they so deformed and maymed? if doctours be so necessary, why are they more in one parish then another?

8 Finally, to say that doctors ought to be in euery parish, is to giue a rule to poore parishes most burthensome, litle profitable, & through this realme impossible. To maintaine doctours beside pastorus, were burthensome: and seeing the doctor doth nothing which the pastor ought not to do, vnprofitable: and to find doctors to supply all parishes through the realme, is impossible. Wherefore, vnlesse they can shew where doctors are first instituted; secondly, where appointed to be in euery parish; and thirdly, how it may be possibly, we will neuer allow them for doctors of discipline in our schoole.

I doubt not, but some disciplinary doctour will be angry when he seeth his dignity thus annihilated. therfore to refrigerate the heat of his choler, may it please him to consider two or three colde reasons which *Th. Cart.* bringeth forth, if he can not procure him triumphant entrance into the whole Church, at least to helpe him to intertein-ment in some few parishes.

Answere to the arguments of the aduerse partie.

Doctors (saith he) had their name of churches, *ergo* doctors ought to be in euery church. what if I deny his antecedent, as *Iunius* & his friend *Beza* doth, who say doctors are called of schooles? then is this argument quassed: but denying both antecedent and consequent, much more will the friuolous weaknesse of it appeare. for admit we haue doctors of Diuinity in the church of *Cambridge* and *Oxford*, yet he himselfe knoweth that they are not in all parishes. The church of the *Iewes* had a high priest, had inferior priests teachers of the law: yet had they neither high priest nor priests that taught the law in

euery

euery village or parish.

But (saith he) there is some signe yet remaining of ancient doctors placed in euery church, in that in our Cathedral churches there is one that readeth a lecture. Admit in all Cathedrall churches there were readers, therefore in euery church resorting or depending of the mother church? these readers they came in by late statutes, and were not alwayes, nor in any thing resemble the new doctors, for that they are ministers of the word and sacraments, and vse exhortation.

Thirdly, where *Titus* was left to appoint elders, city by city, he beleeueth that he appointed doctors also; for that they in the new deformation are accounted a kinde of elders: which must needs proceed of a strong conceit, or of a bad conscience. for if he thinke euery place that commeth in his way to make for him, he hath a strong imagination, as had he that beleeued all the ships that came into the hauen of *Athens*, to be his owne goods. If he doe not beleeue that which he allegeth, with what conscience doth he vse so friuolous proofes, and manifest misallegation of texts? to allege one office for another, is not to prooue, but to confound, and trifle. We deny that doctors are termed elders in Scriptures; and though it were granted, yet the common phrase of speech, where it is said that *Titus* was left to ordaine elders, and where the Euangelist saith that *Paul* and *Barnabas* appointed elders, will not admit that he should speake of all sorts of elders, seeing in affirmatiue propositions the word pronounced of another is taken particularly and confusedly, saue where the termes are conuertible. οὐδεμία κατάφασις ἀληθὴς ἔσται ἐν ᾗ τοῦ κατηγορουμένου καθόλου, τὸ καθόλου κατηγορεῖται. And though he regard neither phrase of speech, nor rules of Logike, yet the words folowing in *Tit. 1.* declare that the apostle speaketh of bishops, such as exhort. And *Acts 14.* vnlesse pastors be meant only, one word must signifie doubtfully diuers things of diuers kinds contrediuided one against another. But what shuld I contend against him any longer, that contendeth not only against al authority & antiquity, but the light of the text and himselfe also? In his first treatise he passed this worthy doctor in silence, vsing the word in great contempt against his aduersary. Only this last reason discussed lightly, and the defects of their discipline concerning doctor, noted, I will leaue the doctor to those that are enamored of him.

Act. 14.

Aristot. περὶ ἑρμην. c. 5.

The Church (saith *Th. Cartwr.*) can not be interteined without exhortation and doctrine: therefore there must be a pastour and doctor in euery parish. A reason like to this, that the Church must haue praier, preaching, and the administration of sacraments, *ergo* there must

 be

be diuers miniſters to do theſe things. The ſequell is leud and looſe. And falſe it is, that *Th. Cartwr.* affirmeth, theſe things to be parted betweene the doctor & paſtor: for it is the paſtors duty to teach and exhort; and were the partition made, yet are not doctours required in euery pariſh: for the church gouernment is parted betwixt the ciuill magiſtrate and biſhops, yet neither requiſit in euery pariſh: yet hath this better reaſon, for we know that the prince is Gods miniſter: what this new doctour will prooue, neither they nor we know.

A briefe repetition of the ſumme of this chapter.

Wherefore, ſeeing neither the preheminence of doctours, nor diſtinction from paſtours, nor the limitation of his office, nor the commiſſion for the doctours gouernment, nor the neceſſity of doctours in euery pariſh, which are the principall points of their doctorall diſcipline, hath any inſtitution, confirmation, or allowance of Chriſt or his apoſtles: where they tel vs their diſcipline is drawen from ſcripture, let vs holde this rule: Firſt that their mouthes are no meaſure of trueth, and that they haue no Scripture for their doctour: next, that they haue neither allowance of antiquity nor reaſon: and laſt of all, that their plats are rather bubbles of fantaſy, then rules of Church policy.

Theſe be arguments ſufficient to reiect their doctorall deuiſes. but that you may perceiue the wiſdome of theſe law-makers, you ſhall ſee, if all were granted vnto them they deſire, yet how many things they want, and into what diſorder they would throw this Church and Commonwealth.

Their platformes defectiue in the office of doctor.

What time of ſtudy is required in him that ſhall haue the name of a doctor, and what age he ought to be of, (which is a neceſſary matter, conſidering that boyes are not for gouernment) and what knowledge he ought to haue, they ſay nothing. Concerning his office, they tell vs not whether a doctour may teach in two places, or the ſame man be a doctour in one place, and a paſtor in another, or whether he ought to teach priuately, as the paſtour is to exhort priuately: nor whether the doctours of Philoſophy and arts, be doctours of the Church, as *Iunius* would haue it, nor prooue that arts ſhoulde be taught out of the Vniuerſitie: they tell vs not whether a doctour muſt proceede at the Vniuerſity, or in the pariſh, at the croſſe in the Church-yard, that is, as a man ſhould ſay, at Dawes croſſe: nor whether he muſt haue impoſition of hands, or that it is ſufficient that the pariſh nominate him doctour, without other ceremony. Likewiſe, whether the doctor remoouing from the Church, loſe his title or no, and whether he may ſupply the paſtors office in exhorting, or whe-

ther

ther he may be president of the consistory or no, they leaue it in suspence. What hospitality the doctour is to keepe, may be put *inter insolubilia Petri de Alliaco:* for considering the basenesse of his pension, it is to be feared least he rather gnaw his nailes, then keepe any hospitality. Whether a doctour may be the maister of an hospitall, which is the deacons office, is a great question; for they say that *Th. Cartwright* wil rather suffer this confusion of members of the church, then giue ouer his hospitall. It is moreouer doubtfull whether a doctour, being maister of an hospitall, may gouerne by orders, which had their originall from the pope. Further, how the doctour shall recouer his pension, being denied, and before whom; and whether falling sicke, so that he can no more execute his function, he shall reteine his stipend: and whether he haue freeholde in his pension or holde it at the will of the lords of the consistory, they say nothing. For what defects and defaults he shall lose his stipend, they speake doubtfully: whether hauing appealed from those that deposed him, he is to continue in possession of his office or no, they determine not. But the greatest question is this, seeing the drudgery and seruility of parish doctours is so great, and so intollerable, the reward so vilde and miserable, the pride of the people and consistory so lordly, where learned men can be gotten that will liue in such slauery.

Seeing then, so many matters of importance not resolued, neither by our disciplinarians that are but learners; nor by the great maisters that first deuised their discipline: let them tell vs no more of the perfection of their plats, nor vse any more commendation of it. We tell them, nay we will prooue it to their faces, if they dare abide the incounter, that, compared with our gouernment, it is but a piece of raw and vndigested policy.

That the doctour and his office, which is a great part of their discipline, is but a new inuention, hath bene declared: therefore setting a marke on his forehead, for a new creature of discipline; let vs passe forward to speake of the pastour, which is an office of greater credit and authority, yet not a litle stayned and disgraced with the disciplinarians nouelties.

Of the Pastour, and his office.

Chap. 3. Sect. 1.

In this section first, is declared the state of the controuersie betweene vs, concerning the pastor and his office, and what the aduersaries do holde, and how they leudly confound bishops and inferiour ministers, election and ordination in the ministery, and any office in the minister. Secondly, the election or necessary consent of the people in election of pastors, is disprooued by the examples of Paul, Timothy, *&* Titus, *by ancient councels, fathers, histories, reasons, and the allegations of the aduersary answered. Thirdly, the election of pastors by the consistory is ouerthrowen, for that there can no proofe be brought of any such, much lesse of any such power it had, by testimony of* Chrysostome, *and antiquity, and also by diuers reasons.*

FOr the name of pastor, be it metaphoricall, or howsoeuer, we will not striue: neither will we greatly contend about the office of the pastor, which we confesse to consist especially in praying, preaching, & administring of the sacraments. and I would to God that some pastors, curious in finding faults in others, & carping & controlling matters, which they neither vnderstand, nor can amēd; would look more diligently to their office, & not weaken ẏ hands of others, that diligently attend on their charge. But how can others moderate their tongues, & restraine their malice, seeing they haue nor keepe nor moderation of their tongues and affections themselues? About the name & office we contend not, but rather by whom pastours are to be chosen & ordeined, and how to be qualified, and for what causes to be deposed. Likewise, whether all pastors be of equall degree, and whether they may beare ciuill offices, and haue ciuill titles attributed vnto them, and whether they be strictly limited and restrained to one parish; and finally, whether two pastors may be appointed for one parish or no.

The state of the question concerning ministers of the word, and their office.

They holde concerning election of the pastor, diuersly: some holde, that the people is to chuse: some say that the eldership chuseth, and the people onely consent. they teach that the eldership ought to ordeine, & further, that none is to be ordeined but such as haue the qualities required in a bishop, *1.Tim.3.* and that those that come in otherwise, or entring the ministery, cease to haue those qualities, are to be deposed. The degree of bishops they condemne and remooue; and teach that all pastours ought to be equall. they debase them so, that they thinke it not lawfull for them to haue the title of lord; and disfranchise them so, that they may not beare ciuill office, no, not committed to them by the prince. they will not allow one minister to haue two benefices, as we call them, or two parishes vnder his charge, but yet can indure, nay thinke it very conuenient that one parish should haue two pastors. Against which strange & vaine assertions

The opinions of the disciplinarians, in the cause of the pastor.

.ons we are now to dispute,beginning with the election of the pastor: wherin that you may the better vnderstand both the controuersie & the decision thereof,we are in this question to distinguish,first of pastors,then betwixt election & ordination,lastly,betwixt orders,or ordination, or inauguration of ministers,and their other offices. which the platformers not doing, haue abused others, and confounded themselues as in a labirinth of matters,and resolued nothing.

Pastors or ministers of the word and sacraments, all the ancient fathers haue diuided into bishops, and priests, or elders. whether bishops & elders be equall by the word of God or not,we shall dispute hereafter: sufficeth here,that all antiquity hath distinguished bishops from priests. there can be no instance brought contrary,and therfore I need not here to proue it:that which shall be sufficient,shall be spoin his proper place. Now as ancient fathers,and councels haue giuen the appointment of priests to bishops onely, so in the nomination of the bishop, ancient practise hath either required, or at least vsed the acclamations,or els the silent consent of the people. According to antiquity, the bishop in this realme is chosen by the presbytery of the Church, consisting not of blinde and vnlettered dolts,but of learned men and ministers of the word; we call it the Chapter. After the election made by them, the bishop is brought forth before the people, and by them allowed; of which a solemne act is made: so that first, the disciplinarians fault in confounding bishops and inferior ministers of the word,whose case in this matter of election differed much. For to prooue that the people ought to chuse their minister, they allege authorities that testifie that they did chuse by acclamations their bishop, which made nothing to the purpose. This distinction taketh away all *Cartwrights* reasons from authority of fathers, which he either in this point vnderstood not or marked not, or els, that I do him no wrong, dissembled his knowledge. Next they do vs wrong, that say that in England a bishop is imposed vpon the people without their knowledges, and better consent then in the French churches. And lastly, they do you wrong, to persuade you that bishops might not chuse priests: for both they ordeined them, or, as we call it in more vsuall English,ordered thẽ,which was by imposition of hands, and prayer: and also they sent them from the mother city abroad into villages to teach, as is apparant by that authority that is giuen to bishops, *Conc. Nic. can. 16. & 17.* and infinit acts of councels.

Two degrees of the ministers of the word.

Conc. Nic. and generally all councels and fathers.

Therefore betweene the orders and office of preaching, praying, and administring of sacraments, both of bishops & priests there was no difference:for both receiued one orders and office to preach,pray, and administer the sacraments: but the difference was, that a bishop was ordeined by more bishops then one, priests were ordered by one bishop: the bishop was elected and ordeined, the priests had no election, but first an ordination, and then a designment to a place, which improperly is called election. Here likewise, the disciplinarians fault, that they conceiued that no priests were ministers of the word: secondly, that all ministers of the word were chosen by the people; for so they should neuer haue beene taught: thirdly, that where there is a generall order set downe by the whole realme, whereto all particulars are supposed to giue their consent, by which ministers are appoynted to their places; they notwithstanding giue out most vntruely, that ministers are thrust vpon parishes by the bishop without their consent, whereas all their consents was to the law: & any one man may except against him that is instituted,within tenne dayes, and the bishop hath no more to do, but to see whether the party that is presented, be sufficient; and if he be,to put him in possession; and if not, to heare those that will obiect against him, and repell him.

Can.Apost.
Text.de baptis.
Ignat.

Ordination of a minister, I call the imposition of hands and designation of a fit person to the ministery. Office of a minister, I call whatsoeuer is imposed vpon him, either by vertue of his first ordination or other lawful authority. The ordination of the priests & Leuits was their first inauguration, and presentation before God, in which respect they were priests and Leuites: the same being made iudges by *Moses*, *Dauid*, and *Iehosaphat*, had by a new authority, the office of a iudge imposed on them. So had the bishop of *Arles* by *Constantine* the office of a iudge imposed in the cause of *Cecilian* bishop of *Carthage*. Here the disciplinarians erre, first in that they distinguish not the office of a minister from ordination,or the office of the ministery: and because ciuill offices are not the office of the ministery, thinke he may do nothing but that of the ministery, which you see otherwise in the examples alleged, and shall (God willing) see the same sufficiently prooued, when we come vnto the place assigned to it. Secondly, where they allow him no office but that whereto he is ordeined: they forget he is a subiect, a friend, a father, a husband, which impose diuers offices vpon him. But I maruell not,if they that vnderstand neither duety to their prince, nor to their brethren, doe leudly dispute about offices, either of ministers or others.

This premised, let vs nowe come to the proofe of matters in question.

stion. First I will (God willing) shewe that the people did not, nor ought to chuse their ministers, against that which *T.Cartw.* did first hold: then, that the Consistorie did neuer chuse them, against that opinion which nowe he holdeth. that the people ought to vnderstand of the choyse of the bishop of the Diocesse, and in some sorte yeelde consent, is not in question: for it is the practise of this Church. ordination of ministers I will shewe also that it neuer belonged to the Consistorie, but to bishops, and that not the Consistorie, but bishops, designed or appoynted ministers to their places.

The first point I proue first by testimonie of Scriptures, then by attestation of antiquitie, lastly by diuers reasons drawen from both these, and their owne practise. Of *Paul* and *Barnabas* the Euangelist giueth testimonie, that hauing conuerted diuers to Christianitie in *Lystra, Iconium, Antioch, Derbe* and other Cities, they appointed ministers vnto them: the words are playne, that they appointed, and that the people had ministers appoynted to them. for the wordes are χειροτονήσαντες δ' αὐτοῖς, wherein by a plaine relation the action of the Apostles is separated from the rest of the people.

That the people did neuer chuse their ministers. *Act.*14.

That is, when they had ordeined vnto them.

Of *Timothie* it is plaine, that he was sent to *Ephesus* by *Paul*. therefore saith the Apostle. as I exhorted thee to continue at *Ephesus*. for so the word προσμεῖναι doth signifie. Let the aduerse party shewe where the people did chuse him: nay it appeareth hee was there appoynted against some of their willes, for he was to command some, that they should teach no other doctrine, then that of the Gospel. That which they say of his office of Euangelist, shall then be refuted, when wee come to examine whether he was a bishop or no.

1.*Tim.*1. To continue.

The Apostles wordes are plaine, that *Titus* did appoynt ministers to euery Citie: yea, that himselfe was appoynted to that place by the Apostle. that he was chosen thither by them of *Crete* it is not sayde, neither is it probable: nor can there bee any suspicion brought, that they of the Iland did chuse their ministers, *Titus* moderating the action as they obiect: for although a captaine may bee sayde to doe that, which he doth with his souldiers: yet is there not like reasons in elections that be popular. for there the whole commaundement is in the generall and chiefe Captaine: in popular elections the people claimeth freedome, and chiefe autoritie. and seeing the speech is improper, that maketh one to doe that, which he doth not by himselfe: what reason haue the disciplinarians to forsake the proper phrase, to seeke out another, of which they can yeelde no reason? be it that the Consul is sayde to chuse, when the Senat chuseth (of which not-

*Tit.*1.

 withstanding,

withstanding I finde no example, whatsoeuer *T.Cartw.* vntruely fathereth vpon *Liuie*, vpon whom he looked not, but followed his master *Caluin*:) yet why it shoulde be so construed in this place, hee can alledge no proofe, neither is it vsuall by profane autors to expounde the scriptures: nor hath that reason any sequele, It is sometime so taken, therefore here so taken.

The ancient fathers, they continuing in the steppes of the holy *Can. Apost.* Apostles, obserued the same order which the ancient Canons of the Church confirme by lawe: πρεσβύτεροι ὑφ' ἑνὸς ἐπισκόπου χειροτονείσθω, καὶ διάκονος, καὶ οἱ λοιποὶ κληρικοί. Priestes let them be ordeined by one Bishop, likewise Deacons, & the rest of the clerkes. if the ordination to the ministerie was made by bishops: then surely the appoyntment to their places much mor, eseeing ancient Canons excepting in certaine cases forbid absolute ordination (as they cal them) or ordinations without designement to a place or assignation of a pension in title.

Can. 16. et 17. The councell of *Nice* decreed that it should not be lawfull for any minister of the Church to bee appoynted to another Church, then where he first serued, without his bishops consent: & that he should not depart from his place where he was appoynted, without the bishops leaue; which plainely argueth that the designement of priests to their places, was by bishops onely: of which I neede not longer dispute, seeing al antiquitie giueth the gouernment & placing of priests *Ad Tarsen.* to bishops, οἱ πρεσβύτεροι ὑποτάσσεσθε τῷ ἐπισκόπῳ, that is, let priestes obey their bishoppes sayeth *Ignatius*, ἄνευ τοῦ ἐπισκόπου μηδὲ πρεσβύτερος, μὴ διάκονος, μὴ λαϊκός, *Ad Magnes.* without the bishop neither doth the priest, nor deacon, nor lay man any thing in the Church, saith the same *Ignatius*.

Epist. 3. lib. 1. The gouernment of the bishop is called by *Cyprian* a diuine and high power, which appeareth partly in that he hath the gouernment *Lib. 3. epist 14.* of priests committed vnto him, as *Cyprian* likewise witnesseth.

Chryso. de sacer. *Chrysostome* speaking of the bishop that shoulde appoynt him his charge, hath these words: τοῦ μέλλοντος ἡμᾶς χειροτονήσειν ἐλθόντος, when he came that should ordeine vs.

de baptism. *Tertullian* giueth chiefe place to the bishop aboue priestes, for the honour & peace of the Church. looke the whole course of Ecclesiasticall stories; you shall finde that bishops alone ordeined & appointed places to priests. *Euseb. eccl. hist. lib. 6. c. 35.* of *Nouatus* it is reported, that the bishoppe made him priest, against the will of the whole clergie. Nothing more famous, then how *Arrius* was made priest, & deposed by the bishop of *Alexandria*.

Ierom was made priest by *Paulinus*, *Paulinus*, by *Epiphanius* bishop

of

of *Cyprus. Ierom epist.61. et epist.62. gaudeat episcopus iudicio suo, cum tales Christo elegerit Sarerdotes:* let the bishoppe reioyce (saith *Ierom ad Nepot.*) in his iudgement, when he hath chosen such priestes vnto Christ. *Hæc spectet sacerdos et quod cuique cõgruat, id officij deputet.* let the bishop (saith *Ambrose*) consider these things, and assigne vnto euery one that office whereto he is most fit. and least any man might conceiue that any elders concurred with the bishop, he saith; no man can giue that hee hath not receiued, speaking of officers of the ministerie: *Nemo tribuit quod non accepit.* *Ad Pammach.* *Ad Nepot.* *Offic.lib.1.c.44.* *In 1.Tim.3.*

Basill was ordeined of *Eusebius*, and *Gregorie* of *Basill*, as *Nazianzen* testifieth of him selfe. neither can they alledge any word for the election of priestes by people, or Church aldermen, nor bring an instance against the ordination of priestes by bishops onely. these reasons make equally for election and ordination, for that priestes serued in the Church wherein they were ordeined. *In Monod.*

I say againe, that the disciplinarians cannot shew one priest (for so I interpret *Presbyterum*) that was chosen by the people to any one place. I speake not of bishops, but of priests: for albeit for manifold inconueniences the election of bishops by the people, was forbidden by the counsell of *Laodicea*, and although there bee no commandement of it, nor example in scriptures: yet it appeareth, that the people haue vsed acclamations or approbation at the election of bishops.

So is it nowe continued in this Church, and is not in their discipline: by the which, most disorderly and absurdly, they haue remooued both bishops, and their election out of the Church, whatsoeuer they prate of election of Bishops.

Yet doe I finde, that euen in the election of bishoppes, wherein to incourage the people, more libertie was graunted vnto them, the suffrages of the people were not alwayes necessarie, as appeapeareth first in the examples of *Timothie* and *Titus*, and after in those who succeeded the Apostles, as *Marke* at *Alexandria*, *Linus* succeeding *Paul* or *Peter* at *Rome*, *Dionysius* at *Athens*, *Symeon* succeeding *Iames* at *Ierusalem*. Not the people, but the Synode had the chiefe sway in the Ecclesiasticall elections, as appeareth in Constantines letters to the Synode, that they shoulde not translate *Eusebius* from *Cæsarea* to *Antiochia*. *Euseb.eccl.hist.* *De vita Const. lib.3. c.6.*

The Synode of *Antiochia* deposed *Paul* of *Samosata*, and substituted *Domnus*. *Euseb.eccl.hist. lib.7.c.24.*

The Synod of *Ephesus* deposed *Nestorius*, & placed another. *Acholius* was chosen bishop of *Thessalonica* by other bishops, *Amb.epist.59.* and

and all those placings and displacings, that fell out during the trobles of *Athanasius* and the contention betweene *Epiphanius* and *Chrysostome* and others, were done by bishops and synodes, by the consent and voyce for the most part of the soueraigne magistrate. *Valentinian* committed election to bishops. *Theodoret. Hist. lib. 4. c. 5.*

All which things make nothing for popular elections vsed by the disciplinarians, who I thinke will blush to challenge that power which the people had, and shame to followe their example. they may remember the bloodie broyle betweene *Damasus*, and his competitor, of which a heathen writer maketh mention, the disorder and slaughter was so notorious. betwixt *Boniface* the second likewise, and *Dioscorus* there fell out a foule stirre: he that cōmendeth popular elections, let him consider the tumultes raysed at *Constantinople* about the choyse of their bishop, and howe many seditions, hurliburlies, schismes, and deuisions fell out about the elections of the bishops of *Antiochia, Alexandria, Rome* and other places. Of these schismes and diuisions about the election of bishops made by popular fauour, the fathers haue oft complained: wherefore let them not thinke that antiquitie doeth speake any thing in fauour of popular elections. whatsoeuer by tumult or faction hath bene of the people practised, many reasons make against it.

Ammian. Marcel.

Sozom. lib. 3. c. 4.

Socrat lib. 5. c. 9. et Euseb. histor.

The gouernment of the Church, whether it bee Monarchicall, in respect of Christ the chiefe head, and ruler of the Church, and the chiefe magistrate Gods minister; or Aristocraticall in respect of bishops of diuers Churches consenting; or mixt of these two, I will not argue. But this is apparant to all that haue any knowledge of religion and state, that it is not democraticall or popular: for the scriptures do expresly distinguish the gouernors from the people, giuing commandement to gouernors, & commanding the people to be subiect, as *Tit. 3. 1. Heb. 13. 17.* Of which ground this conclusiō ariseth: To chuse the principall officers of the Church is a principal poynt of soueraigntie, but the people haue not the soueraigne gouernment of the church. *ergo.* The *maior* is euident by the examples & precedents of all gouernements. The princes of the *Iewes* did elect their chiefe Iudges and officers: and the gouernment of *Rome*, and *Athens*, which were popular states, were declared to be popular in nothing more, then in the choyse of the chiefest magistrates. the *minor* is notorious and confessed in part by the disciplinarians, who begin nowe to be almost ashamed of their *Anabaptisticall* popularitie.

T. Cartw.

Further, if the people shoulde haue interest in choyse of their pastor,

pastor, and other ministers, in respect they are Christians, and to bee ruled by those officers which they chuse: then not onely housholders (as full learnedly and politically saith *T.Cart.*) but women and seruants and yong men, and all that are the people of God, should haue voyce in the election. for all these haue like interest in their pastor with housholders: and with God there is no differenee of man, nor woman, master nor seruants. and oft times the seruant is wiser then the master: but this *T.Cart.* thinketh to bee absurd, and therefore it may please him to thinke the like of his popular elections too. nowe why only housholders should giue voyce in church elections, seeing in ciuill elections all Citizens that be of yeres & discretion, may giue voyce in ciuill elections where the state is popular; I expect resolution from his wisdome the next returne of answere.

2.reply. p.226.

Gal.3.

This inconuenience likewise followeth of the election by voyces of housholders. seeing in euery Church there are in the externall societie of it more called then chosen, and more temporizors, and colde professors then true Gospellers: that these will ouerrule all causes by pluralitie of voyces; which they cannot allowe of, and therefore haue little cause to stande so stiffe for their popular elections, especially seeing the scriptures so much mislike them, as hath bene shewed, and may further appeare by this reason.

Those are to chuse which haue aucthoritie to depose: but reade all scriptures and fathers, you shall neuer finde any deposed by the people: and therefore if election and deposing proceede by equall degree and pace, the people is not to chuse their pastor.

The Apostles they excommunicated notorious offenders: the godly bishops they examined ministers causes, as did *Timothie*, whō the Apostle willed not to receiue an accusation against an elder vnder two or three witnesses. and *Titus* is enioyned after once or twise admonition, to reiect an heretike: which could not be done effectually, vnlesse he also coulde cause others to anoide him by displacing him. the Synodes deposed heretickes, and excommunicated them. *Theognis*, and *Maris* were deposed in the Synode of *Nice*, *Nestorius* in the Synode of *Ephesus*, *Dioscorus* in the councel of *Calcedon*, *Paul* of *Samosata* in the councell of *Antiochia*. And lightly in euery councell some one or other was deposed. *Ambrose* deposed one for his insolent demeanour in his going, refused another for his indecent gesture. *Alexander* deposed *Arrius* and others: which power being a part of the keyes, must either be kept from the people, or else they will encroch very farre vpon the Consistorie.

To answere all our authorities and reasons, they say that this election by the people, was an order prescribed by the Apostles, & commanded inuiolably to be kept: when we desire to see the place where this order should be set downe, they bring vs forth two or three places of Scriptures racked from their meaning. First they alledge the
Act.1. maner of proceeding in the election of *Matthias*: then, ỳ of the electi-
Act.6. of the deacons, & that of elders appoynted *Act.14.* the first place, the more it is pressed, the lesse it speaketh for them or against vs.

First, the election *Act.1.* both in respect of the officer chosen, being an Apostle, and the maner of proceeding, the matter being decided by lot, is not to bee followed in the election of an ordinarie officer, and proceeding ordinarie. and no conclusion can bee drawen from the one to the other.

Secondly, in the election of *Matthias*, the whole number of beleeuers, not onely that were in the territorie, but also that were then in the worlde was assembled: but in the election of their pastors, the consultation of the Consistorie, and consent of the people (say they) is sufficient. if they take any aduise of the magistrate, or other ministers, that seemeth to be a worke of supererogation.

Thirdly, in this election the people did present two to the Apostles: by the rules of discipline, the Consistorie chuseth and causeth some minister to present him that is chosen, to the people to view him.

Fourthly, the Apostles in the election of *Matthias* gaue no voyce: in the newe discipline, the Elders clayme to haue the only deliberatiue and deciding voyces, the people they haue a poore consent, so litle as nothing can bee lesse: yea, lesse then that which the people haue in the parishes of England. For here within tenne dayes,
Ordon. de Gen. any may obiect sufficient matter: at *Geneua* they must speake within fiue dayes, or else they are for euer precluded. Thus while the people looke for a feast, they are fedde with faire wordes, and shewes without substance: neither is the word συγκατεψηφίσθη that is, *he was reputed*, any argument of the peoples consent or suffrages, but of a common liking or allowance, which may be sayde to bee in those that are absent, and whome the matter concerneth not, yea of vs that liue nowe.

Fiftly, here the Apostles and people concurred in the action, no eldership was present: but in the election of pastors, the Consistorie or Synode doth all, the people is inuitted to behold the goodly works of the Consistorie, and to come when dinner is ended.

Sixtly,

Sixtly, here God did chuse by lot, ἀνάδειξον ἐκ τούτων τῶν δύο ἕνα ὃν ἐξελέξω. that is, shewe which of these two thou hast chosen &c.in pastorall elections,the Presbyterie chuseth by voyce,neither the voyce of God nor the voyce of the people is expected.

Seuenthly,here the people present two to the Apostles:the disciplinarians make their Consistorie, or some deputie from it to present but one to the people,which either they must haue, or else stay the Consistories good leasure.

Eightly, here was no fasting vsed: the disciplinarians make great accompt of fasting in these cases. 9 this election was not to a place, but to an office: but here the controuersie is about the appoyntment to a place, and therefore the disciplinarians can haue no helpe of this place,seeing their elections be to a place. neither if the man be a minister els where,needeth he any newe ordination hauing receiued the same alreadie, vnlesse the marke of his ministerie was made either in water,or in a watrie braine, that receiueth no impression. Let them turne this place which way they will, the poynt of it (as you say) is still against them, not against their aduersaries.

Al the fathers condemne double ordination to one office.

The election of Deacons, is not so fitly alledged to prooue the Consistoriall election with consent of the people, as they weene.

First, for that the office is diuers, and respecteth externall matters,not onely internall: and further needeth no such curious ordination. finally, all offices haue not one forme of election, which hath bene shewed already in bishops & priestes,and is verified likewise in deacons. For the office of bishops is most weightie,and not to be permitted to a popular canuase. Secondly, the deacons had the managing of the Church stocke, wherein euery one pretended priuate interest; and therefore there was more cause the deacons shoulde bee chosen by common consent, then the pastor, whose office concerneth no mans temporall interest nor commoditie.

The forme of this election of deacons is farre different from the pastors election by the Consistorie. First, here the people did first chuse, & the Apostles confirme: in the election of the pastor,the conference & Consistorie,or one of them,doth first and alone chuse,and the people consent and confirme,or rather weakely allowe.

2 Here the *Hebrewes* and *Greekes* ioyne together,& al the church τὸ πλῆθος τῶν μαθητῶν meeteth to chuse deacons: in ye choise of the pastor 6. or 7.ministers, & 3.or 4.elders or elders somtime alone conclude the matter,& then aske the people how they like of their doings,& content themselues if they haue the assent of the greater part of one parish.

Most of their plats require but one, and some no minister at all to chuse ye pastor.

Thirdly, the Deacons here chosen were not limitted to a certaine place: nay, it appeareth they went afterward abroade preaching in diuers places. but pastors are sent to one certaine parish, there to abide vntill hee heare further the pleasure of the Consistorie, vpon whose will his poore pastoralitie doth depend.

1,ag.part.3. Fourthly, here is an election made without Consistorie: for the first mention of Elders is *Act.11. Daneau* confesseth that the Consistorie was not yet erected. but it is not materiall what hee saith, for it was neither then nor afterward erected. nowe in the new church policie, it were absurd to make an election of pastors without Eldership, which *Daneus* maketh to be the eyes of the church.

Lastly, the Apostles onely appoynted Deacons, and gaue them autoritie. καταστήσομεν (saith *S.Luke*) speaking of the Apostles: but that bishops should giue autoritie to pastors, they cannot abide, and some of them in great choller calleth it Antichristian. And therfore I must desire them to lay off their holde of these places, for they will cutte the sinewes of the Consistorie asunder, if they be too hard griped.

The greatest force of all their defence is placed in the word χειροτονήσαντες. to helpe at a pinch, *Stephanus* translateth *quum creasset per suffragia*. The *Geneua* translation sauouring both of the *Geneuian* interpretations, and discipline, hath, *when they had ordeined by election*. whereby they woulde insinuate that the people did chuse by lifting vp of handes while *Paul* and *Barnabas* moderated the action. This word therefore shalbe wrested out of their handes, and the place turned vpon those that produce it. let no man bee offended that I disprooue the translations: wee are to adhere to the word of God, and not to translations.

Whosoeuer therefore considereth the wordes, hee shall see that there is a relation betwixt *Paul* & *Barnabas*, and the people: and that as preaching, teaching, and the word χειροτονήσαντες is spoken of them, so αὐτοῖς is referred to the people. so that in construction of

Or, to chuse. speech, the people could no more be said χειροτονεῖν, then to preach and teach; nor then *Paul* & *Barnabas* could be said to be the people. the word χειροτονήσαντες is spoken of them actiuely, αὐτοῖς is spoken of the people passiuely. For what the other did, that the people had done vnto them. therefore it is absurd to giue that to the people, which *Paul* and *Barnabas* did, or to take that from the Apostles which the word χειροτονήσαντες doth giue vnto them. Let any man that vnderstandeth the *Greeke* bee iudge. The Apostles are sayde to appoynt, the people to haue Elders appoynted to them.

Secondly,

Secondly, the word χειροτονεῖν in no Greeke authour is taken for election by other mens hands, as our braue platformers would haue it, but by the hands of them of whom it is spoken, ἀρχὰς ἃς ὁ δῆμος χειροτονεῖ, *κατὰ κληρωθέντες* saith *Æschines.* And in another place, ἃς εἴωθε χειροτονεῖν, that is, the officers which the people appointed, and which the people was woont to appoint. the word is manifestly spoken of those that lifted vp their owne hands, or that did chuse themselues, not of them that chose by others: which exposition hath no sence; for these Greeke words are not transitiue like those that are in the Hebrew coniugation *Hiphil.*

Some will reply that χειροτονεῖν doth signifie sometime, to chuse by lifting vp of hands; which I yeeld: and yet they shall gaine nothing, vnlesse they prooue that it signifieth not otherwise. for sometimes it is taken generally for any appointment or choice by one, as μάρτυσι τοῖς *Act.10.41.* προκεχειροτονημένοις ὑπὸ θεοῦ, that is, to witnesses ordeined of God. οἱ τοῦ θεοῦ χειροτονοῦντος παραιτησάμενοι, those which refuse when God appointeth (saith *Chrysostome.*) And in *Thucydides*, of one contending against an *De sacerd. lib.4.c.1.* order made by the people, ἀντιχειροτονῶν is affirmed. sometime I confesse *Thucyd.lib.6. Step.p.206.* that it is taken properly, especially, where it is ioyned with a nowne collectiue: but that χειροτονεῖν should signifie to chuse by the hands of others, as the disciplinarians leud grammarians would affirme, it can no where be shewed.

Thirdly, seeing no ancient father doth otherwise interpret it then as I haue done, for the appointment of priests made by *Paul* and *Barnabas*: who, not hauing either his nose stuffed with preiudice, or his head with new Commonwealths, will follow those that digresse not onely from ancient fathers, but from the common vse of all that euer spoke Greeke?

Fourthly, this new interpretation is contrary to their disciplinarian practise: for the people doth not chuse by holding vp their hands, but consent in deepe silence, hanging downe their heads, and shrinking in their shoulders, in token they can not do withall. Secondly, not the ministers do moderate the people as here, but one *quidam* felow doth moderate the elders; of which sort here was none.

Lastly, it is contrary to reason, that these being newly conuerted to Christianity, should be permitted to chuse their pastours. If they that were to be chosen, were of their owne city, they should not do *New Christians.* well to chuse νεοφύτους, if of *Pauls* company, what acquaintance could they haue with them, being scarce yet Christened?

I am not ignorant that diuers other places are alleged to prooue the election and choise of the minister to be in the people; as where the apostles are sent on message, *Act. 8.* which concerneth election nothing: for it was onely a calling and commission for a speciall seruice, and not to serue in any place of the ministery: and the place where *Timothie* is exhorted to stirre vp the gift which he had receiued by the imposition of hands of the eldership: which is meant of ordination, and performed by bishops, as *Chrysostome* expoundeth it, and not of the eldership, much lesse of the people. but neither these nor any other speake to the article, vpon which they are produced.

Daneus Isag. lib.2.c.18. Defence of French discipline.

But I need not longer stand to dispute against popular elections, whom now the disciplinarians do abhorre, and detest as much as we; and *Th.Cartwr.* very gently is come home, and hath eaten vp his former opinion. I trust he will eate diuers of the rest, if he come forth in disputation. In the meane while, the eldership may doe well, to make him confesse his fault publikely, that sometime made popular election a piece of that liberty that Christ purchased with his bloud; most impiously and shamefully matching a circumstance or ceremonie with deliuerance from hell, death, and damnation. Well, now he speaketh all for the election of the consistory; against which, we haue likewise somewhat to say, although they say not much for it. for in the Scriptures there is no place to prooue any inkling of such matter.

1.Tim.4. *In 1.Tim.4.*

Of consistory, they doe not so much as finde the name in Scriptures: therefore, although very loth, yet must they be beholding to the Canonists for it. After much seeking, they finde the word *Presbyterium*, with which they intitle their consistory: but he is a simple fellow in Scriptures and stories, that will thinke that the presbytery did consist of such patchery, as their new found aldermen, and parish doctors. *Chrysostome* interpreteth presbytery, bishops, which is farre from their reckoning. wherefore, before they tell vs that election of pastors belonged to the consistory, let them proue that euer there was such a consistory, either instituted by Christ, or practised by the apostles. Secondly, let thẽ shew that election of officers of the church belongeth vnto them, which I haue alredy shewed to belong to others. The apostles as they receiued general cõmission of gouernment of the church, so they deliuered the same ouer vnto bishops their successors, as *Paul* did to *Timothy* & *Titus*. The apostles designed pastors to euery place. And absurd it were, if vnlettered elders should be placed iudges of doctrine, and of other qualities of ministers.

Matth.28. Iohn.21. *Act.14.*

In all antiquity there is no step of the consistoriall elections, no, not of the consistories themselues. Of a number of ministers of the word.

word, which had the name of presbytery, we read in *Ignatius*, *Cyprian* and others. Of the addition of dumbe elders and doctors, we can vnderstand nothing. Secondly, the gouernment was euer in the bishop and not in the presbytery, as they conceiue it: which shalbe shewed in his place.

Lastly, the election by consistories, is subiect to faction & diuision, vndiscreet and partiall choise, slow proceeding. The same is preiudiciall to the lawes of the realme, to the patrons right, princes prerogatiue, & all good course of gouernment, which cannot stand where there be so many lords without controlment, and the iudges and the parties are the same persons.

Of the Pastour, and his office.

Chap. 3. Sect. 2.

Wherein is declared that ordination of ministers belongeth not to the consistory: First, by the examples of Paul *&* Barnabas, *and testimony of Scriptures. Secondly, by the witnesse of ancient counceils and fathers. Afterward, it is shewed that iurisdiction and offices of gouernment in the Church or Commonwealth are not to be committed by pastors, but by the soueraigne magistrate, that is prooued both by example of the Iewish and Christian church.*

HAuing thus spoken of election, let vs now intreat of those points, which are in controuersie betwixt vs, concerning ordination; which the aduersary (as I said before) not distinguishing from election, nor making difference betwixt ordination to the ministery, and any other office imposed on the minister, hath proceeded confusedly, and taken one for another, and alleged that which maketh for ordination to proue election, and contrariwise that which concerneth ordination to the ministery, against any other office in a minister. which hauing distinguished, we are to shew first, that ordination of ministers belongeth not to the consistory: secondly, that although the magistrate ordein not to the ministery, yet that he may appoint offices of gouernment, and make choise of such ministers, as he shall thinke fittest, for decision of matters, and execution of lawes ecclesiasticall.

The first is euident, both by testimony of Scriptures, and of antiquity. The apostles *Paul* and *Barnabas* as they assigned places vnto ministers, so they laid their hands vpon those that were chosen, and made them ministers. I thinke the aduersary (howsoeuer they giue election to the people) will not say that the people imposed their hands, and ordeined them ministers. If they say the consistory imposed hands, let them shew where the consistory was at the time of this

Act. 14.

Hierome so interpreteth it.

 action,

action, and what it did, and how it could be framed before ministers of the word were appointed there.

Timothie was chosen minister by the imposition of hands of the a- *2.Tim.1.6.* postle *Paul*: which office the apostle calleth τὸ χάρισμα τοῦ θεοῦ, that is, the gift of God, and sheweth that he had it by imposition of his hands, διὰ τῆς ἐπιθέσεως τῶν χειρῶν μου. As for consistory of elders, there was none present at the action: for although he make mention of the imposition *1.Tim.4.* of hands of the presbytery vpon *Timothie*, yet both was that presbytery of another sort then this new consistory, for it consisted onely of the ministers of the word (as the fathers interpret it) and the imposition of hands was to another purpose; for it was διὰ προφητείας, that is, that *Timothie* by their hands might receiue the Holy ghost, and power of miracles, and prophecy. And although interpreters referre *Chrysost.* the place to *Timothies* ministery, yet would the apostle neuer haue ascribed the same to himselfe, nor in phrase of speech altered the persons, if the matter had bin one in both places. And that this interpretation is true, the authority and commandement which *Timothie* receiued of *Paul* alone, to teach at *Ephesus*, doth declare.

Further, where *Paul* commandeth *Timothie* not to put his hands suddenly vpon any, it is euident that ordination belongeth vnto ministers of the word: for seeing the charge is committed to the ministers of the word, who is so presumptuous to take the same vpon them without authority?

2.Tim.2. *Timothie* was likewise willed to commend that to faithfull men which he had heard of *Paul*, which is nothing but to appoint preachers.

Can.4. The councell of *Nice* decreed, that bishops should be ordeined of bishops; will they then still speake for their aldermen, that can say nothing for them?

The ancient Canons of the church giue ordination onely to bishops. The ancient fathers digresse not from the Canons. What *In 1.Tim.4.* *Chrysostome* saith, I haue shewed. *Cyprian* saith, that bishops ordeined *Cornelius* bishop of *Rome*: for so I interpret *Sacerdotes* in that epistle *Lib.4 ep.2.* of *Cyprian*. *Hierome* was ordeined by *Paulinus*, *Paulinus* by *Epiphanius*. *epist.61.& 62.* *Basil* of *Eusebius*. *Gregory Nazianzene* of *Basil in monod.* See all the fathers in *1.Tim.2.& 5.*

They themselues confesse, that the ancient presbyteries had power to ordeine: but they only consisted of ministers of the word, as shall be shewed. Let them shew where one of their aldermen is called *Presbyter*, or admitted of the presbytery, or where their do-

ctours

ctours made vp a part of the presbytery.

Finally, seeing those that ordeine, are to make diligent inquisition of the parties learning and maners, that is to be ordeined minister; who with reason can giue the ordinatiō to merchants, & men of occupation, such as are the vnlettered lay elders? δεῖ μὲν οὖν τὸν χειροτονεῖν μέλλοντα πολλὴν ποιεῖσθαι τὴν ἔρευναν. Diligently ought they to inquire, that are to ordein ministers, saith *Chrysostome*. Wherefore, vnlesse, committing the dis- *Chrys. de Sacer.*
position of matters to the vnlearned sort, we will debase all learning, *lib.4.c.1.*
and goe against the apostolicall order, and ancient customes of the church: such elders as they would haue, are not to intermeddle in ordination of ministers; especially, seeing in the making of ministers, they giue them all power of iurisdiction, and externall church-gouernment: wherin they preiudice the Christian magistrate to whom that belongeth, and pretend to giue that they haue not themselues.

Moses commanded the *Israelites* to appoint iudges and officers in *Deut.16.*
all the cities of the promised land. now then, seeing the execution of the law perteined to the chiefe magistrate; who doubteth, but that the magistrate by this law is authorized to appoint iudges & officers for gouernment of Church & Commonwealth? So *Samuel* appointed iudges. *Dauid* and *Salomon* appointed officers to iudge both in the causes of God & the king. *Iehosaphat* appointed iudges both at *Ie- 2.Chro.19.*
rusalem and in all the cities of *Iuda*. *Ezra*, according to his commis- *Ezra 7.*
sion, gaue what parts of the gouernment it pleased him, to those that he thought fittest for the charge.

The same authority Christian princes reserued to themselues; they appointed and called synods, to decide controuersies. *Constantine* *Socrat. l.1.c.34.*
himselfe iudged in the cause of *Athanasius*: and committed the cause *Euseb.lib.10.c.5*
of *Cecilian* to certeine bishops, & others of his court. *Valentinian* sent *Eccl.histor.*
Ambrose twise in ambassage to *Maximus*.

That which the disciplinarians suppose, that all ministers being ordeined, by vertue of their ordination, had equall iurisdiction and authority in the externall gouernment of the church, is an absurd opinion of men ignorant of the gouernment of the church. for in the ancient church of the *Iewes*, all priests were not of the Sanedrin, but such as were appointed by law, or the prince: and that bishops *Deut.17.*
did iudge with authority, it proceeded from the authority of the *2.Chron.19.*
prince in Christian gouernment, when the prince was Christian: neither can there be any consent in the church of a realme, if euery minister be appointed gouernour, but euery particular parish church will be a body of it selfe: then which nothing can be more absurd

and inconuenient. That paſtors are alſo called ἡγούμενοι, is in reſpect of their teaching; as doctors are called gouernours of ſchooles, becauſe they teach. That in externall gouernment, euery miniſter is to deale with ſoueraigne power; is not meant by the Holy ghoſt: as ſhall be more at large diſputed hereafter. This, to declare their abſurd conceits of election, and ordination of miniſters, is ſufficient. Now let vs examine their lawes, concerning the qualities which they require in paſtours.

Of the Paſtour, and his office.

CHAP. 3. SECT. 3.

In which ſection is prooued that the rules of the apoſtle, 1.Tim. 3. *&* Tit. 1. *concerning the ſufficiency and integrity of biſhops, are not ſo to be expounded, as if all that were not anſwerable to the ſame, were to be reiected out of the miniſtery, but to call men ſo nere to thoſe rules as is poſſible, conſidering the frailty of men and ſtate of things: which is declared by the ſtory of the Church before Chriſt, by the example of the apoſtles and ancient ſynods and fathers: and reaſons drawen from ſome impoſſibilities, and compariſon with other rules in like caſes. The reaſons to the contrary are anſwered, and our defence iuſtified by the practiſe of thoſe that make theſe new expoſitions.*

OF paſtours, they require of neceſſity, that they be iuſt of the leuell of *S. Pauls* rule, *1.Tim.3.* If a man be not anſwerable in all points to his rules, they will not haue him choſen miniſter: if he being a good miniſter when he is choſen, afterward fault through infirmity, they will haue him depoſed without remiſſion. if they would haue the miniſter to come ſo nere to theſe rules as may be conueniently, then they ſay nothing, but that we allow, wiſh, and deſire: if they will allow none to be choſen, but ſuch as are iuſt with that rule, and all depoſed that fall from that rule; I ſay they ſpeake contrary to the apoſtles meaning, precedents of apoſtolike churches, to antiquity, and to reaſon, and go not about to chuſe a good miniſtery, but to thruſt all men out of the miniſtery.

For who is without blemiſh? who doth not ſometimes paſſe the bonds of ſobriety, modeſty, and ſuch vertues as *Paul* requireth in the biſhop? Is *Th. Cartwr.* (whoſe railing and ſcoffing euill agree with this rule,) Is *Beza,* Is *Caluin* anſwerable to this touch? No, the ancient biſhops had their faults: the holy apoſtles of Chriſt were not vnblameable, they contended ambitiouſly for ſuperioritie, as do the diſciplinarians ſometime moſt eagerly. *Peter* denyed his maiſter, he diſſembled, and walked not aright; and therefore was reprooued of *Paul.* Let vs aſcend higher, and conſider the gouernment of the

Iewiſh

Iewish Church : we shall finde that the whole family of *Aaron*, although diuers of them had faults, were chosen to the Priesthood; the tribe of *Leui* to the seruice of the Church, and were not put of their ministery for euery transgression. Diuers of them, in the time of the iudges, fell to idolatry. *Heli* himselfe sinned so, that after him God translated the priesthood from his posterity. In *Achaz* time, the high priest was minister of publike idolatry : yea, *Aaron*, the man of God, was not free from the peoples sinne. yet do we see none of them deposed or refused. Where was the ecclesiasticall consistory this while, with their thunderbolts of excōmunication & deposition?

Ministers not to be deposed or refused for euery transgression.

Neither can any say, that there was more lenity vsed then vnder the law, then now vnder the gospell : or deny that the same was practised vnder the Gospell. Our Sauiour *Christ* chose *Matthew* from the toll table, a calling among the *Iewes* most infamous. *Paul*, of a blasphemer was chosen an apostle. And *Onesimus*, that ran from his master, was made (as Ecclesiasticall stories witnes) a bishop. And of those that offended, we reade not any that for light causes was deposed. *Iohn*, the writer of the *Reuelation*, declareth that ministers of the churches, which fell through frailty, and were not answerable to their calling, were to repent, and not presently to be deposed. The bishop of *Pergama* bore with the *Balaamites* and *Nicolaitans*. He of *Sardis*, was almost dead. He of *Laodicea*, neither hoat nor colde. What should I speake of the bishops of the first church after *Christ*? Reade the stories, consider what men were chosen, consider who continued in their calling : some were in opinion wauering, some erred, some taught strange positions, some commited offences : yet neither for light offences were they refused, nor for the same deposed. Who can excuse *Origen*, *Tertullian*, & *Cyprians* errors? Was *Epiphanius* and *Chrysostome*, *Hierome*, *Ruffin*, *Augustine*, and *Ambrose* blamelesse? I will not name those of our time : but take the best, he is not answerable to the perfection of the apostles rules. the which discourse I will comprehend in the compasse of these reasons following, that the aduersary may know whereto to answere.

Ignat.

Apoc.2.& 3.

The Gospell is not more rigorous then the law, nor the orders of the church of Christians more extreme then the lawes of the church of the *Iewes*: but in the time of the law, diuers were chosen to office in the church, and continued in the same, notwithstanding imperfections condemned in the apostles rules : therefore the same are not to be applied to election or deposition, but set before the minister as a glasse, to come vnto them so neere as he can. The assumption is 1

euident by the story of *Aaron* that was not innocent when he made the goldẽ calfe: in the posterity of *Aaron*, who were priests, notwithstanding some imperfections: in the priests, during the time of the iudges, and of idolatrous kings in the times of the prophets, who cry out against their wickednesse, and yet were they not deposed. Nay, it appeareth manifestly, that there was a sacrifice, as well for the
Ezr.10.19. priests offence as the people, & that the priests that had defiled themselues in the dayes of *Ahaz*, and in the captiuity, were sanctified:
2.Chr.2.30. those when *Hezekias* reigned, and these when *Ezra* returned, and afterward serued the Lord in the temple and sacrifices. *Nehe.10.28.*

2 If none be to be allowed and accounted for good ministers before men, but they that perfectly answere the rules of the apostle: neither are any to be accounted for good men, but those that fulfill the law of God. for the lawes morall and ecclesiasticall are pretended to be deliuered equally, and with like reason to both: but good men are they accounted, that in some sort liue well, and commit no crimes, and are ἐν πλατεῖ, that is, in a common vnderstanding, as they say, righteous: or els there is none good nor honest in respect of men, which is absurd, *ergo, &c.*

3 If none are to be chosen ministers, nor suffered in the ministery, but such as answere the apostles rules concerning ministers; then no princes nor gouernours are to be chosen or suffered but such as answere the rule of Gods law, *Exo.18.Deut.1.& 16.& 17.* and *Rom.13.* Let the disciplinarians shew a diuers reason, if they can: but I hope they will not haue all princes deposed, nor say that they deserue to be deposed, if they answere not the rules prescribed to princes in Gods word. they may easily conclude of these premises themselues, that these rules are not be wrested to election or deposition.

4 *Christ Iesus* departing the world, instituted a ministery of men: neither may we thinke that the apostles meaning was other, then that the ministery should be instituted in all churches: but if none be instituted nor tolerated, but such as haue the qualities required by the apostle; there will be no ministery in the world, much lesse will sufficient numbers of such be found, as must serue in the ministery: for who can say, he is vnreprooueable, righteous, holy, that he hath alwayes kept his hands and tongue in temper? who is not selfe-willed, and opiniatiue in some matters? if *Th. Cartwr.* would say he were a man of those qualities, he would prooue himselfe a presumptuous hypocrite: and yet he maketh no question, but that he is a man well and sufficiently qualified to be president of the consistory. Wherefore

fore let these talkers of discipline cease to deuise these trappes for other men. if others fall into them before, they will not long after keepe themselues from falles. let them consider the weakenesse of mens nature, and howe that the Saintes of God haue fallen: yea, *Moses* the man of God, and the holy Apostles could not cleare themselues, and yet vnlesse these men dare doe it, no man euer thought otherwise of them then of good men, and sufficient ministers.

Wherefore then is this rigour brought into our Churches, which is not seene in the practise of the lawe, nor was vsed of Christes holy Apostles nor ancient fathers? the councell of *Nice* decreed, that *Nouatian* heretikes returning to the Church should be receiued, in the degrees and orders which before they had taken in the church: so farre were they from putting offenders out of the ministerie for light offences, that they receiued heretikes vpon repentance. *Can.8.*

Ierome in a whole treatise against such wayward fellowes as now trouble our Church, disputeth that bishops returning from *Arrianisme* are to be admitted as bishops into the Church. wherefore then doe wee not followe the moderation of graue and auncient fathers of the Church experimented in gouernment, rather then rash yong doctors, whose heads are twined about with euery fancie? *Aduer. Lucifer.*

The ancient Counsels made deposition the extremest punishment of the Church, and vsed it not but in cases subiect to excõmunication, and for grieuous offences: these men pretending to follow the Apostles rules, say that ministers for euery light fault are to be deposed. to bring in this rigour into the Church is a notable practise of *Satan* to driue all yong men of hope from the ministerie, that such sory hyndes as these may ouerthrowe all by their misgouernment.

To excuse themselues, and to seeke colour for their new practise, they say the Apostles wordes are plaine, that a bishop ought to bee such, as they set downe. sure he is blinde that cannot see the Apostles wordes, and reade what he saith: but hee is more then sharpe sighted, that can see that the Apostle speaketh of election or deposition, which interpretation is repugnant to the practise of the Apostles. but when a bishop is chosen, these rules are to be set before him, that he may therein meditate and striue to obserue them, not that he shall be deposed, if he cannot keepe them: for then shoulde he be deposed for his sonnes faultes, for his wiues faultes, and more adoe there woulde be about electing and chusing of ministers, then about teaching of faith and maners; and the minister should be forced to haue a wife, whereas mariage is a matter indifferent in it selfe.

S.Ierom saith that the description of a bishop *1.Tim.3.* is a glasse of priesthoode, and requireth almost things contrary to nature. Nowe where the word δεῖ (that is, must) is vrged, we are to vnderstand, that it importeth not alwayes necessitie nor force, but sometimes decencie, whence τὸ δέον, that is, that which is conuenient: hath his originall, sometime, it signifieth profite: therefore let it be decent and profitable that the minister be such as is described, or let him come so neere as may be, so that all be not refused or deposed that haue not atteined to the high pitch of this perfection. *S.Ierom* saith, that if one or two things be wanting in the Catalogue of bishops vertues, yet that he shall not therfore want the name of a iust or fit bishop. *Hierom lib.1. aduer.Pelag.c.8.* But alas, why should the disciplinarians require such perfection in manners, and excellencie in learning? doe they (trowe you) execute the same rules against themselues? sure no. for who is more insufficient for learning, or defectiue for maners, then the principal of this packe? but they are so bent to put out others, that so they may hurt those whom they cannot fancie, they care not if ẇ the same engins they strike those through, whom they greatly fauour. and besides, while men are rauished with contemplation of the sublimitie of their rules, they meane to steale away the hearts of men from a moderate and quiet gouernment. as for the practise, they hope that men will not looke into it. but let them not abuse themselues, for their consistoriall recordes will come to light by one meanes or other, and their ignorance, lewdnesse and insufficiencie cryeth loude though I holde my peace.

Fr.disc.art.34. Tit.de minist.

I haue stoode vpon this poynt the longer, that you may see what gouernment we are like to haue, when leauing the course of the primitiue Church, yong striplings will prescribe lawes out of their studies, as if *Diogenes* should speake out of his tub.

Of the Pastor and his office.

Chap. 3. Sect. 4.

The superioritie of Bishops is therein declared to proceede from diuine authoritie by reasons drawen from the practise vnder the law, from Christs and his Apostles gouernment: wherein diuersitie of degrees in ministers of the word was obserued: Likewise from the example of Timothie, Titus, Siluanus, Marke, *and the Bishops of the seuen Churches.* Ap. 2. et 3. *The exception that they were Euangelists, is answered. The same is proceued by the practise of the aduersarie in the superioritie of their Consistories and their presidents, and by diuers inconueniences and schismes which otherwise would insue, by generall consent of fathers, and for that the contrary was alwayes holden heresie. and finally, obiections to the contrary, are refuted and retorted.*

When

WHen they haue cleared the rankes of the ministerie with the rigour of their lawes, they hope to range the rest more easilie by teaching *æqualitie*, if the equalitie of degrees in the ministerie which exalteth euery base companion, and debaseth men of great excellencie, and confoundeth all orders, deserue to be called *æqualitie*, especially being voyde of reason and equitie. this poynt by course of our treatise, commeth nowe to bee considered, which may be beter resolued, if we recal to mind how ÿ same amongst vs came first in controuersie. Certaine there were among vs, which as *Diotrephes* desired preheminence, but either for want of meanes, or consideration of their wantes despairing to obteine the highest places, they nowe striue to bring downe others lower, and to make them equall to themselues.

To effect their purpose, ambition and disdeine to be ruled, is coloured with reformation: and therefore they affirme, that it is the order appoynted by God, and an Apostolicall institution, that all ministers be equall, and that the platformers may haue a stroke with their fellow bishops. This I say, and doubt not to proue it, is a vaine fancie rising of discontented humors, which hath neither authoritie from God, nor commendation of practise, & a disorder repugnant to order and quiet gouernement of the Church, and neither allowed by scriptures nor fathers.

So a certaine tyrant entertained his ghests: those that were too long for his bed, he cut shorter. Those that were too short, he racked to the iust measure of his bed.

1 When God gaue lawes to his people, of which *Moses* giueth *Deut.4.*
this testimonie, that all nations should admire the *Iewes* for their gouernment, he not only appointed a hie priest, but amongst the priests
appointed diuers rankes & degrees, the gouernours whereof were cal-
led *Sharei hacohanim*, or ἀρχιερεῖς *principes sacerdotum* or chief priests. be *Ezr.c.8.*
sides those that by their place & course had ordinarie preeminence, *et Mar.14.*
some were chosen by the prince, iudges & gouernours, as appeareth *et Act.19.2.*
both in the historie of *Dauid*, when he setled the affaires beyond *Ior-* *1.Chr.26.*
den, & in the proceding of *Iehosaphat*, who out of the order of priests
chose such as he deemed most sufficiēt for gouernmēt. now then if the
disciplinarians notwithstanding that ÿ papists vse the same reason for
the pope, doe borow some helpe from the high priest, to proue their *I B.*
consistorial president: then much more reasō haue we to deriue the e-
quity of diuers degrees from priests to ÿ ministers of the Gospel, forasmuch as the same causes (that is for auoiding of schisme, cōtention &
disorder) do stil remain: & if as he ÿ made a certain defence against *Br.*
slāders (for so it pleaseth him to miscal ÿ good mans modest dealing)

 affirmeth

affirmeth, the equitie and common reason of Church gouernement is alwayes the same: then can there bee no equalitie among all the ministers, but still there must be some placed in higher degree to moderate the rest: for that was the cause why God appoynted that order in the Church of the *Iewes*: which gouernment, who so misliketh, presumptuously aduanceth himselfe against the wisedome of God. which reason *Ierom* in plaine termes confirmeth & saith, that this superioritie of degree was an Apostolical tradition taken out of the old Testament. *Ut Sciamus* (saith he) *traditiones Apostolicas sumptas de veteri Testamento, quod Aaron et filij eius atque Leuitæ in templo fuerunt, hoc sibi episcopi et Presbyteri et Diaconi vendicent in Ecclesia.i.* that we may vnderstand that the Apostles take rules or traditions out of the olde Testament, let bishops, priestes and deacons challenge that in the Church, which *Aaron* and his sonnes and the *Leuites* were in the Temple. I vse *Ieromes* testimonie the rather, to shew that when he would make bishops and priestes all one, he meaneth not to make bishops a humane constitution, but opposeth Apostolicall constitution to Christes owne commandement.

Hierom ad Euagr. epist. 85.

Howe much this superioritie and order in the priestes vnder the law, and ministers of the Church did please our Sauiour Christ, he declared in his owne gouernment when he chose twelue Apostles, according to the nomber of the twelue princes of tribes, and seuentie disciples, according to the number of *Moses* helpers or counsell. If then the degree of Apostles was aboue the seuenty disciples, as is manifest, in that Euangelists (which were these seuenty) are placed after Apostles; and twelue princes excelled the seuentie: then was not distinction of degrees forbidden, nor equalitie enioyned. that which they alledge that among the Apostles, equalitie was obserued, answereth not our reason concerning the diuers degrees of ministers of the word shadowed & shewed in the preheminence of Apostles aboue the seuentie disciples: and therefore, either let them denie that the example of Christes gouernment is to be followed, or yeelde vs difference of degrees of ministers preaching the word.

Whosoeuer taketh exception against this order, for that it was not continuall, and that the high priest was a type of Christ; may easily be satisfied, if he consider the equitie that is permanent, and that beside the high priest there were diuers degrees of priestes: or else that the same course was continued, when with his corporal presence Christ left his Church: for he left diuers degrees & functions of ministers of the word. *Some he gaue Apostles, some Prophets, some Euangelistes, some Pastors*

Ephe. 4.

Pastors and teachers: he left it not to be gouerned by a confused multitude of pastors, but distinguished the gouernours into degrees. Neither can it auaile them, to alleage that this diuersitie of degrees was betweene Apostles, Euangelistes, Prophets, and Pastors: for if the gouernement of the Church be alwayes the same (as they affirme) or if the equitie of that gouernement be continuall (which they cannot denie,) then must there alwayes bee one degree of Ministers, to commaunde, the rest must obey: for that without order, the Church can not be maintained. *Caluine*, I knowe, distinguisheth order from superioritie. as if order could bee, where all are equall, or as if his consistoriall president had no superioritie, when he can commaunde, impose silence, and hath a negatiue voyce.

That order which Christ Iesus prescribed, the Apostles diligently obserued and maintained. For they did not onelie keepe an Apostolicall dignitie themselues, and shewed their authoritie in their actions, but in the Ministers which they appointed, they set notable marks of difference. to some they gaue charge of one Church onely, as to those whome they appointed *Actes* 14. to others they gaue the charge of diuers: Of *Timothie* the ancient fathers reporte, that he had the care and charge, not of *Ephesus* onelie, but of diuers other Churches in that tract of *Asia*. The wordes of *Saint Paul* witnesse of *Titus*, that he had the ouersight of the Churches of *Candie*. *Siluanus* had charge of a great parte of *Greece*. The seuen Byshops of the Churches to whome *Saint Iohn* wrote, had the chiefe gouernement of the Churches and the territorie: *Apollos* of *Corinth* and *Achaia*, *Dionysius* of *Athens*, & the territorie about it, *Crescens* of *France*, *Marke* of *Alexandria*. To cast a mist ouer our eyes, that they should not see the trueth; the disciplinarians doe saye, that *Timothie*, *Titus*, and the rest were Euangelistes, which they make a diuers degree from Pastors: which if it were graunted, is the ouerthrowe of their cause. For if Euangelistes be a degree superior to Pastors, then is there superioritie of degrees in the Ministerie of the worde. And though Euangelistes be ceased, yet the equitie of the difference can neuer cease, which is, that there be superioritie for remedie of contention, and disorder.

Chrys. Theodoret. in Tim. 1.

Euseb. lib. 2.

The obiection is of no force. for neither were they Euangelistes, nor if they were, would it helpe their cause. Why *Titus*, *Siluanus*, *Crescens*, *Dionysius*, *Appollos*, should be Euangelists, they cannot bring anie pregnant presumption. *Marke* was an Euangelist in writing the Gospell, but that is nothing to the conceite of these men. onely of

Timothie they haue some little coniecture, ỷ he should be an Euangelist, because the Apostle exhorteth him to do the worke of an Euãgelist. which God wot worketh nothing: for not the worke, but the ordination maketh an Euangelist. Neither doth the worke of an Apostle make an Apostle, for the Apostle *Paul* had many felowes in his
1.Cor.16. worke, which yet were not Apostles. Of *Timothie* he affirmeth, that he wrought *the worke of the Lord as well as he.* They knowe that the preaching of the Gospell was a worke common to Apostles, Euangelists, and Pastors. How then can that which is common, make a difference betweene those to whome it belongeth alike? Philosophers can tell them that not the worke, but Art doth shewe an artificer: and that he is not a good man that doth a good worke, which may be done against his will and by chance; but doth well accor-
Arist.eth.2. ding to the habit and rule of vertue. δίκαιος δὲ καὶ σώφρων ἐστὶ, οὐχ ὁ ταῦτα πράττων, ἀλλ' ὁ οὕτω πράττων ὡς οἱ δίκαιοι καὶ σώφρονες πράττουσι. That is to say, he is iust and temperate, not that doth the worke, but doth them as iust and temperate men doe them. The Iewes did the worke of the diuell, yet were they men.

Timothie no Euang. but a Byshop.

That hee was no Euangelist, in that signification (which they take it) these reasons declare. First for that he was called ordinarilie by imposition of handes, which agreeth not to an Euangelist, which (they say) is extraordinarie, and hath no ordinarie charge. They themselues, when they consider that he was ordeined by the presbyterie (as they say) will retract their error I trust. For albeit their presbyteries (as they hold) haue power to ordeine Pastors, yet they haue not power to make Euangelists. Secondlie, Euangelistes *Ephes.4.* are the 70 disciples, or else are they omitted, but *Timothie* was none of the seuentie. Hee was appointed to watch and take charge of
προσμεῖναι τῇ ἐφέσῳ. *Ephesus*: but the charge of Euangelists (as they say) is not limited, but generallie extended, either to a whole nation, or to the whole world, as that of the Apostles.

Contrariwise these reasons shewe, that he was a Byshop. First, for that he had ordinarie imposition of handes. Secondlie, for that he continued there (as stoies say) & died there; whereas the Euangelists office was to goe from place to place, as themselues say. Thirdlie, for that hee did the office of a Byshop in ordeyning Ministers, de-
Euseb. Chrys. Theodoret. ciding of causes, and all this onely in the Church of *Ephesus* and that quarter. Fourthlie, for that the ancient fathers doe saye that he was there Byshop, whose vniforme consent, I maruell with what face these felowes can deny. *Paul* did by imposition of handes

ake

make *Timothie* a Byshop, saith *Ierom.* in *2.Tim. 1.* Lastlie, the subscription of the Epistle, wherein hee is called first or chiefe Byshop, doth witnes it.

If they denie the witnes of fathers, yet (I trow) they wil not raze the words of the booke of God, which were a boldnesse wel beseeming their hastie zeale, but not becomming modest Christians. That it is not in the *Syriak* copie, is a strange allegation, seeing as originalls are not tryed by copies, but contrariewise. The same copie is otherwise much faultie, both in that it wanteth some parte of the Gospell of *Iohn*, and also in diuers places digresseth from the Greek. That these wordes are put after the Epistle, is a friuolous allegation: seeing in transcribing copies of letters, the superscription is sometime put before, sometime after. That it is sayde in the third person (ἐγράφη) ἀπὸ Ῥώμης, that is to say, it was written from *Rome*, it is yet more friuolous. for why? are not dates written in the thirde person most commonly? But seeing there is great consent for this title, why shoulde they goe against so manie witnesses without reason? Well, were it supposed that hee were an Euangelist: was there such a difference betweene Byshops, and Euangelistes, and Apostles, that they coulde not bee spoken of one person? What is thē the reason that the fathers make these diuers functions of one person, as doeth *Ambrose*, and make them one, as doeth *Eusebius*, as generallie doe all the fathers, that affirme *Peter* to haue bene Byshop of *Antioch* and *Rome*, and *Iames* to bee Byshop of *Ierusalem*, as appeareth also by the anthoritie of the Euangelist, *Act.15.* where according to his sentence, when hee sayde κρίνω, matters were determined, and where wee reade of Priestes first established vnder the Byshop? Wherefore, vnlesse they can alleage other *Act.11.* answere, this reason will stand firme against their equalitie of Ministers.

Further if they saye true, when they tell vs that we must striue to come so neere as maye be to the orders of the Apostolike and first Churches; then ought wee to haue some degree of Ministers to commaunde inferiour Pastors, and to keepe them in order. for that was the manner of the Apostolike Church, that had not onely Apostles, but Euangelistes also (by their owne confession) that had iurisdiction ouer other Pastors. If they denie this, then is not the Apostolicall gouernement necessarie in our Church, as hitherto they haue borne vs in hand. If they saye the order of Apostles is ceased, yet all the Apostolicall function in gouernment is not ceased. First for that the Apostle telleth vs, that Apostles and Euangelistes are giuen for the consummation of the Church to the worldes ende. Secondly, for that the care of common vnitie, & common procuration of manie Churches is not ceased: for it hath grounde of morall and politicall equitie that ceaseth not. And thirdlie, our Sauiour promiseth to continue with his Church in Apostolike gouernement, to the worldes end. *Matth. 28.*

Ephes. 4.

Now what reason haue they, why seeing Doctors differ in degree, and some are rulers of schooles, some of one forme, some professe Diuinitie, some Lawe, some Philosophie; there should not be degrees among Pastors likewise? These (say they) may not haue diuers degrees, for that they are comprised vnder one name. as if a generall worde might not comprehend manie particulars: and as if that which they holde in Pastors, themselues did not ouerthrowe in their Doctors, which they distinguish into degrees: and make the Doctors of Diuinitie to goe before the teachers of tongues, and those before their Regents.

Ordon. de l'esch de Geneue.

Further, how can they teach equalitie, that allowe gouernours of Consistories, chosen sometime perpetuallie, sometime for a yeere, sometime for more, sometime for lesse? How can they allowe their Presidents of Synodes, and their goodly visitors of Churches, an office new founde? For if all superioritie and authoritie be forbidden to Ministers (as full soberlie they tell vs, and alleage Christ for author of their opinion) then is not anie superioritie for anie time to be allowed. for that which is simplie euill, is not tolerable for one moment. For there is no moderation in sinne, as they may learne of diuines, the which Philosophers can tell them, to bee true in vices. And if the moderate rule of Byshops be forbidden, which notwithstanding can make no lawes, nor doe any thing without warrant of lawe; what shall wee esteeme of the tyrannicall dominion of the Consistorie, which not onelie can set orders, but whose worde is a lawe, and whose will is not restrained almost by any lawes? Thus all men may see, that they condemne not superioritie, but they would haue it themselues.

Disci. de France.

For if superiorite of Ministers ouer Ministers bee vnlawfull; then may not the Consistorie, consisting for the most parte of Ministers, exercise anie authoritie, or rather dominion ouer Ministers. and if they may punish, excommunicate, depose the Minister; then is not superioritie forbidden of Ministers ouer Ministers. For if it bee vnlawfull simplie, then may neither one doe it, nor more, neither by him-

himselfe, nor with companie. When *Tho. Cartw.* (obseruing the rules of his platforme) answereth these reasons, he shall be fed with birdes milke.

Moreouer in taking away superioritie, they take away not tyrannie, but gouernement and order from among the Ministerie. For what gouernement can bee deuised, where none is bounde to obey, nor anie hath authoritie to commaunde? And order is among things distinct, which followe one after another, of which degrees, and sequences, order taketh his name.

Ordo est rerum præcedentium & consequentium. Philo de mundi opificio.

Wherefore if all Pastors of this Churche, meane to march all in one rancke, although the way be plaine, yet will they often fall in disarray. Neither doeth it helpe the matter, that they giue a prioritie, and superioritie for a time to some one, or more: for as that office faileth, so order and gouernement faileth. And (which of all others they had neede to take heede of) there entreth superioritie, and a higher degree, which ouerthroweth their rules of discipline and confused equalitie.

Further in making all Pastors equall, they take away all iurisdiction, and in the darke, cutte the synewes of their owne Consistorie. For no man hath iurisdiction ouer his equals: and in termes of lawe it is resolued, that *par in parem non habet imperium.* And hee that hath iurisdiction, in the acte of iurisdiction, is superior to him that receiueth doome or right at his handes. Therefore in the Consistorie they make a president, in the Synode a moderatour, and change them at pleasure: and make the Synodes and Consistories iudges of Pastors. which is no way to worke equalitie, but in stead of one gouernour, to make a number of lordes and gouernors, with authoritie not to be controled, and affections vnstayed and vnbrideled. and making the Consistorie and Synode continuallie to change their president, they make it a verie deformed and strange bodie, sometime with a head, sometime headles, sometime with eyes, sometime without eyes, but alwayes without order of lawe, or constant gouernement. Equalitie is the nurse of negligence. for that which is cared for of all equallie or in common, the same (as the prouerbe teacheth vs) is neglected of all. If rule teach them not, yet experience of other Churches that haue this discipline (which is a mistresse to teach the most senceles) may instruct them. For while euerie one streined curtesie who shoulde beginne, and would not take on him that which belongeth to all; the calamitie came vpon them, before they began to consult for remedie. For nothing goeth more slowlie forwarde, nor is longer

Equals ouer equals haue no iurisdictiō

Guerres ciuiles de France.

delayde, then that which is in the deliberation, power, and execution of many. and that which *Demosthenes* sayde of a Monarchie in matters of warre, sure is founde true in matters of peace: τὸ γὰρ εἶναι πάντων ἐκεῖνον ἕνα ὄντα κύριον καὶ ῥητῶν καὶ ἀπορρήτων, καὶ ἅμα στρατηγὸν, καὶ δεσπότην, καὶ ταμίαν καὶ πανταχοῦ αὐτὸν παρεῖναι τῷ στρατεύματι, πρὸς μὲν τὸ τὰ πολέμου ταχὺ καὶ κατὰ καιρὸν πράττεσθαι πολλῷ προέχει. *Philip* (sayth he) for that he being one, is chiefe disposer of matters publike and secret, and is generall, and leader, and treasurer, and is alwayes present with the armie, to dispatch thinges quickelie and in season, hath great aduantage of vs. So in Church gouernement. wherein one hath the care of the Churches of a prouince, dangers are more easilie preuented, matters dispatched, orders established and executed: and therefore the poets saying hath here place, οὐκ ἀγαθὸν πολυκοιρανίη: this multitude of laye lordings, and consistoriall commaanders is not good.

Olynth.1.

[Iliad. 2.]

Finallie the equalitie of Ministers is the cause and original of schisme and contention: *Hinc scismata & hereses* (sayth *Cyprian*) *dum Episcopus qui vnus est, superba quorundam præsumptione contemnitur.* Here hence grew schismes and heresies, while certaine presumptuouslie contemne and despise the Byshop. For sure this is the cause of that contention that is growen among vs, that certaine base companions presumptuouslie haue perched aboue Byshops. what doe I saye, aboue Byshops? Nay like princes, like *Lycurgus*, or *Numa*, they haue taken on them to prescribe to the parliament and the realme, lawes, and orders. *Inde hæreses* (sayeth *Cyprian* in another place) *quod non vnus in Ecclesia ad tempus sacerdos, aut vnus Iudex vice Christi.* Here hence are heresies, that there is not one Byshop in the (particular) Church for the time, nor one Iudge in Christes stead. Which albeit absurdlie alleaged for the Popes vniuersall gouernement, yet is verie fit to proue the Byshops gouernement ouer a diocesse, and direct against the throng of these new Elders, which of late haue striuen to come into the Church. *Ierome* sayeth that the order of Byshops and their superior authoritie was generallie receiued throughout the worlde for remedie of schisme, and that if this superioritie were not, there would be as manie schismes as Priestes. Where are thē these presumptuous platformers, that taking themselues to know more then all the fathers of the ancient Churches, haue pronounced that to bee Antichristian, which they tooke to be the onelie remedie of schisme, & which proceeded of the holy ghost, or els it would not haue bene so generallie and vniuersallie receiued? Doe they not blush

[Lib.4.epist.9.]

Lib.1.epist.3.

ad Euagr. epist. 85.

Aduers. Lucifer.

[Zanch. conf.]

blush to oppose themselues against generall consent, in matters of gouernement? No, for they haue hardened their faces, and commaunded their tongues to speake any thing.

All ancient writers, all stories doe speake for the degree of Byshops aboue Priestes, and condemne this new deuised oligarchie, or rather anarchie of Ministers, of equal authoritie. τί γὰρ ἐπίσκοπος (saith *Ignatius*) ἀλλ' ἢ πάσης ἀρχῆς καὶ ἐξουσίας ἐπέκεινα πάντων κρατῶν; For what is a Byshoppe, but hee that hath commaundement and power in the Church aboue all? And that Elders clime not so high as the Byshop, hee commaundeth Priestes to bee subiect to the Byshop. The contentious platformers of our Churche, percase haue not read the place. οἱ πρεσβύτεροι ὑποτάσσεσθε τῷ ἐπισκόπῳ. These Elders (which they aduance) hee thrusteth downe in the croud among the laye people. ἄνευ τοῦ ἐπισκόπου μηδὲ πρεσβύτερος, μὴ διάκονος, μὴ λαϊκός. without the Byshop, neither can the Priest, nor Deacon, nor laye man doe any thing. Least any shoulde thinke that the Priestes ruled ioyntlie with the Byshop; as Christ before the Apostles, so hee placeth the Byshop before the Priestes, he calleth the Byshop ἀρχιερέα θεοῦ the chiefe Byshop, or Priest of God.

Ad Trallen. *Ad Tarsen. & Smyrneum.* *Ad Magnes.* *Ad Magnes.*

Dyonisius commonlie called *Areopagite*, but who I thinke was of *Corinth*, for hee was verie ancient, speaketh to the same effect. σοὶ δ' οἱ θεῖοι λειτουργοί, καὶ τούτοις οἱ ἱερεῖς, ἱεράρχαι δὲ τοῖς ἱερεῦσι, καὶ τοῖς ἱεράρχαις οἱ ἀπόστολοι. that is: *Let the Deacons (prescribe to thee) the Priestes to the Deacons, the chiefe Priests or Byshops to Priests, and Apostles to Byshops.* Hee speaketh to *Demophilus* a monke, that in contempt of Ecclesiasticall degrees, was like to the disciplinarians. In which authoritie it maye bee obserued, that hee accounteth none for Elders, which are not ἱερεῖς or Priestes: then, that he placeth Byshops in degree aboue them, and not in equall ranke with them.

Ad Demophilum

Tertullian as he maketh three degrees of Ministers, so he placeth Byshops in the hiest degree, and calleth the Byshop *Summum sacerdotem, chiefe priest:* and putteth priestes vnder Byshops, and Deacons vnder Elders. Which least anie shoulde conceiue to bee laye Elders, he giueth vnto them, yea and to Deacons the Ministerie of sacraments: *Dandi (scilicet baptismi) habet ius summus sacerdos, qui est Episcopus* (sayeth he) *dehinc presbyteri, & Diaconi, non tamen sine Episcopi autoritate:* The chiefe priest which is the Byshop, hath power to minister baptisme, and after him the Priestes and Deacons: but not without the Byshops authoritie. The disciplinarians, when they

De baptismo.

see the Byshop to be chiefe, and Priestes to be vnder him, and to receiue authoritie from him, and that Deacons are part of the Ministerie, I feare will pronounce *Tertullian* an heretike, for speaking against their discipline. Nothing can be more direct against them. Neither *De coron milit.* doth it helpe them, that in his Apologie and other Treatises, he mentioneth more presidents and gouernours then one of the Church. for he meaneth none but Byshops, which worde he auoydeth, writing to the heathen that did not vnderstand the worde, that was peculiar to Christians. Which is the reason also, that *Iustine Martyr* doth *ἀποκρ. πρὸς ὀρθοδόξ.* call him προεστῶτα and not *Episcopum*, for that he likewise writ to a pagan Emperor, vsing the worde ἐπίσκοπον writing to Christians.

Iustin. Apol. 2. ad Anton. pium. The same *Iustine* is a cleare witnesse for the preheminence of Byshops: forasmuch as hee calleth the Byshop προεστῶτα or Ruler, the rest hee calleth ἀδελφοὺς or brethren, which were gouerned. Of which sorte Priestes must be, or else they were not among the number of brethren. προσφέρεται τῷ προεστῶτι τῶν ἀδελφῶν ἄρτος. The bread saith he, is brought to the gouernour of the brethren. Where was the gouernement of the presbyterie in his time? Those that referre it to the president of *Beza conf.* their Consistorie, either marke not, or are wilfully blinde and wil not see, that the Byshop is called προεστὼς not in respect of the Consistorie, but of the whole people. Well, now let vs heare *Cyprian* speake, of whome they make no small account, supposing him to bee a deare friend of their Consistorie. But it is to be doubted, they will spare him *Lib. 1. epist. 3.* no more then others, if they heare his iudgement. If (saith hee) the whole brotherhood would obey the Byshop according to the commandements of God, &c. yea, according to Gods rule? And must all the brotherhood, Priestes and all, obey the Byshop? You see, he saith so, therefore must the Consistorie be packing, & Bishops be accoun*Cypri. lib. 2. epist. 7.* ted the institution of God. The cleargie of *Rome* writing to *Cyprian*, acknowledgeth the bishops gouernement ouer priests, & the whole Church within one precinct. *Post Fabiani excessum non est constitutus à nobis Episcopus qui omnia ista moderetur.* Since *Fabians* death we haue not appointed a Byshop, whose office it is to moderate & gouerne all *Lib. 4. epi. 9.* these matters. *And hence* (saith he) *are heresies sprong*, as hath bene before alleaged, while the Byshop which is one, is by presumption *Lib. 3. epi. 9.* of certaine contemned. *Apostolos* (saith he in another place) *Episcopos & praepositos dominus elegit.* where hee accounteth Byshops a diuine institucion & the Apostles successors. *Gregi pastor, plebi rector, naui gubernator Episcopus*: The Byshop is gouernor as the shepheard of sheepe, the master of ÿ ship. And that you may see that the B. ruled the Elders,

he

he calleth the bishop *præpositum Presbyteris*, gouernour of priestes. and where he saith, *Presbyteris et diaconis non defuit sacerdotij vigor &c. vt comprimerentur*. that is, the bishops diligence and authoritie was not wanting, that priests and deacons might be kept in order, he sheweth the bishops authoritie ouer Elders. where was the Consistorie then, that nowe keepeth bishops, yea princes and all in order? *Lib.3. epist.14* *Lib.3. epist.5.*

The appointment of bishops in churches *Ireneus* doth deriue from the Apostles practise and tradition, and saith it was receiued in the whole world. The canons called of the Apostles, decree those priests worthie to be deposed, that contemning their bishop, doe (as our disciplinarians) make conuenticles apart. The ordination and gouernment both of priests and the whole clergie is committed to bishops. they cannot denie but the authoritie of bishops is confirmed and established by diuers Canons of the councell of *Nice*. In the generall councels throughout the worlde, nothing more receiued then superior iurisdiction and authoritie of bishops ouer priests. all the fathers that liued about those times, giue testimonie of it. I except not *Ierom*, who albeit he thinke the beginning not to be from any law of God: yet did he neuer say as our foulmouthed deformers of religion, that it is an abuse brought in by antichrist. nay contrary (he saith) it is an Apostolicall tradition, *epist ad Euag. 85.* *Lib.3.c.3. aduers Hereses.* *Can.32. Apost. c.54.40. &c.* *C.14. et 17.*

What the opinion of *Basil* is concerning the autoritie of bishops, it appeareth by his Canons and gouernment. himselfe in his life obserued Ecclesiasticall canons, & caused them in his diocesse to be obserued. *Chrysostome* prescribed, commanded, corrected, and did al the partes of Ecclesiasticall gouernment himselfe, and holdeth the order of bishops and their authoritie to proceede from the Apostles. *Epistola ad Amphil.* *Greg. Naz. in laud. Bas.* *In 1. ad Timoth.*

S. Augustine declareth that bishops succeeded the Apostles. By common consent of the fathers, they that thought otherwise, & hold that there is no difference of degrees among pastors, & that bishop and priest is all one (as do the platformers) are condemned for heretikes, *Epiphanius* calleth that opinion of *Aerius* wherby he holdeth bishops & priests to be one, to be λόγον μανιώδη a furious speech, scarce beseeming a modest & sober man. Of the former discourse, these conclusions may be inferred. *In Psal.44.* *In Heres. Aerii.*

1 Seeing the fathers with one consent throughout the world receiued the constitutiõ of bishops, that it came from the spirit of God by the ministerie of the Apostles: for it is not the power of man, that on a sudaine can moue mens hearts generally to receiue one order established, but the effectual worke of Gods spirit: wherein the autho-

L ritie

De eccles. Christ. obseruat. ritie of the learned father *Zanchus* may sway somewhat. *Credo* (saith he) *quæ à pijs Patribus in nomine Dom. &c.* I beleeue that those things that were by godly fathers gathered in Gods name, and consenting together, defined & receiued, that they were also from ŷ holy Ghost, although not of like autoritie with scriptures. he alloweth else where the authoritie of bishops. their saying therefore that contend against such a consent, is (as *Epiphanius* saith) furious and frantike.

2 Seeing the holy fathers say it is a diuine institutiõ; the babble of cõtentious felowes against such autority weieth not so much as a peper graine against a woolsacke. If they were not very venturous, they would not hazard ŷ reputatiõ of their discipline against al antiquity.

3 That which ancient generall councels, which this realme do approue, doe decree, that it is not by euery light fellowe to be reproued; and rather doth he deserue stripes then wordes, that wil disallow that which all generall councels haue allowed, not being contrariant to the word of God, which of those councels cannot be presumed.

4 Lastly, in taking vpon them the patronage of *Aerius* & his opinions condemned by the holy fathers for heresies, they discredit their discipline much, in acknowledging that it is condemned for heresie, and themselues for heretikes: which although (because they haue seared their faces) they are not αὐτοκατάκριτοι, yet are they κατάκριτοι of Iudges, that in this case cannot be excepted against for partiall. for they spake before these things came into controuersie.

To excuse themselues and defend their opinions, they vse diuers shifts, and make many obiections. they alledge diuers textes of scriptures: they vse *Ieroms* autoritie, and the testimonie of late writers. In the vauward they place a text much of thẽ abused, but yet neuer framed sufficiently to their purpose. Our sauiour Christ (say they) forbad dominion to his disciples, and willed those that were greatest, to be as the least: wherby they would inferre, that one minister may not haue iurisdiction ouer another. but therein they deale wisely that they doe not frame the argument themselues, but leaue the place to the reader to be framed at pleasure. for answere whereof, I say first, that whatsoeuer our Sauiour here forbiddeth to his disciples, he forbiddeth to al Christians, that is, tyrannie & ambition, which neither in Christians is tollerable, nor in heathen cõmendable. for we may not thinke that Christ allowed the strict dominion of heathen princes ouer their subiectes, or their vaine glorie and pride. the word κύριος hath relation to δοῦλος, so that κυριεύειν is to rule their subiects as slaues, which among the heathen was vsuall: but among free people vnsufferable, in so much

much that a certaine *Romane* Emperour is saide to refuse the title of *Augustus.*
Dominus although hee desired others more hie and hautie in our iudgement. and if this be not the interpretation of the place: then will it follow, that it is lawful for princes κατακυριεύειν and κατεξουσιάζειν, that is, to *Matth.20.*
rule at pleasure without lawes, as doe the lordes of the Consistory. which equall gouernment cannot permit, nor can they grant, vnlesse to bring in their discipline, they can be content the people shalbe oppressed with any tyrannie. But admit that were true, that our Sauiour doth forbid that gouernment to his disciples which he allowed in the Gentiles, yet can no other sence be picked out of it then this, that the gouernment of ministers shalbe diuers from that of the Gentiles. for we may not thinke that in these wordes he forbiddeth greatnesse: for then would he haue said, Let none be great among you. now saying, *He that is greatest*, he doth plainely allow a greatnesse amongst them, which he woulde haue tempered with humilitie. and of the same the Apostle maketh mention, where he saith he was not inferior to those that were chief or were pillars: much lesse may we thinke the Apostle taketh away gouernment & superiority. for then were their consistories, & their Synodes & their moderators gouernment dashed in pieces, which cannot be without superioritie: nay which is more absurd, then might not the Apostles exercise iurisdictiō ouer inferior pastors, and *S. Paul* was not wise to say *I haue determined*, if he had no autority *1. Cor. 5.*
to determine; nor make mention of a rodde, if he had no Apostolicall *1. Cor. 4.*
correction: and *per consequens Bezaes* long discourse of excommunication, should be but a drousie tale in a winters night.

The place vos non sic rebeaten vpon the disciplinarians by diuers reasons.

This argument may thus bee retorted vpon their heads, that bring it to proue equalitie of ministers: if (notwithstanding the prohibition of our Sauior) the Apostles had superior autority ouer other ministers, which the truth sheweth, & all interpreters consent to be lawful: then may superiour autoritie of ministers stand ouer other ministers, notwithstanding Christs prohibition in that place: for he did not forbid autority ouer some, & grant it ouer others; but generally denieth it al, *vos autem non sic.* and in things simply denied, there can be no qualification that will serue. 2 Againe, if all superioritie be forbidden by these words of Christ vnto ministers of the word ouer other ministers, then doth the president of the Consistorie vsurpe dominion ouer his brethren: then doe the ministers of the Consistorie vniustly conuent, examine, punish, excommunicate ministers: and in summe, the whole deuise of their discipline is a packe of iniustice: nay further, if these haue no iurisdiction ouer other ministers, then shall the miniſters of the newe Conſiſtorie liue like Kinngs ſubiect to no controlment.

3 Laſt of all, if Chriſt did not prohibite dominion to princes, then is it lawfull for them to vexe and oppreſſe their people, that is, κατακυριεύειν καὶ κατεξουσιάζειν. which if they be matters to hote to be lifted: let the diſciplinarians lay downe this place, & abrenounce their wreſted interpretations without reaſon or authoritie.

The admonition, to relieue the diſtreſſed arguments grounded on the words of our Sauiour, brought two other places: the firſt out of the *2.Cor.10.* the ſecond out of *Col.1.1.* but for that *T.Cartw.* with his tooles cannot hewe them to his purpoſe, he hath left them to ſpeake for themſelues. and therfore ſeeing they can conclude nothing them ſelues, I wil not buſie my ſelfe with anſwering nothing, but wil come to certaine places deuiſed ſence to ſerue this turne, which he ſuppoſeth to make more to his purpoſe. Out of the Epiſtle to the *Philippians* he alledgeth that the miniſters of the word are called biſhops. which were it ſo, yet it is no argument to proue all equall: for that vnder the
Dan. Iſag. par.3. name of deacons are elders compriſed as they ſay: yet elders are a degree (as they make them) aboue deacons. the communitie of names is no argument of cõmunitie of natures & offices, Apoſtles are ſometimes called elders, ſometime deacons, ſometime biſhops: yet they confeſſe the degree is diuers. all iudges haue one common name, ſo haue magiſtrates, ſo had the prieſts vnder the lawe, & the Leuites; yet are there degrees among them. *T.Cartw.* ſhould haue framed his argument as *S. Ierom* doth: becauſe all biſhops are called prieſts, & contrariwiſe; that therefore they are one. but hee durſt not, for feare hee ſhould batter his lay or vnteaching elders with it: for if *Ierom* ſay true, then away muſt we cut our newcome elders: for ſaith *Ierõ, Epiſcopus* & *Presbyter* were one. but neither theirs nor his reaſõ can paſſe for good: for although theſe names be enterchanged, yet there is a certaine ſuperiour iuriſdictiõ deriued from the Apoſtles to certaine, which is not made cõmon to all elders, but to ſome. for if Chriſt do continue with his church in Apoſtolike gouernment to the ende of the world, as he
Matth.28.20. promiſeth: & if Apoſtles, prophets & Euangeliſts & paſtors are to laſt in their doctrine & gouernment to the perfectiõ of the church, which is not accompliſhed before the end of the world, as the Apoſtle teſti-
Ephe.4. fieth, μέχρι καταντήσωμεν οἱ πάντες εἰς τὴν ἑνότητα τῆς πίστεως, vntil ſuch time as we meet al together in the vnitie of faith: then is not Apoſtolical autority that
Ephe.4. then was, ceaſed: and this is the opinion of the fathers. *S. Ambroſe* ſaith that biſhops are Apoſtles: which is more then if hee had ſayde,

they

they had apoſtolicall gouernment. *Eos qui nunc vocantur epiſcopi* (ſaith *Theodoret) vocabant apoſtolos*. Thoſe which are now biſhops *In 1.Tim.3.*
were in times paſt apoſtles. And *Cyprian* plainely affirmeth, that biſhops ſucceeded as lieutenants to the apoſtles: *Epiſcopi & præpoſiti* (ſaith he) *apoſtolis, vicaria ordinatione ſucceſſerunt*. Biſhops and preſidents ſucceeded the apoſtles,& were ordeined in their places. Now, *Ep.9.lib.3.*
if that doctrine and gouernment be alwayes neceſſary, to the worlds end: then, as there is a ſucceſſion of doctrine, ſo there muſt be alwayes a ſucceſſion of gouernment. but theſe elders, that like moules are new crept forth of the earth, for that they can ſhew no ſucceſſiõ, they can not abide to heare talke of ſucceſſion. and therefore whatſoeuer the ancient fathers ſpeake concerning the ſucceſſion of the apoſtles at *Ieruſalem, Rome, Alexandria, Epheſus, Antioch*, and ſuch like places; becauſe it is a declaration againſt their freeholde, they heare it with ſmall pleaſure, and deny it with a leud grace.

The authority of *Ierome* in this caſe weyeth not much: firſt, for that he ſpeaketh againſt all antiquity, which calleth the degree and order of biſhops a diuine order: and ſo himſelfe elſewhere ſaith.

Dionyſius calleth it θεοπαράδοτον παράδοσιν, a diuine tradition or doctrine. *Epiſtola ad Demoph.*
Cyprian deriueth it from *Chriſtes* rules, which he calleth *Magiſteria diuina*: and no man (ſaue *Ierome*) ſaith contrary. Nay, they condemne *Ieromes* opinion in *Aerius* for hereſy. Secondly, he is contrary to himſelfe: for he calleth that an humane conſtitution, which himſelfe confeſſeth to haue bene receiued through the world: and affirmeth that to be humane, which he confeſſeth to haue ſucceeded the apoſtles. Thirdly, he ſpeaketh in his owne caſe, being a prieſt, and no biſhop; and yet not cleare of all ſpots of ambition. Laſtly, if it be an humane tradition (as himſelfe affirmeth) why doth he call it *Ad euag.ep.85.*
Apoſtolicam traditionem, an apoſtolicall tradition? why doth he ſo religiouſly obſerue it; for humane traditions and ceremonies, haue no authority to binde the whole church as this did: why doth he commend it ſo highly? and why, ſeeing the time of the originall being in the apoſtles time, who then gouerned the church by direction of Gods holy ſpirit (for *S. Iohn* liued long after this order) and the *Euſeb.lib.2.*
cauſes being ſo neceſſary for auoiding ſchiſme, could he conceiue that it had a humane beginning? as if man had not ſet order, the church had bene without remedy of ſchiſmes. Why did not the apoſtle *S. Iohn* reforme this order, if it had not bene apoſtolike?

They allege further out of *Cyprian*, that he chargeth *Pupian* for *Ep.9.lib.4.*
making himſelfe biſhop of biſhops; which they litle vnderſtand, or

els dissemble their great skill. for *Cyprian* taketh bishop there as we take it; not as they fondly conceiue, for euery minister of the word. so that speaking against the challenge of *Pupian*, he leaueth the authority of bishops ouer priests, which is euident in euery second epistle, almost throughout. This *Pupian* was a schismatike, and tooke on him, as the disciplinarians doe, to controll *Cyprian*, a lawfull bishop, himselfe being but a counterfect bishop, without lawfull ordination. And this is it that *Cyprian* complaineth of, that by proud presumption bishops were contemned, which was the originall of schisme and heresies. and we finde it very true, to the disturbance of the peace of many good mens consciences.

They allege diuers other places, as *Acts 14.* where *Paul* and *Barnabas* is said to ordeine elders. and *1.Peter 5.* where he calleth himselfe an elder. and *Heb.13.* where pastors are called ἡγέμενοι. All which places are of small value for their purpose, and receiue one answere, that community of names taketh not away difference of degrees, as is euident in magistrates, iudges, priests of the law, and Leuites, and ministers of the word in the apostles time. They themselues confesse inequality in doctors; wherefore then should not the like reason be in pastours? Thus when all is come to all, they flie to *Caluin, Beza, Daneau*, and certeine other petit quidamets, and the articles of *French* discipline. of whom I will say no more, but that they are affectionate to their gouernment of *Geneua*, and speake what they can for their owne cause, and therefore their witnesse not woorth a rush in this case, especially, deposing against Scripture and antiquity, yea, against themselues, (for if *Beza* in the gouernment of the *French* churches, doth not deale as archbishop, what calling hath he?) and that without any graine of reason. but so violent are their affections, that they condemne all other churches for not reformed, that sauour not of the smoke of their discipline, newly forged.

Their reasons are examined. if they can answere ours, let them do it. in the meane while, let them forbeare to make vant, that as our discipline is antichristian, so theirs came all from *Christ* and his apostles. For maintenance of common peace, they haue bene hitherto forborne: but if they cease not to practise and to raile, there shall such a wracke be made of their *French* articles of discipline, and *Geneuian* ordinances, that they shall repent that euer they began this quarrell against our church.

Wherefore, seeing they will haue the moderators, and consistoriall superiority to haue diuine allowance, although no testimony of antiquity,

quity, nor reason can be brought for either; let them not deny the superiority of bishops ouer inferiour pastours, to haue witnesse of the word, seeing stories giue the same his originall in the apostles times, and all fathers and councels affirme it, and their reasons that are brought against it, are weake and friuolous.

Of the Pastour, and his office.

Chap. 3. Sect. 5.

In this section, the lawfulnesse of the title of Lord in some ministers, is proued by examples of the priests & Leuits vnder the law, called by farre greater titles by God himselfe: by Christs example, & his apostles: by the practise of the ancient church, & of the disciplinarians them selues: by law of nations, and instinct of nature, that euer thought honorably of the priesthood: lastly, for that the reasons of the aduersary haue more affection then efficacy, and hurt their owne stile, as well as the stile of our ministery.

Hat which they can not do with reason, that some haue attempted by sleight, some by faction. There is nothing that more mainteineth the state of church-gouernment with vs, then the iurisdiction & authority, which lawes giue to bishops. and therefore, meaning the ruine of the state, to effect their purpose, bishops must be brought into contempt. to which end, some of them haue spred abroad most leud and infamous libels: the very best of them are still yelling and crying against their titles and offices: some litle whelps there are, that are yalping against their liuings. for as long as bishops continue their reputation and dignities, neither can faction preuaile, nor lawes & orders want patrons. if they were once abased, they hope with more ease to worke all their confusion. What is the reason that *Cartwright* can not abide that ministers of the word should be cōmissioners in causes ecclesiastical vnder her Maiesty? forsooth because he cōdemneth her Maiesties supreme authority in causes ecclesiasticall, and giueth the same to his elderships: wheras they withstand the factious gouernment of elders, & defend her Maiesties lawful authority. They would not haue bishops iustices of peace, because they would haue none, that mislike their proceedings, in authority; that with more ease they might take peace frō among vs. & this they colour with certeine weake argumēts, which conclude nothing; & pretend to seeke equality, where they seeke nothing more thē rule & dominion. They of the admonition complaine ẏ bishops wil haue the stroke without their felow seruants. so ẏ if of felow seruants they were made felow rulers, the cōtrouersy were almost at an end. These their clamors & simple conclusions I thought good here to answere, and

Admonition to the Parliament.

and to ſhew that the title of Lord in a miniſter (which they enuy ſo much) is neither to be enuied, nor condemned as vnlawfull. Of their offices we ſhall haue occaſion to ſpeake afterward.

The miniſters of the word, eſpecially thoſe that labour and take
1.Tim.5. extraordinary paines, are worthy double honor; and if they deſerue honour, which is the thing, ſure they can not iuſtly be debarred of the title, vnleſſe this honour muſt be in minde and conceit, and yet not
Auth. quomodo oportet episcopos col.1. l.maxima. named; which is a ſtrange conceit & fancy. *Maxima in omnibus ſunt dona Dei à ſuperna collata clementia, ſacerdotiũ & imperium.* The prieſthood and magiſtracy are two ſingular graces, granted to men by Gods mercy (ſaith a *Romane* emperour.) If ſuch be the honour of prieſthood, how can they be thought vnworthy of titles of honour? By the law of nature, prieſthood, among all nations, hath bene ho-
Ierom.in Iob.1. nourable. Before the law, kings and princes, and the greateſt and wealthieſt were prieſts. and in the Scriptures, men of great honour
Diodor Sic. lib.1.et.7. Ceſ.com. were called by the name of prieſts, as *Kimhi*, *Lyra*, & *Hugo* vpon the 98.Pſalme teſtifie. Among the *Ægyptians* the prieſts had the ſecond place after the kings. The *Druydes* among the ancient *Gaules*, had
Cor.Tac. de mor. Ger. Pro domo. moſt matters, both publike & priuate, committed to them: *Stra.li.4.* The prieſts among the *Germans* were iudges in martiall cauſes. *Tullie* doth take it, that it was a diuine ordinance, that the ſame men were gouernours of religion, and the Common wealth. *Diuinitus inſtitutum quod eoſdem religionibus Deorum immortalium et ſummæ Reip. præeſſe voluerunt.* *Ariſtotle* doth place them among the moſt noble ci-
Ariſt.polit.7.9. tizens: ὔτε γὰρ γεωργὸν ὔτε βανάυσον ἱερέα καταστατέον. neither husbandmen nor baſe men are to be prieſts. This I ſhew, not wanting proofs out of Scriptures; but that you may ſee, that theſe froſty bearded hypocrites, in debaſing the miniſtery vnder the meaneſt, ſtriue not onely againſt order, but againſt the law of nature and nations, that neuer thought baſely of religion, or of the teachers of religion, and accounted thoſe
Ariſt.polit.7.9. atheiſts, that debaſed the prieſthood, πρέπει γὰρ τιμᾶσθαι τὼ θεὼς. Neither is it the meaning or practiſe of Gods law, that the miniſtery ſhould be debaſed, much leſſe diſhonoured.

Vnder the law the prieſts had not onely great honours, but alſo ti-
Ezra.8. tles of honour: of prieſts, ſome were called *Sharei hacohanim*, that is, Princes of prieſts; then which, no title was more honourable in that ſtate. *Eleazar* the ſonne of *Aaron*, was called *Neſhi neſhiei*, that is, Prince of princes. *Num.3.* The teachers of the law were called
3.Reg.18. *Rabbi*, and the prieſts, fathers. *Iudic. 17. & 18.* The ſeruant of king *Achab*, meeting with *Elias*, calleth him Lord. And *Elizeus* is called

Lord

Lord by the *Sunamite. Eliasaph, Elizaphat, Suriel*, are called *Neshiei*, that is, princes and heads. Yea, all priests were called elders : which name, although it seeme not so high and glorious as the titles that now are vsed; yet was it the greatest that was then vsed to princes, and men of great state. Vnder the law the priests had as great titles as princes, giuen by God himselfe.

Numb.3.

Num.3.et Iosf.c.21. Roshei abot.

In the primitiue church, when magistrates beganne to professe Christianity, the bishops then were not inferiour to any lord of the empire, in their names and titles, being called *Religiosissimi, Sanctissimi, Deo amabiles, domini papæ, patres patriæ, patriarchæ, clarissimi, spectatissimi.* that is, Patriarches, fathers of their country, lords most religious, holy, &c. and in our times, some giue the title of *Clarissimi* to ministers, then the which, *Iulius Cæsar* had no greater. Since Spanish brauery and Italian flatery (saith one) began to broch copie of titles, euery petit companion taketh vpon him great names : therefore the king of *Spaine* decreed that none should haue the title of *Altezza*, but himselfe. whereupon it was written vpon *Pasquil, Tu solus altissimus.* Now then, that generall custome is so lauish in titles to others, will they of the new discipline make a law, that none but such as they allow, shall haue titles, and be called *Altissimi*, or Lords? if they can not make lawes, this custome of honorable titles will neuer be left in the ministery, as long as the same standeth; nor seeing they are words of courtesy, is it conuenient. and therefore they had best to conceale their affections, & not declare that they enuy bishops both the things & the names, & can neither afford thē good turne, nor good words.

Bez. ep. Cor. ep. ad Bez. de pol. Iudaic.

The disciples of our Lord had their titles, not onely concerning their ministery, but also their other actions and dignity; some wherof were giuen and allowed by *Christ* himselfe. some were called *Boanerges*, or sonnes of thunder, *Peter* was called *Cephas*. and *Iames* the bishop of *Ierusalem* was called *Iustus*, a title which a certeine *Athenian* could not abide, and therfore would haue *Aristides*, surnamed *Iustus*, banished. Titles therefore, are no marks of ambition, as some pretend, nor forbidden as vnlawfull, so the minde be meeke & humble : otherwise, the proud minde of men is to be condemned, euen in the vagrant doctors of reformation, that like *Diogenes*, liue by earth, water, and the aire : τὸ δὲ πῦρ δεξίωμα κάλλιστον (as saith *Pindare*) that is, the fire which is kindled by charity, though neuer so precious, they want, and liue not by it. a woondrous matter, that such vnder pretence of beggery, should waxe so rich and fat, and purchase : see, see what it is to liue in persecution.

Plutarch. in Aristide.

Nay, our Sauiour *Christ*, who is an example of all humility and meeknesse, refused not titles of Maister & Doctour, then which, the greatest of the *Sanedrin* among the *Iewes* had no greater; whose action may be warrant for all that do as he did.

Petr. Galat. they were called *Rabbi.*

I need not long argue against titles: for the aduersary is not so rigorous in this point, but that he can allow of titles. nay, which is worsse, like Pharisees they loue highest places at feasts (which they seeke after greedily) and glorious titles, most ambitiously, and if you call them not maister and doctor, they will looke big and sowre, and depart malcontent. *Daneau* calleth the ministers and doctours of *Heidelberg, Clarissimos. Beza* refuseth not the title of *Vir clarissimus,* and *Doctor fidelissimus.* a most famous man, and a most faithfull doctour. *Daneau* is called a most reuerend and learned man by a certaine platformer. and our platformers are woont to scratch one anothers ambitious galles with *Maister* and *Most learned,* and refuse not the title of worship. If then titles be lawfull, why not the title of Lord? if lofty titles are onely condemned, why doe they not define which titles passe for lofty, which for base?

Isag. part. 4. epist.
De polit. Iud. epistola.

Further, if that be true, that those that enter the ministery, loose no nobility; then if a lord enter into that function, as in *France* hath bene done, and may be done, some minister may lawfully be called lord. and if the elder, which they make a degree vnder pastour, may be a lord, as they confesse; then haue they no reason to debase their learned pastors, and despoile them of their titles.

Names and titles of honor, are termes of humanity and courtesie, wherin, if there be any abuse, it is principally in those that giue them; and therefore quarrelling with bishops titles, they not onely quarrell with the common vse of speech, but contend against common humanity and courtesie. A strange matter, that they that haue no ciuilitie, should now take on them to reforme our mother tongue, and teach termes of courtesie.

Yea, but this title of lord is (say they) too lofty. why? forsooth they cannot tell, but that they haue a longing to make bishops the scumme of the people, that such hindes, as themselues, may triumph as lords in the consistory. The reason that I haue alleged of honors, and honorable titles giuen to the ministery, vnder the law, vnder the gospell, by instinct of nature, yea, by *Christ* himselfe, and their owne practise, they can not answere. euen this title of κύριος or lord, is giuen to *Paul* and *Sylas*. they say it is not so large nor lofty as lord with vs. I say, considering the diuersity of times, that it was more lofty, being giuen

Act. 16.

giuen of slaues to their lords, and being condemned in princes, *Luke 22.* where our Sauiour missliketh κυριεύειν or lordly dominion in them. it is the title that *Augustus* refused. and therefore considering those times, it is a great title: for those that were but *milites* then, or plaine souldiers, are now *caualliaros* and knights, and lords of great dignitie.

Neither doth our Sauiour, *Luke 22.* condemne the title of Lord in ministers, where he saith οἱ βασιλεῖς τῶν ἐθνῶν &c. εὐεργέται καλοῦνται: ὑμεῖς δὲ οὐχ οὕτως. that is, the kings of the nations, &c. are called bountifull benefactors, but it shall not be so with you. For declaration of which place, we are to vnderstand, that this precept, *It shall not be so with you*, concerneth all Christians, represented there in the person of the apostles. My reasons are these: For that the opposition betwixt the Gentiles and Christians is more fit, then betweene the Gentiles and the apostles: neither can the contrary exposition stand, which maketh it lawfull for other Christians to follow the maners of the Gentiles, and excepteth onely the ministers. Secondly, for that pride, and vaine titles are condemned in euery Christian. Thirdly, for that *Christes* humility is not to be followed of the ministers onely, but of all Christians: and if that were materiall, so diuers learned men expound it. and (which I respect) the words will beare it, and almost inforce it. for seeing the words, Bountifull benefactours, are an exposition of the words, Beare dominion, and are put ἐξηγητικῶς, that is, expositiuely, which must needs be, or els it must be said, that *Matthew* is defectiue, and leaueth a necessary instruction concerning titles (which driueth *Caluin* to confesse the same) then I say, that as dominion is forbidden, so the pride of dominion and tyranny is forbidden to all Christians. But suppose that in the person of the apostles our Sauior instructeth onely ministers, and that εὐεργέται or Bountifull benefactours signifieth more then κυριεύειν or Dominion, that went before: yet all that can here hence be gathered, is that the ministers may not be called εὐεργέται or Bountifull benefactors: that is, that they may not take vpon themselues to be called by singular titles of Bounty, as did the Gentile kings, which otherwise, being tyrants, yet would be called Benefactors of the world, or of countries, which is a proud title.

The word εὐεργέται doth not make against the title of Lord.

And that our sauior alludeth to thẽ, it is euident, for that he calleth thẽ not kings only, but kings of the Gentiles, & mentioneth a proud title vsurped only by one or two *Ptolemeys* kings of Egypt, and *Cleomenes* king of *Sparta*; of whõ I read only, that they were called εὐεργέται. for vnlesse men appropriat this title to thẽselues, & chalenge it as belonging to thẽ, as benefactors of coũtries, εὐεργέτης is a term of no great

Arist. polt. 5. c. 3 ἅπαντες εὐεργετήσαντες ἢ δυνάμενοι τὰς πόλεις ἢ τὰ ἔθνη εὐεργετεῖν ἐτύγχανον τῆς τιμῆς ταύτης. i. βασιλείας.

 excellency,

cellency, and spoken of meane persons, and alwayes in the best part.

To presse and racke this place, that it may say somewhat against the lordship and titles of ministers, they helpe it with a translation, making εὐεργέται to signifie gratious lords; which is very simple, and not answering our Sauiours meaning. for the title of εὐεργέτης is a stile reprehended by our Sauiour, and scoffed at of the Gentiles themselues, as too too ambitious, which can not be said of lords, or gracius lords, being a title vsuall in diuers, and not disallowed, but in some, & that by those that like nothing. Secondly, for that the stile of εὐεργέτης appropriate to themselues, is onely found in two or three, and those great princes, the title of lord being giuen to many of meane estate, in respect of them. That the ambitious chalenger of the title εὐεργέτης is reprehended, and not the word, I proued by this, for that the word is of a base signification, and giuen to simple men, and is taken in good part. which to auoid, *Th.Cartwr.* saith that munificence is more then liberality; which he would prooue out of *Aristotle:* but he coineth a piece of mony of his owne stampe, for he hath no such thing. he saith that μεγαλοπρέπεια or magnificence is more then liberality: so is it more then εὐεργεσία, which is spoken of euery small benefit. but what is this to purpose? he allegeth further, that εὐεργέτης is a word of empire, which is a ridiculous ignorance of the Greeke tongue. The title was proud in *Ptolomey*, for that he tooke to himselfe by excellency, that which was common to infinite, or made himselfe a benefactor of mankinde or of great countries, like another *Hercules.* So *Philadelphus* was a fond title in another *Ptolomey*, and εὐπατὼρ in another, and *Sage* attributed to *Charles* of *France*, sauoureth somewhat that way: yet are the words in their owne nature of a meane and base signification.

Ethic.4.c.2.

To expound εὐεργέτης as *Th. Cartwr.* doth, with *nubîm*, is a weake course, and strange: for the vse of words is not to be declared by other languages, but by the same. *Th.Cartwr.* hauing ended his part, and hauing no more to say; in commeth one, and vrgeth further, that lawfull dominion is opposed to a ministery: then which, what more absurd? for who euer would imagine that our sauiour *Christ* allowed the tyranny, and vanity of the Gentiles? but so blinde they are in running against the ministery, that rather then they will allow lawfull titles in the ministery, they can be content to subscribe to all the tyranny & folly of the Gentiles. This therefore let them receiue for finall answere, that our sauiour *Christ* condemneth not modest titles of honour, so they be neither ambitiously sought, nor proudly stood vpon; but he condemneth the tyrannous rule, and vaine and proud

Defence of the godly ministers.

proude titles of the Gentiles, some wherof were called εὐεργέται: some σωτῆρες: some θεοί, as *Antiochus*, some ægles, as *Pirrus*. Likewise he condemneth pride, and presumption, euen in the meanest titles: as for example, of Master, Doctor, of which title some are more brag then others of their lordship. Benefactors, Sauiours, Gods.

I say lastly, that he condemneth tyrannous, and lordly rule, wherby we say that the bishops of this land are not touched, for they cannot make lawes nor prescribe orders, but according to lawe: but the lords of the Consistorie are iustly noted, who calling themselues the lords seruants and ministers, as the *Pope* calleth himselfe *Seruum seruorum Dei*, yet taking vpon them to conuent, condemne and censure princes, to ordeine and depose ministers, and to gouerne in all matters of maners and doctrine, so farre as doth apperteine to conscience, and finally to make lawes, and abrogate them at pleasure, and not to bee subiect to controlment; are not onely lordes, but proude and absurd tyrants, if they might haue what they seeke. this they cannot excuse with infirmitie of the brethren, which serueth them nowe and then for a buckler. for it is a plaine doctrine, and notorious presumption of theirs. Therefore let vs heare no more of the bare title of lord, which the bishops haue not, as they are ministers, but as they haue Baronries annexed to their liuings and dignities, the lawfulnesse whereof they cannot disprooue: but let them hereafter looke better to moderate the infinite and vnbridled dominion of their Consistories: in which albeit they haue not title of lords, yet they practise both lordship and tyrannie.

Of the Pastor and his office.

CHAP. 3. SECT. 6,

The authoritie and title of Archbishop is approued by the Councell of Nice, *by the Councels of* Ephesus *and* Calcedon, *and practise and sayings of diuers ancient fathers, long before the Bishops of* Rome *sate in the seate of Antichrist. The exceptions against the name are declared to be weake and friuolous.*

IT is not ynough for them to quarrell with the common sort, and their common vse of speech, that giueth the title of lord to bishops: but they must also challenge counsels and fathers, for vsing the title of Archbishop. let vs therefore consider their reasons. Archbishop is the title of Christ (as they say) and therefore is not to be applyed to any man: of which reason, I denie both antecent and sequele. the antecedent I denie, for that they can no where ſhew where Chriſt is called Archbiſhop. the title of chiefe ſhepheard, or ὁ ἀρχιποίμην prooueth it not: for they muſt remember that the ſtrife is about the word and title, not about the thing, if then they can proue ὁ ἀρχιποίμην that is chiefe ſhepheard, to bee as Archbiſhop of one prouince, or to bee the ſame with that word, then that title ſhall be granted to belong to Chriſt.

Nowe as they deale, their courſe is abſurd: for one word prooueth not another, nor two titles differing can bee ſaide to bee the ſame. The ſequele I denie, for that many titles that are ſpoken properly of Chriſt in reſpect of the whole Church, are not vnfitly applied to men, in reſpect of particular Churches. Chriſt is called the true ſhepherd, or paſtor, hee is likewiſe called our doctor, he is called our maſter. he is called the biſhop of our ſoules: likewiſe in reſpect of their Churches, miniſters of the word are called paſtors, and which is more, true paſtors, doctors, teachers. and maſter, it is a common title of curteſie applied to miniſters & others: matters which can not be denied. if titles that are proper to Chriſt cannot be applied to men, why are theſe titles applied to them? if they had ſayd that the titles that belong to Chriſt in the ſame reſpect belong not to men, we had yeelded that they ſay true: but then they ſay nothing to purpoſe: for in that reſpect that Chriſt is called chiefe ſhepherd, doctor, and maſter and paſtor, no mortall man can iuſtly take vpon him to be chiefe ſhepherd, doctor, or maſter.

They ſay further, that the title of Archbiſhop being compounded of a word that betokeneth principalitie and gouernment, to wit of ἀρχὴ or ἄρχων, ioyned to biſhop, that it is too loftie a title to fit the lowe degree of miniſters, & alledge that the councell of *Carthage* decreed that no biſhop ſhoulde be called ἔξαρχος τῶν ἱερέων ἢ ἄκρος ἱερεὺς, that is *prince of prieſtes or the high prieſt*. To the firſt I anſwere, that titles are not vnuſuall nor vnlawfull in miniſters. Secondly, that Archbiſhop is not ſo loftie a title as they conceiue, or ſuch, but that greater titles haue bin giuen to biſhops of the learned godly fathers. the Canons of the Apoſtles call the biſhop prince of the people *can. 54. Ignatius* maketh

Ad Trall. the biſhop πάσης ἀρχῆς καὶ ἐξουσίας κρατοῦντα, that is, one that hath all principalitie and power in his handes: hee meaneth in Church affaires, and maketh him Gods lieutenant, προκαθήμενον εἰς τόπον Θεοῦ. *Ierom* calleth bi-

Lib. 3. epiſt. 1. ſhops *Eccleſiarum principes*, princes of the Church in *Iſai. 1. Cyprian* calleth biſhops pilots, gouernours: the power of biſhops hee calleth

Lib. 1. epiſt. 3. *Sublimem et diuinam*, that is, high and diuine. *Origen tract. 12.* In *Matth.*

Matth. calleth biſhops *principes populi Chriſtiani.* that is, princes of the people of Chriſt. *Tertullian* calleth the biſhop *Summum ſacerdotem,* that is, the chiefe prieſt. *Ambroſe* giueth him the title of prince of *de Bapt.*
prieſtes in *Ephe.4.* neither doth the ſcripture abaſe them beneath the common ſort. among the prieſtes ſome were called *Roſhei Abot*: and *Neſhei*, that is, prieſts, the new Teſtament entitleth them προεστῶτας, ἡγουμένους, and προϊσταμένους, that is, rulers and preſidents, and gouernours, which are ſo farre aboue the title of Archbiſhop, as gouernours are aboue ouerſeers. for theſe wordes ſignifie the gouernment. the word ἐπίσκοπος ſignifieth inſpection or ouerſight onely, and may be without authoritie or rule. Thirdly, I denie that the word Archbiſhoppe is compounded of a word betokening rule & empire. why do they ſay it, & are not able to proue it? ἀρχὴ in ἀρχιεπίσκοπος is taken as in ἀρχίατρος or ἀρχίφυλος *Ioſh.21*. for one that in order and ranke is firſt. and as it is abſurd to thinke that ἀρχίφυλος or ἀρχίατρος is gouernour of Phyſicions or of all his tribe; ſo to conceiue that Archbiſhop is ſo called, becauſe hee is gouernour of all biſhops, is to conceiue without reaſon. and the very name of Archbiſhop ioyned with the name of a Citie, doth ſhewe that he is nothing but firſt biſhop, of and in that prouince: in which reſpect Archbiſhop is called Metropolitan in the Councel of *Nice*, and Archbiſhop by that name in the Councell of *Calcedon.* at which names while ſome doe ſcoffe, what doe they but ſcoffe at Councels, fathers, orders and religion?

Numbers.3.

In tranſlat.70.

The reſt of their reaſons are trifling; as that among the giftes that our Sauiour gaue to his Church, Archbiſhop is not founde. no more is biſhop nor prieſt, but yet all comprehended ynder the name of paſtor. but their presbyteries, conferences and Synodes are neither there found nor vnderſtoode. Archbiſhop, Biſhop and Miniſter haue one miniſterie to preach the word and miniſter the ſacraments, which doth not take away difference of degrees, that things may be done in order.

For euen of things belonging to the miniſterie, all cannot doe all things at all times, but euery thing muſt bee done in his time and place, and by perſons conuenient, and ſo it was among the prieſts and Leuites, which had diuers orders among themſelues. *Nomb.3.* To thinke that all the Prieſts in the *Iewiſh* Church did iudge & gouerne, is a fancie becomming men of their iudgement in matters of ſtate to affirme.

That Archbiſhop is a name inuented by Antichriſt cannot bee

prooued. It is boldly affirmed and maliciously repeated, but neuer prooued. who will affirme *Cornelius*, *Cyprian*, *Basil*, *Epiphanius*, *Chrysostome*, *Ambrose*, *Gregorie*, & other godly fathers, to haue names and titles and offices from Antichrist, or who can endure those that in great rage, no reason, doe call these godly fathers limmes and members of Antichrist? for so they must needes, if Archbishops bee the limmes and members of Antichrist as they sticke not to affirme: will they also charge the generall Counsel of *Calcedon* with Anticristianisme? but were the name giuen by the *Pope*, what is that, if the gouernment be from God, and confirmed by the ancient Councell of *Nice*, *Calcedon*, and *Antiochia*, that confirme the autoritie of Metropolitans practised by the godly fathers continued from the beginning, not gainesaide by any but such as *Aerius*, and his complices, which compared with the gouernment of the Consistorie and the presidents of Consistories, and their new vpstart Elders, shall appeare to be of God, when those shall appeare to be fancies of men?

Can.6.

Why they should call Archbishops the inuention of *Popes*, being so long before the authoritie of the pope did shewe it selfe, they haue no reason: why they should condemne all orders of gouernment proceeding from the pope, they haue lesse reason: seeing their proceeding in excommuuication, their banes in mariage, their authoritie in their censures is papal, if not of a newer stampe. It sufficeth that speaking against archbishops, you see that they speake not against vs onely, but against the councels and fathers also.

Can.Ephes.et Calced.

Wherefore, seeing these that condemne the autoritie of Metropolitans, and title of Archbishop, doe striue against the autoritie of generall councels, against the ancient gouernment of the Church without reason: their bold audaciousnesse is rather to bee censured by a iudge, then longer refuted wieh words. Neither can it excuse them, that *Caluin* and *Beza* and others haue condemned Archbishops and bishops: for neither are they so violent against our bishops as these hot braines are, nor is that they speake being intended against the papists, to be extended against the ministers of the Gospel. nor though it were so extended, were they to be credited, speaking great words in commendation of a new gouernment erected by themselues. If any will alledge & vse their reasons against Archbishops, the same shalbe answered. and if any be in loue with the Consistorie, the same shalbe disproued, & the gouernment of Archbishops compared with that of the consistorie shalbe proued more godly, ancient & profitable, both for this land and others.

In what respect *Caluin* and *Beza* haue condemned Archbishops.

Of

Of the Pastor and his office.

CAP. 3. SECT. 7.

Therein by lawes and examples of gouernement, both in the Church of the Iewes, and Christians, is proued, that it is not vnlawfull for some Ministers to vndertake ciuill charges, and that being citizens and free borne, they may not refuse them, being imposed on them, nor are to be declared vncapable of them. the same is proued likewise by the practise of the disciplinarians. All those reasons that are alledged to the contrarie, are answered.

THis dispute is not concerning the office of a Minister, whether it consist in doing of ciuill offices: for there is no question, but the office of a Minister of the worde, is diuers from the office of a Magistate. But the question is, whether that person which is called to the Ministerie, may also beare some ciuill office, if for his abilitie he be thereto called? or whether a Magistrate or inferior ciuill officer, taking vpon him the Ministerie, doe presentlie loose, or ought to forgoe his ciuill office? they say that the offices are so distinct, that one person may not meddle with both. We hold that some are of that sufficiencie, that they manage both better, then some accounted of the aduersarie sufficient, doe manage eyther: & that there is no lawe, why in a Christian common-wealth a Minister may not (if he be able and called lawfullie) deale in ciuil charges. which opinion is true, as the other is false, and iniurious.

And truelie may I call it iniurious: for it taketh from the Ministers all right of borgesie & freedome of citizens in the common-wealth, which is a way to discourage manie from the Ministerie. For he deserueth not the name of a citizen, or free subiect, that in a common-wealth is excluded from all partes of the gouernement: πολίτης δ' ἁπλῶς οὐδενὶ τῶν ἄλλων ὁρίζεται μᾶλλον ἢ τῷ μετέχειν κρίσεως καὶ ἀρχῆς. A citizin (sayth *Aristotle*) to speake plainely, cannot be defined in any termes better, then when he is sayde to be a citizen that hath part in the offices that manage iurisdiction, and haue commandement. Thinke it not strange (good reader) to heare the name of *Aristotle* or his politikes in this discourse, for we are now talking, not of the Ministerie onely, but of ciuill offices. And therefore seeing the Ministers that are occupied about the seruice of God, haue had alwayes the reputation of citizens, and bene thought of honorably of all nations; they should haue wrong to be excluded from ciuill offices, and declared vncapable. I could shewe by lawes of all nations, that they haue not onelie had this right, but enioyed it. but what neede we the testimonie of men, hauing such light in the lawes of God?

Politi 3.c.1.

The Lord purposing to meete with the ignorance of inferior iudges, appointed an order of iudges to sit in the head citie, consisting of the high priest, & of inferiour priests & leuits, as men most skilful and learned, afterward some chiefe men were adioyned to them, to iudge of causes capital, or of blood & other hard controuersies. If God (notwithstanding the office of ÿ priesthood, more troublesome then, by reason of the multitude of Sacrifices and ceremonies) did notwithstanding thinke thẽ fittest to iudge in ciuill causes of greatest weight; then is it not against the nature of the Ministerie, to deale in ciuill causes. I am not ignorant that some distinguish and say, that the Priestes gaue sentence of lawe, the magistrate sentence of fact: which proceedeth of palpable ignorance of state. For who euer sawe, in one cause, one bench of Iudges to set downe lawe, another bench to set downe fact? the parties shewe the fact, the Iudges determine. *Ex facto ius oritur: therefore he that wil rightly iudge, must know the fact precisely.* Secondly, it is too cõtumelious, to make the prince Minister of the priests sentẽce. Thirdly, were it granted, that the Priests set downe lawe concerning ciuill causes: yet that is as much as we neede in this disputation: for we are to proue, that Ministers by the lawe of God, may deale in ciuill causes. *Philo* sayeth, the Priestes iudged of fact aswell as lawe.

Deut.17. Vatablus ex rabb. Philo de creatione principis. 2.Chr.19.

De creat.princ. & lib.3.de vita Mosis.

But that they dealt not onelie in matters of iudgement, but also in other offices, and that not in lawe onelie, but in fact; it appeareth further by the historie of *Dauids* gouernement, who numbring thirtie eight thousand Leuites, appointed twentie foure thousand to hasten the worke of the Lord. sixe thousand hee appointed to be rulers and iudges. which, least anie man conceiue to be Ecclesiasticall officers, he must remember, they were appointed by the king, whome the disciplinarians exclude from commandement in Ecclesiasticall causes: and dealt for the kings causes.

1.Paral.23. & 26.

He also appointed *Hasabia* and his brethren, and *Ieria* and his brethren leuites, rulers, and gouernors of the *Iewes* beyond Iorden: not in Ecclesiasticall causes, but both in the causes of God, that is for the execution of Gods lawes, and for all the kings busines. so that we must vnderstand, some were of counsel, some for the warres, some for the treasures, some for other causes, for these bee the kings affaires. *Eleasar* the Priest was the chiefe of those that deuided the land of *Canaan* among the tribes: and *Benaiah* a priestes sonne, was captaine of a parte of *Dauids* armie: *Azariah* was chiefe of *Salomons* counsell. *1.Reg.4.*

1.Paral.26.

Iosua.14.

1.Paral.27.

Iehosaphat, he likewise apointed Priestes and Leuites iudges in *Ierusalem*,

rusalem, and in all the cities of *Iudah*, not that should seuerallie dispatch ciuill and Ecclesiasticall causes, but that ioyntlie they shoulde iudge the causes of God and the king : although the principal iudges of these causes were seuerall. Whosoeuer list to see further of these distinct iurisdictions : let him looke that Latine treatise which I made against a certaine *Italian* in that argument, where the conceites of two distinct tribunals is at large refuted.

Consider the commission which the *Persian* king gaue to *Ezra*, and which *Ezra* gaue to others. you shall see that the Iudges he appointed, iudged not in Ecclesiasticall causes, but generallie in all matters, whereof there were Priestes and Leuites that had the principal charges. The sonnes of *Samuel* were the chiefe Iudges of the land, yet were they priests. the which practise (as it should seeme) stil cōtinued. *Ezr.7.*

Ioseph testifieth, that in euerie citie, there were seuen chosen out of the chiefe men for Iudges, which had likewise two Leuites ioyned vnto them for Ministers. *Antiq.lib.4.c.7.*

That the Iewish sanedrin at *Ierusalem* consisted of Priestes, and that they handeled ciuill causes of life and death, warre & peace, both the scriptures, talmudists, and iewish histories testifie: that it was done onelie by vsurpation, is sayde, not proued. For both the institution of the order of Iudges, being to beare the burden together with the prince, & to iudge in causes of bood, and that ẏ same was neuer reprehended for dealing in ciuill causes, may shewe that it was by right. *Pet. Gal. lib.4. cap.3.* *Deut.17.4.* *Numb.11.*

But what neede I speake of Priestes dealing, in inferior offices, seeing the same did oft times susteine the greatest charges of that common-wealth? First *Moses* was both gouernour of the people, and a Priest that had the chiefe care of Gods seruice. after him, both *Heli* and *Samuel* were Iudges and Priestes. When the people returned from *Babylon*, *Ezra* a priest was the chiefe leader and ruler of the people. and after *Nehemias*, the gouernement continued in the stock and familie of the Priestes. I neede to saye nothing of *Azariah*, that was of *Salomons* counsell, and *Iehoiadah* that was the kings tutor. This they say was extraordinarie, and they haue often saide it; but they neuer yet could proue it. That is called extraordinarie (as themselues say) that is contrarie to common custome or rules. but that a Priest shoulde bee gouernour, is not contrarie to custome, being done so often; nor rule, seeing I haue shewed the institution to bee of God, both by the lawe of *Deuteronomie*, and practise of iudges, kings, and continuall gouernement of that state: wherein the Priestes were employed in greatest matters of

 state:

ſtate: as namelie *Zadok* in the time of *Salomon:* whoſe chiefe capteine alſo was a Prieſtes ſonne, and a Prieſt: a matter more repugnant to prieſthood. and *Iehoiadah* was the kings gardian in the time of *Ioaſh:* πρασσέτω μηδὲν δίχα τοῦ ἀρχιερέως. ſayeth *Ioſeph* of the king; that is to ſaye: Let him doe nothing without the chiefe Prieſt.

Ioſeph.lib.4. anti.c.7.

Let vs deſcend downe vnto the times of Chriſtian Emperors, at what time the Church and common-wealth were one bodie onelie diſtinguiſhed in reſpect, and then we ſhall ſee, that they accounted it not abſurd for Byſhops to beare ciuill offices. The Emperors, *Honorius*, and *Arcadius* gaue iuriſdiction to Byſhops in all ciuill cauſes, wherein the parties that contended did chuſe them arbitrators. What they determined, the Emperors ratified, ſo that no appeale was admitted from their iudgement. The Emperors *Valentinian*, and *Valens*, gaue Byſhops power to ſet prices vpon things ſolde in the market, leaſt by hard prices the poore ſhoulde bee grieued. By the grant of *Honorius* and *Theodoſius* the archbyſhop had iuriſdiction in cauſes of ſuch as returned out of captiuitie. All cauſes that belonged to the clearkes of the Church of Conſtantinople, were decided by the archbyſhop. *Iuſtinian* in certaine caſes, gaue Byſhops iuriſdiction in cauſes of account, and debt. *L. Si preſens. ibidem.* How they dealt in cauſes of marriage, teſtaments, of pupils, orphans, ideots, that title doth at large declare. all which time, the Byſhops of Rome had no iuriſdiction nor authoritie more then other like Byſhops. *Ambroſe* was ſent ambaſſador by *Valentinian* to the tyrant *Maximus*. The Emperor likewiſe ſent *Maruthas* in ambaſſage to the king of *Perſia*. Of *Conſtantine*, *Euſebius* reporteth, that he had Byſhops cōtinuallie preſent w^t^ him, and aſſiſtant to him. τοὺς τοῦ θεοῦ ἱερέας ἐπιύγετο συνεῖναι τῷ αὐτῷ, καὶ παρεῖναι. *Baſil* for his graue aduiſe, and authoritie with magiſtrates, is by *Gregorie Nazianzen* called *princeps Magiſtratuum*, the prince of Magiſtrates. *Ambroſe* ſaith, it belongeth to the duetie of byſhops to keepe ſuch things, as by widowes, & orphans are committed vnto them. Of himſelfe he teſtifieth, that he compoſed diuers matters in lawe, and controuerſies by his arbitrement. What ſhould I ſpeake of the iuriſdiction of *Theophilus* and *Cyrill*, the Archbyſhops of *Alexandria*, which dealt in the greateſt affaires of the common-wealth, all which, *Th.Cartw.* with one worde thinketh to wipe away, when he ſaith, that this was more then could be tolerated in Byſhops? but it is not words nor lookes, that can encounter with the authoritie of ſo many lawes, fathers, reaſons. He ſaith that it is not tolerable: but *Auguſtine* hoped to receiue reward at Gods hand, for his paines

L.Si qui. Cod. de epiſc.aud. — *L.epiſ. iudicium Cod.ibidem.* — *Cod: eod. L.negotiatores.* — *L.Chriſtianos. ibidem.* — *L. Decernimus. ibidem.* — *Epiſt.27.l.5.* — *Soc.l.7.* — *Epiſt.Conſtanti. lib 2.* — *In Monod.* — *Offic. lib.2.c.29.* — *Ambroſ.epiſ.24. lib.5.* — *Socr.lib.7.c.7. & 32.*

paines taken, in hearing ciuill causes. Whether are wee to folow the word of God, the practise of ancient Churches, & authoritie of most wise princes & graue fathers, or the rash opinion of him, that in his foolish conceit will condemne whatsoeuer himselfe misliketh: nay, which condemneth him selfe & his owne friends, & their platforms? Himselfe, for that being a pastor or a Doctor (as he accounteth himselfe) he taketh on him the mastership of an hospitall, a meere ciuill office: his friendes, for that being Ministers, they take on them ciuill charges. *Beza* is of the counsel of state at *Geneua*, & nothing hath bin done these manie yeares without him. *Villiers* was of the counsell of the prince of *Orenge*; whose malice the English nation felt, in requital of ẏ good they did vnto him, while hee liued a banished man in England. & their owne platformers, for that where they make Elders an Ecclesiasticall office, they are notwithstanding ẏ principall gouernors of the state. *Caluin* maketh no bones to make a syndik, which is the chiefe magistrate of *Geneua*, president of their Consistorie. And *Beza* sheweth that at *Geneua* ẏ chiefe counsellors of state, are chosen continuallie Elders of the Church, and that ciuill iudges which are there, *le petit conseil* are also Elders. And in his preface before the new Testament, he would haue Church officers chosen of the most sufficient noble men. So ẏ a leader of men of warre may (putting off his armes) be one day an Elder, and putting them on the next day, a warriour & commander. The articles of *French* discipline make a special prouiso, that such may be admitted Elders. If then magistrates may be Ecclesiasticall officers, & both at one time; why may not Ecclesiastical officers be magistrates likewise, which followeth by the rules of conuersion? for albeit *Th. Cartw.* lay downe new rules of discipline, yet I trow he hath no commission to breake the lawes of Logike, and frame vs new principles of conuersion. There is a certaine thriftles and witles pamphlet, called a *Learned discourse*, that would haue Deacons to be chosen of the most worshipfull & sufficient gentlemen: he excepteth not such as haue charge in the common-wealth. If then he can of his liberalitie, bestow the basest charges of ẏ Church of men most worshipful, making iustices of peace, slaues, & seruants to their Consistorie; (a matter ridiculous) then let thē not thinke it so strange a matter, for Ministers to beare certaine offices imposed vpon thē in the common-wealth, by those that haue authoritie. If *Th. Cartw.* were made an officer, as an ambassador, or counseller of state by ẏ prince, I doubt whether he would, sure I am, that (consider his allegiance) he could not refuse it. Some percase will say, he would giue ouer his Doctor-

August. de oper. monach.

Summa cap. discip. Geneu. Put among Caluin. epist.

Beza epist. 20.

i. The streit or little counsell.

ship, and Mastership of his hospitall, in case anie such matter should be, for auoyding of confusion of offices, and resume it againe afterwarde: but it is but a fiction and a dreame of their discipline. For I haue knowen many that haue forsaken their platforms for their profite: but those that forsake their profite for mainteining of their platforme, are *tanquam rara auis in terris*, a bird appearing verie rarelie.

Now let vs see how clearklie they reason, both against themselues and against vs. First they alledge the example of our sauiour Christ, who (as they say) refused as a thing vnmeete for his ministerie, the office of a iudge, and whereas one desired leaue to burie his father, would not permit him. First, I denie that *Christ* refused this office by him to be performed as vnlawfull for the Ministerie, but to shewe that *Christs* calling was to be obeyed and followed, although priuate duties were neglected. For that no man (I thinke) will denie, but that Ministers may compose the controuersies of their friendes, which is a worke of charitie enioyned vnto all men: or holde that they may not accompanie their friendes to buriall, or see them enterred decently. For *Christ* doth not take the affections that be naturall, from Ministers, nor doth he make them *Stoikes*, or like some of the disciplinarians: who (though full of affection, or rather furie to set vp discipline) yet are altogether without mercie, against those that resist thẽ. neither would he haue Ministers vnlike to other men. At *Geneua* the Ministers deale in the controuersies of friends, and followe bodies to burial. Secõdlie I answere, that these examples of our Sauiour are not to purpose: for ẏ question is of publike offices; these are priuate duties. and if *Cæsar* had imposed this charge vpon him, he would not haue refused. Againe, the question is not, whether all Ministers are to deale in ciuill offices (for we thinke it absurde) but whether a charge imposed by the prince may be refused of anie Minister. besides this, these examples are of such duties, as (they themselues knowe) Ministers are not of ciuilitie to refuse. This argument therefore may thus be beaten vpon thẽ. If (notwithstanding *Christes* refusal) Ministers may be arbitrators, and compose matters betwixt friendes, and accompanie their friendes to their buriall (which they cannot denie, vnlesse they will condemne the practise of their Consistories, in which, the Ministers meddle in all matters of brabble; and the fact of the Ministers of *Geneua*, that followe the bodies of their friendes and others being dead to the buriall) then doth not this example make against ciuil offices in Ministers: but that is a worke of charitie, and thought lawful by them. *Ergo, &c.*

Againe,

Againe, if all ministers be subiects, they are not to refuse any ciuill charge laid vpon them, notwithstanding Christes examples here alledged. *Ergo,* they make not against ciuil offices in ministers. the sequel of the *antecedent* is proued, for that Christ did neither dissolue the moral law, and lawes of charitie, nor take away or exempt any frō ciuil gouernment: for not onely lay men, but ministers are commanded to be subiect to princes, as saith *Chrysostome.* and that free immunitie which Popish priests claime, is derogatorie to the Princes auctoritie, and not supported by any commandement of Christ.

They alledge also out of *S. Iohn,* that our Sauiour refused to iudge the harlot taken in adulterie. which as it concerneth not the matter they woulde proue, so it may be vsed to disprooue their opinion. the Pharises do not bring her before Christ to be iudged (for they knewe he was a priuate man, and had no auctoritie to put any to death) but to know Christs opinion concerning the law, that they might entrap him, if he should mislike of *Moses* law. Where they say that Christ refused to be iudge, they speake against the text: for Christ called for the witnesses, and gaue absolutorie sentence that shee should depart. Wherefore thus I enforce their owne place against them. if notwithstanding this example, any minister of the Gospel may declare and teach what he thinketh to be Gods lawe, which the disciplinarians take to be ciuil iudgement; then is not ciuill iudgement forbiden vnto ministers by this place: but that is apparant, for that it is the ministers duetie to declare the law of God, and to teach it, *Ergo, &c.*

To presse the matter further. If what our Sauiour did here, the same may be done in ciuil causes; then may ministers call for witnesses, and discharge the parties that come before them to be iudged in ciuil causes, especially when the prince imposeth that charge vpō them. Lastly, if our Sauiour Christ whipped the exchangers and marchants out of the Temple, which is a matter mere ciuil: then Christes example is rather a cōfirmation for ministers to take ciuil offices vpon them, then a president to refuse them. Neither can they escape out by saying that this was extraordinarie, and not by vertue of Christes office: for it is blasphemous to say that Christ did contrary to lawe, and absurde to make Christ to haue any other office here vpon earth, then of the ministerie by which he taught, ruled, and redeemed his Church. *T.C.* in his pleasant humour, would by this example make ministers tortors, which iest rebounds on our Sauiour Christ: but iesting cannot elude the argument, that ciuil offices may be in ministers.

Secondlie, they obiect against vs the practise of the Apostles that dealt not in ciuill causes, but relinquished their office of Deaconship,

which they were not able to exercise,(as they say) together with the Apostleship. which argument, as it may in some sorte serue against the disciplinarians,that(as did *Caluin* and *Beza*)take vpon them to be pastors and doctors: so it can not be applyed with anie reason against our cause, vnlesse they wil make the Deaconship a ciuill office, as in
Ordon.de Gene. deede they do at *Geneua*,and call them *Procureurs de l' hospital.* That which they saye that they were not able to exercise the Deaconrie with their Ministerie, & that therefore they gaue it ouer,is vntrue:for if they might not haue bene ioyned together, then would the Apostles neuer haue taken the Deaconship vpon them. the murmuring of the *Greekes*,& that it was not so thought meete:(the worde is ἀρεστόν. was cause they gaue the office ouer, because they would not incurre their disfauour,nor alienate their mindes,& attend their office wholy. That the Deacons office was not so troublesome as the office of iusticeship,is vntruth.The multitude of loue-feasts,ỹ multitude of pore, the great summes that were collected of mens possessions,declare the infinit trouble of that office then;whereas this in two or three houres a weeke, and sometimes lesse, may easilie be discharged,of him that vnderstandeth what he doth. Now then let vs see how this example of the Apostles doth make for ciuill offices.

If the Apostles notwithstanding their Ministerie dealt in the sale
1.Cor.6. of landes,distribution of goods, & set downe orders for ciuill iudgements,for masters,seruants,husbands,wiues,matters mere ciuil; then is there no such disagreemēt betweene the Ministerie, & ciuil offices, as is pretended: but ỹ is apparant by the whole course of their acts, & ỹ story of the Church,*Ergo,&c.* And further,if it be lawful to cōsult,to care & prescribe in ciuil causes, thē is it also lawful to execute orders. for there is ỹ same reasō of both. Lastly,if ỹ Apostles, notwithstādiug their offices,did gouerne their houses and families,and prescribe the same to be done of byshops and Ministers: then ciuill offices are not forbidden ỹ Ministerie. for the house is a part of the citie, & domestical charge part of a ciuill dutie.That which they say that the Apostles gaue ouer ỹ Deacons charge, is not altogether true. for they had still
Act.11. the care & ouersight,so that Deacons were rather ioyned with them as helpers,then erected as a new office to take the whole charge vpon them.But admit the Apostles did beare no publike office in the common-wealth,when the Church was a bodie separated from the common-wealth:shal Ministers be now excluded,when the Church and common-wealth is one body,differing in respect?That were to continue a practise, when the cause of it is remoued. Wherefore, seeing the

the Apoſtles did deale in ſome ciuill charges, then much more is it lawfull for Miniſters now.

Neither is the diſtinction of Ciuill and Eccleſiaſticall cauſes and iuriſdiction ſuch, but that both Eccleſiaſticall and ciuill offices may concurre in one perſon, ſeeing the ſame perſon in diuers reſpectes is a member of the Church, and a member of the common wealth. If by reaſon of the cauſes of the Church, the miniſter coulde not deale in ciuill cauſes, then might not miniſters looke to the gouernment of their houſes, their wiues, their children, their glebes, if happily the diſciplinarians doe allowe them any glebe (for theſe cauſes are ciuill) then muſt the miniſters be caſt in a newe mold, and be deſpoyled of affections, and almoſt of humanitie, and be made of wood & ſtone.

The French diſcipline alloweth none.

Secondly, graunt this diſtinction of cauſes in that ſort they craue it; the prince could no more deale in cauſes of the Church, then the miniſter may deale in cauſes of the common wealth. for if the gouernours of the church may not deale in the cauſes of the common wealth, no more may the gouernours deale in cauſes of the Church. for the ſame reaſon is in both. ſo while they ſtriue to ſhut out the miniſters, like ſtrangers out of the common wealth, their reaſons eſtrange & ſequeſter the prince from the gouernment of the Church.

Thirdly, they exclude their right honorable Aldermen, whom they make Church officers, from their lordſhips, Iuſticeſhips, prouoſtſhips, and from their occupations and trades. ſo that if once the Conſiſtorie preuaile in England, we are like to looſe many good marchants, apotycaries, taylers and retailers, ſhoemakers and ioyners: all which ioyne together to make a Presbyterie. for if the cauſes be diſtinct in the perſons, then if they will be Church officers, they muſt giue ouer their trades. but this the French diſcipline thinketh not conuenient that (in deſpite of our diſciplinarians) ſaith, that their elders may ſtill keepe their tēporal offices & trades. thus you may ſee that our platformers are like the *Lamiæ* whom Poets faine to haue had no eyes to looke into their owne cauſes at home, though they had Eagles eyes, & were very ſpeculatiue in other mens matters abroad. ſo that while they ſought by a traine, to ſet their enemies corne on fire, they are not aware howe they ſet their owne houſe on fire, that ioyned hard to it.

The Allegoricall ſence is not Argumentatiue. *Lir. in Heb. et Scolaſt. Doct.*

Their fourth obiection drawen from the weight of the miniſters office, the compaſſe and nature of it, for that it is a ſouldior fare (as they ſay) that ought to be attended vpon, is to no purpoſe. for the duetie of a miniſter may be done although the duetie of a ſubiect, maſter, husband, father, friende (which perſons the miniſter ſuſteineth oft times) be not neglected. vnlesse they proue that the ministers duetie ought onely to be attended, they say nothing to purpose, but wander in a Labirinth of wordes without finding issue: but this they doe not indeuour to proue, nor can proue. for that I haue shewed that both offices haue bene susteined of one person with great allowance and commendation, both vnder the lawe and vnder the Gospell. and as souldiers oft times in respect of their places, susteine diuers offices, as of a souldior abroade, a Iustice at home, a father, a friende, a iudge in warres : so it is in the office of the ministerie, wherein the ministers by reason of diuers respects, the principall duetie not neglected, are bound to discharge many ciuill offices.

5 But saith *Cartw.* further, as one member encrocheth not vpon another, no more ought ministers of the church to encroch vpon the gouernment of the cõmon wealth : in which similitude there is at all no likenesse. for the Church & common wealth being two bodies, in diuers respects are vnfitly cõpared to one naturall body, & the members of two naturall bodies likewise to the members of one. and if the members of a common wealth were like to the members of a naturall body, then as a foote is alwayes a foote, and an eye an eye in a naturall body, so he that taketh an office vpõ him in the church, could neuer leaue it nor take higher nor lower office: which they see to bee absurd. in some, things comparatiue are not argumentatiue : and if in the common wealth, great men for their sufficiencie haue diuers offices, why should a poore minister (that is a subiect also) be debarred from any dignitie in the common wealth? but what stirre is this that these fellowes keepe about encrochment of offices & distinction of causes, seeing the aldermen of the Consistorie(whom they make notorious members of the church) are great stirrers, and busie officers in the cõmon wealth: and seeing that vnder colour of distinction of offices, the Consistories doe call to their cognition, all ciuill causes, and examine Iudges, and controll Princes?

6 That the magistrate may by the same right inuade the office of a minister, that the minister occupieth the roume of a magistrat (which is also obiected) is vntrue. for the matter is vnlike: for there was a flat prohibition, that none should take vpon thẽ the priesthood, but those that were of the stocke of *Aaron*; and a cõmination against those that should presume to doe it without calling. but no cõmandement can be shewed to exclude ministers from ciuill offices. nay, the contrary both in law & fact hath bene shewed: and yet if a Iustice of peace, or Maior, or other ciuill officer were fit & able to execute the ministerie, I doe thinke that his ciuill office is no impediment to his calling. but

A stranger that approcheth nere, shall die. *Nomb.* 3.

what

what ſhould *T.Cartw.*odiouſly tell vs of M.Maior taking on him an office in the Church: ſeeing in the Churches (whoſe gouernment he commendeth) not only M.Maior, but M.Alderman from the tribunal ſeate of iuſtice, & from the fiſhmongers ſtall, & tailers ſhop-board, or marchants banke, leape vpon a ſudden into the conſiſtorie, where all matters of Church gouernment are handled, and preſently againe to their former trade & occupation? we reade of *Matthew* that from the tolbanke was called to an eccleſiaſtical function: but we read of none that forſaking the miniſterie returned with any cōmendation to the tolbanke, ſay *L.T.* what he can in it, & let *T.C.* helpe him. but yet let him (ſpeaking of magiſtrates) next time diſtinguiſh betwixt ſoueraigne, & inferiour magiſtrate: for we ſay not that a miniſter may be ſoueraigne magiſtrate, but may haue autoritie deriued from him.

7 Their laſt obiection is grounded vpon the practiſe of ancient churches & autoritie of councels & fathers out of the councel of *Carthage*, that a biſhop ought not to meddle in the execution of Teſtaments, or tutele of pupils, widowes, & ſtrangers: which although it be rigorous, yet will we not ſticke to admit, in caſe they will (according to rules of law) admit ẏ ſame councel for iuriſdiction & gouernment of biſhops, & for diſtinction of apparel and ſuch like: howbeit in the ſame councell there are ſo many ſimple conſtitutions, as that biſhops ſhall not looke to their houſholds cōmanded by *S.Paul*, nor reade the bookes of the heathen, of cutting of beards, & labouring in an occupation, that I vſe the ſame only to ſhew what was then as a record of hiſtorie, rather then to ſhew what ought to be as a lawe. *Carth.4.*

The Canons of the councel of *Calcedon* are not to be vſed of them which refuſe them againſt themſelues in the autoritie of Archbiſhops and biſhops, & in this very cauſe of diſtinction of offices. for if Eccleſiaſticall officers may not followe gaine, what ſhall become of their aldermen ẏ are marchants, which gaine nothing ẇout great leaſings? *Cicero offic.*

The councel is alledged to proue that biſhops may not take on thē the care of orphans, or tutele of minors. but cautelouſly *T.C.* leaueth out the exceptiō ẏ they may take on them thoſe charges which law or kindred caſteth on them; which ſheweth that a miniſter may take on him a charge impoſed ſo he ſeeke it not. finally ẏ tutelſhip was none honour, but a burden troubleſome & perilous to the tutor, being ſubiect to all actions for the pupil, & to a ſtrait account. therfore a greater gratification could not be vſed towards miniſters, then to excuſe thē hereof. whereby appeareth that thoſe fathers did not accompt ciuill offices cōtrary to the office of a miniſter, nor ment to preſſe miniſters, but to gratifie them.

Hillary, he findeth fault with *Constantius* for aduancing bishops aboue the degree of bishops, which maketh neither hote nor colde to this matter: for who would imagine that a meane ciuill office should make a man exceede the degree of bishops?

lib.5.epist.33. *Ambrose* saith that worldly gouernment was the weakening of the priest, which is true, if he giue ouer his calling, and betake himself to the worlde as some disciplinarians doe: which is the weakening and death of many, that might otherwise doe good seruice in the Church: but if executing his charge, the bishoppe doe otherwise seruice to his prince and countrey, he deserueth double commendation.

Caluin, *Beza* and *Daneau* speaking against the honours and offices of Ecclesiasticall persons, confusedly dissallowe that in bishops, which they allow not onely in their consistoriall aldermen, (that are magistrates, nobles, and great men) but also in themselues, *Beza* and *Villiers* and others of them being councellers of state: yea, *T.Cart.* himselfe that condemneth secular cares in others, hath in that small time he hath seated himselfe Doctor (or I knowe not what) at *Warwicke* so scraped and gained, that if he proceede as he hath begunne, yet twentie yeeres, he will bee able not to crye out bishops, but to buye them out.

Bishop *Iewels* sayings are most shamefully wrested contrary to his meaning, to make him condemne that in his writing, which hee allowed in all his life and practise. Hee condemneth the Pope that challengeth the vse of the sword as part of his pastorall authoritie. against those that preach diligently, and doe seruice in mainteining of publike peace, which is the duetie in part of all Christians, neither he nor any other speaketh, saue the disciplinarians that speake ouer.

Howbeit seeing the question here, is what is lawfull, what vnlawful; what a ridiculous poynt is it, leauing the word of God & law, whereby we ought to be tried what is lawe what wrong, to make a tedious, friuolous, fond pelting speake of *Beza* and *Daneaus* fancies, and certaine other authorities of men?

Deut.17. Wherefore considering the lawe of God, the practise both of the ancient *Iewish* and later Christian Church, and the duetie of bishoppes and ministers that they owe to their Prince and Countrey, and (which is not least to bee weyed) the weake and friuolous allegations of the aduersarie; I conclude against the disciplinarians, that ciuill offices in Ecclesiasticall persons, are not absolutely

absolutely vnlawfull. But what neede I conclude against them, that long since (like fauourable disputors) haue yeelded to themselues? As for *Thom. Cartwr.* I conclude hee hath made a very handsome declamation, but a very weake disputation of this argument: which before he proceed further in reformation, he must be desired to reforme.

Disc. de Fr. Tit. du consistoire art. 5.

Of the Pastour, and his office.

CHAP. 3. SECT. 8.

Wherein the iniury of disciplinarians offered to this Church, in charging the same with maintenance of an vnlearned ministery, and non residence, is declared: for that for learning and number of ministers this church may compare with any of theirs: and secondly, that the non residence they condemne in vs, they allow in themselues, which are more iustly to be charged, seeing some of them haue three or foure parishes committed to their cure, and are oftener absent without cause or licence.

TO prooue that the pastours ought to be learned, and that he ought to be resiant at his charge, the disciplinarians (like men that haue leasure enough) make long and needlesse discourses; and *Th. Cart.* hath made a vaine and idle treatise to that purpose. for I know none that simply wil deny either of these two points. but that which is in controuersie, *viz.* what learning or preaching is sufficient, and whether if preachers may not be had, the church should stand voide without reading of Scriptures, publike prayers & sacraments, and what is *non residence*, they themselues define not. nay, they studiously run away in a cloud of generall termes.

The spoiles of the church, the greedinesse of some men, the small number of liuings able to mainteine sufficient preachers (for of almost ten thousand parishes, there are not much aboue fiue hundred that are aboue thirtie pounds in the Queenes books) the contention also of forren and domesticall enemies of this church, I confesse, are causes that we haue not that number of learned preachers, that were to be wished. which is not onely our case, but of diuers of our neighbours, whose condition in this respect is farre worsse. But if any man say, we either allow vnlearned, or that we seeke not to haue learned ministers, he doth charge this church with an vntrue accusation.

The reasons of the want of sufficient ministers.

The end and intent of our lawes, and the desires of the gouernors of the church, is to haue so sufficient and learned a ministery as may be gotten; and for this cause, with prayers sollicit, and with rewards prouoke sufficient men to take vpon them that calling. If others that can not in all points answere the duety of a sufficient minister, be

Vnlearned mẽ not mainteined in this church.

chosen; it is because sufficient men vpon so small liuings can not be mainteined, and for that it is better to haue ministers, such as reade, pray, administer sacraments, and vse such exhortations as they may, and that the church should in some sort be supplied by the helpe of the ministers next adioyning, then that the people should continue without exercise of prayer, or Scripture, or administration of sacraments (as in some places they doe elsewhere) vntill such time as meanes may be found to mainteine a preacher. If they thinke otherwise, and suppose that publike prayers, sacraments, and reading of Scriptures, and the helpe of other ministers adioyning, helpe nothing, and that a sufficient preacher must be had in euery parish, or else none; they thinke absurdly and peruersly, and can not shew reason of their opinions.

The remedy of want of ministers.

Further, if any parish be disposed to mainteine a preacher that is learned, and not contentious; they may not onely do it, but haue encouragement & commendation for so doing. so that where certeine factious supplications haue beene exhibited for a learned ministery (taxing the bishops vnder hand, as causers of the contrary) & whereas certaine not euill affected, cry out for a learned ministery; they doe wrong to blame others, for the fault is in themselues. Let them defray the charges of a learned minister, and a learned minister will shortly be found.

The lawes of our church binde to residence.

Likewise it is the principal intent of the law, that euery minister be resiant at his benefice: yet so, that certaine times & causes be allowed of absence. for the minister is not like a slaue *ascriptitius glebæ.* that is, appendant or regardant to a church as to a manor. and beastly it were to tie him to the church, as forzats be to gallies. the disciplinarians will not be so tied. Now, for that many causes of absence may be pretended, which are not sufficient; the law setteth downe for what causes, and what persons, and how long they may be absent, & leaueth not men to their owne discretion and liberty, much lesse to the willes of a sort of lordly companions called elders. If men be absent for other causes, and for longer time, or otherwise then is set downe; it is not the fault or defect of our gouernment, but of those that do not execute the lawes, which are very penall in that behalfe.

Non residence, both by statutes and ecclesiasticall Canons is condemned. and therefore iniuriously doe they charge the gouernment with maintenance of *non residence.* for although by the lawes of this land, one minister may haue (in certaine cases) two parishes vnder his charge: yet who can account him *non resident* that is continually at his

his charge, or that the lawes allow *non reſidence,* that binde him to be continually at his charge? Againe, ſeeing they that broch vs theſe nouelties can allow themſelues two or three moneths of abſence, yea, ſometimes halfe a yeare, to trouble her Maieſty and the Parliament, with their plats, deuiſes, and ſupplications, and thinke it lawfull to abandon their cures to teach in great townes, and condemne thoſe that lie continually at their charges, and teach continually at the one or the other of their cures; they muſt either put themſelues in the caſe of *non reſidents*, or ſhew better reaſon, why they condemne others. If *non reſidence* or abſence be not lawfull, why are they ſo often abſent? if it be vnlawfull to haue two benefices, why hath one poore miniſter in the Scottiſh reformation three or foure pariſhes committed to his charge? why is it more lawfull to be abſent without leaue, then by licence of the gouernours? when we haue made an account of their words, this is the ſumme of all; that they allow any liberty to themſelues, none to others; challenge any prerogatiue to themſelues, grant none to others. If heereafter they will diſpute formally, they muſt ſhew who are *non reſidents*, who not; who is to be allowed, who to be condemned. and ſo if they can excuſe themſelues, and charge others, their diſcourſe will be more probable and orderly.

Of the Paſtour, and his office.

Chap. 3. Sect. 9.

Wherein the fond deuice of certeine that would haue two paſtours in a pariſh, is refuted by the hiſtory of th: apoſtolike churches, and generall conſent of all fathers, by the inconuenience and impoſſibility: and laſtly their reaſons are anſwered.

LAwes are to be appointed (as *Theophraſtus* thinketh) in matters that often fall out, not in matters rare, and paſſing reaſon, *in his quæ* ἐπὶ τὸ πολὺ, *non quæ* ἐκ παραλόγου *accidunt:* and to ſet downe orders that can not take effect, is rather to wiſh, thẽ to make lawes. what then ſhall we iudge of the politike diſciplinarians, who although (conſidering the want of maintenance and learned men) ſufficient paſtors can not be found, for to place in euery pariſh one; yet haue thought it good diſcipline to appoint in euery pariſh two? what els, but that their diſcipline is like *Platoes* Commonwealth, that is, a goodly deuiſe, that pleaſeth themſelues woondrous well, but can not haue place in any church? Our firſt exception therfore againſt this ordinance, is, that it is impoſſible. Secondly, that it is not conuenient. Thirdly, that the ancient practiſe of the church condemneth it.

ff. de legib. L. iura.

The impoſſibility appeareth firſt,in that charge that is required in mainteining of learned men; if where there is ſome reaſonable portion allotted to the miniſter, no addition can be procured, how may we be induced to beleeue that the people will be perſuaded to mainteine two ſufficient learned men? and if they were willing, how could they doe it? Secondly, where ſhould theſe learned men be found? if there were a muſter made of all the diſciplinarians, the nũber would not be great,and few anſwerable to their touch of paſtors. Few of them be ἐλεγκτικοὶ able to refute, many κατέλεγκτοι, that is,to be refuted and reproued. and of the reſt I know none that will ſerue in ſo diſordered and ſeruile a gouernment,if he be either wiſe or learned.

But to paſſe ouer the impoſſibility, it will not be conuenient. for if one of theſe diſciplinarians doe euill agree with himſelfe, and his neighbours that are farre from him, how would two of them agree

One groue holdeth not two ruddocks.

in one church, as it were vnder one roofe? if *vnum arbuſtum non alit duos erithacos:* one church will neuer holde two biting platformers: as the ſtirres of *Midelberg* betweene *Br.* and *Harriſ.* declare. How will ſchiſme and faction, and the ſcandale thereof ariſing, be auoyded? If in ciuill cauſes multitude of gouernours be not allowed, and

οὐκ ἀγαθὸν πολυκοιρανίη.

multitude of commanders were the ruine (as is ſaid) of *Caria*; how much is this plurality of paſtors & biſhops to be feared in the church? eſpecially, where contention and faction is neither ſo curiouſly looked into,nor ſeuerely puniſhed, as in the ciuill gouernment.

For the third point, we are to vnderſtand that the apoſtles committed the diſpoſing of matters at *Epheſus* to *Timothie*, in *Crete* to *Titus:* and ancient hiſtories giue the preheminence of a biſhop to *Iames* at *Ieruſalem*. The epiſtles mentioned in the *Reuelation* are addreſſed to the angell or paſtor of *Smyrna*, to the angell of the church of *Sardis*, of *Philadelphia*, not to angels; which ſhewed there was but one paſtor in the church, as one head of a body, one gouernor of a ſociety. and as well faſhioned is a church with two paſtors,as a body with two heads, looking like *Ianus*, one forward, the other backward,& contending one againſt another,with diuers motions.When through ambition, contrary to the practiſe of the apoſtles times, diuers contended to be ioyned biſhops together in one church, the fathers in their writings deteſted it,the ancient councels forbad it.

Lib.1.epiſt.8. *Vnum altare* (ſaith *Cyprian*) *vnum ſacerdotium.* that is, There is but one altar,one prieſthood in the church. Againe, *Epiſcopo ſemel facto alius non poteſt conſtitui.* When a biſhop is once ordeined or appointed,

Lib.2.epiſt.11.

it is not lawfull to appoint another. he affirmeth that the plurality of biſhops

bishops is against the law of the gospell : and saith, that as there is but one Christ, and one Holy spirit, so there ought to be but one bishop in a Christian church. and for that there was not one bishop or priest in the church at one time, he imagineth that heresies did take root and spring. And before him, *Tertullian* reckoning vp the degrees of ministers, placeth but one bishop in a church. That he reckoneth diuers presidents and gouernours of the church, belonged to the whole church, for which he made his Apologie, and not to euery priuate congregation. When *Constantius* the emperour would haue had *Liberius* and *Fœlix* both bishops of *Rome* at one time, the people answered with great consent,that as there is but one God and one Christ,so they would haue but one bishop.

Lib.3.epist.2. *Lib.3.epist.11.* *Lib.1.epist.3.* *De baptismo.* *In apol.c.39.*

Ignatius holdeth that as there is but one altar in the church, so there is but one bishop. and *Ierome*, howsoeuer he dissent from vs in the original of episcopal authority;yet ioineth with vs in this,that for auoiding of schisme, one bishop was appointed in one diocesse.When ambition would not keepe it selfe within rule,the councels set order. By the Canons of the apostles he is decreed to be deposed, that erecteth another altar in the church. The councell of *Nice* (as *Augustine* affirmeth) forbiddeth two bishops to be in one church,and acknowledgeth himselfe to be made bishop of *Hippo* in *Valerius* time against the Canons. *Quia ab vno Deo patre sunt omnia, singulos episcopos singulis ecclesijs præesse decreuit*, saith *Ambrose, in 1.Cor. 12.* When the custome of chusing more bishops in one church, tooke place in *Afrike*, *Damasus* bishop of *Rome*, in an epistle to *Prosper*, condemneth the same, and the order of *coepiscopi* or *chorepiscopi*, which he sheweth to haue entred by leud custome, against the decrees of Canons. *Hierome* vpon the *Phil. 1.* saith there can not be more then one bishop in one church.

Ad Philadelph. *Can.30.* *Ep.110.* *Can.8.* *Damas.epist.ad Prosperum.*

To proue that many bishops were of one church, they allege that *S.Paul* saluteth the bishops at *Philippi*. but that these were all bishops of that city, it appeareth not. *Chrysostome* saith, he calleth elders or priests by the name of bishops; which although called of the principall city,yet had not charge in the city,but vnder the charge of one bishop,gathered the church in villages thereabout. The elders likewise that came from *Ephesus*, had not charge of the church in the city,but (remaining in the chiefe city vnder the gouernment of one bishop, which then was *Timothy*) went out to teach in villages, from whence they returned into the head city,of whence they tooke their name sometimes. If we expound it otherwise, it will folow that at

Act.20.

Epheſus and *Philippi* there were not two onely, but many biſhops: yea, ſometime twenty, ſometime forty, for ſo many paſtourall elders were in one city, as appeareth by *Cornelius* epiſtle.

Euſeb. eccl. hiſtor. lib. 6. ſect. 43.

In diuers churches, when biſhops grew olde or weake, not able to diſcharge their duety, they had a coadiutor ioyned to them: which although he were not ſo in proper ſpeech, yet was ſometimes called biſhop there. but the matter was rare and contrary to Canons, ſauing vpon neceſſity. Wherefore, what reaſon haue they to commend theſe dualities of paſtors, but that changing all ancient orders, they will frame vs (without conſideration of impoſſibility, or inconueniency) a famous all new gouernment inuented by themſelues?

Of the Paſtour, and his office.

Chap. 3. Sect. 10.

Wherein the imperfection of their plats, concerning the paſtours office, is diſcouered by rehearſall of many inconueniences, which they haue not remedied nor can remedy: and ſecondly, in that many doubts, which may fall out, concerning the examination, ordination, age, liuing, authority, dignity, office, diet, & apparell of paſtors are not reſolued, nor mentioned by them.

THe diſciplinarians theſe many yeres haue ſought to remoue archbiſhops, biſhops, deanes, archdeacons and prebendaries; and it is their cry & ſong, Downe with them. If *Th. Cartwr.* were not maiſter of an hoſpitall (as *Aerius* the heretike, who thought an elder and a biſhop to be all one, was afore him) they would haue maiſters of hoſpitalles remoued too: and that ſo much the rather, for that it is a more popiſh office then any of the other. But if they will proceed orderly and diſcreetly, it were good before ſo many godly, wiſe, learned, and experimented men be remooued at one clap out of the church of God, to conſider how ſo many places may be ſupplied, and what kinde of men they are that muſt ſucceed. for to depriue the church of ſo many godly, graue, wiſe, and learned men, before we know where to haue againe ſo many, to match them in godlineſſe, wiſedome, and learning, were a point of deformation, raſhneſſe, and confuſion, rather then reformation.

The which not hauing conſidered nor reſolued, let this be the firſt defect of their paſtourall deuiſe; that while they ſeeke to remooue moſt godly and learned men out of the church (whoſe labours, if they had not bene, the platformers might now haue deuiſed plats of pigſties in ſome corner of the world, *à remotis*) they conſider not who ſhall ſucceed them: for they may not thinke that any can indure to ſerue in their tyrannicall and confuſed gouernment.

The

The second is as bad as the first. they would haue lands taken frō bishops,and the liuings and reuenues from Cathedrall churches,and tithes and glebe from the ministery.but how they shall be bestowed, and how the ministery without them shall be mainteined,is a matter passing their capacity,and scarse thought of by them. if they imagine that they shall be imployed in the mainteinance of their scholars,doctors and pastors, they do but dreame, or as frantike men vse to doe, speake ouer.

For if now,notwithstanding the lawes and prouisoes made in that behalfe, a great part be interuerted by sleight, and turned from the right vse; what shall we thinke will become of them,when the orders of this gouernment being dissolued,it shalbe lawfull to imploy them as shalbe thought best to those to whom the ouersight of those matters shall be committed? To dissolue a college is a matter easie, but few are able or willing to build a college. If they conceiue that men will haue more regard of their conscience, then to inrich themselues with the spoiles of the church: they are to vnderstand that some of their best fauorers are greatest spoilers of the church; and that diuers, vpon whose trenchers they attend, and whose zeale they commend, can be content to keepe a parsonage in their hand, that is worth 100 li. and very liberally to allow a minister 40 li. others of them keepe some 2, some 3, some 10 appropriations in their hands, and are notwithstanding,great friends of reformation,& cry out against bishops and Cathedrall churches. and great reason they haue so to do: for by this meanes they hope to swallow the rest,that haue already digested and consumed a great part. but better reason haue all that fauor religion, to preuent and withstand such insatiable mens desires, painted ouer with a faire vernish of reformation.

I cannot compare these men to any,more fitly,then to one of whō *Tully* speaketh in one of his orations; who being taught two points by a certeine philosopher: the first, that pleasure was the end of all actions: the second,that notwithstanding, he must honor vertue: he greedily snatched at the first,and cared not a iote for the philosophers exception. So when the platformers teach that lands are to be taken from ministers & Cathedrall churches,their fauorers allow their saying, they commend them and fauour them: but the second point, to wit, that the same are to be bestowed vpon scholars, doctors,pastors, and needy elders,they will neuer vnderstand,nor see Scripture for it, and then they will tell our new clergy, that if these liuings were not fitting for godly, graue, and learned men, then are they not for them *In Pison.*

that are neither wise nor learned. and if they haue not these lands of the church, what recompense should they haue all this while, for their labour, and losse of those commodities which now they inioy by the church? The conceit therefore of our platformers, that thinke and say, that not only the church liuings that now are, but the robberies of first fruits & appropriations (for so they call them, calling her Maiesty and all their fauourers in a pang of their zeale church robbers) will returne to the church, is but a Lenten fancy. But suppose all should fall out according to their desires, & that the church goods should not be inuaded and spoiled: yet haue they not resolued vs, who shall haue the gouernment and disposing of them, when this law *Agraria* shall be enacted.

Ecclesiasticall discipline, *pag.* 116. by *Wat. Trau.*

They haue not tolde vs who shall be these diuiders or agreemensours. If the synod of the whole realme; there would be no small contention: if certaine persons deputed, where are they to be found that will deale sincerely and vprightly? if after diuision, the deacons shall be made receiuers and disposers; then will they reigne and rule: if the whole consistory; then least portion will come to the pastor, and to the maintenance of learning. so that now, where twentie learned men are mainteined to do the Church and Commonwealth seruice, scarse one poore hungry scholar would finde bread and drinke, and candle light: the rest must be bestowed on the elders and deacons, to buy them clokes to couer their motly ierkins, and lether aprons, and muske balles to wash their beards and hands that sauour so strong of base occupations. and where now many poore men are relieued; the poore should want, and their almes be turned to the maintenance of certeine labourers and artificers, as taylers and retaylers called elders, which neglecting or disdeining their occupations, on which they liued, will now liue on that for which they neuer laboured nor swet, nor was euer meant they should enioy. All this while the pastour which hath wrought vs this goodly worke, must stand content with his allowance, and (as in some other countries of the pretended reformation, where the ministery is ruinated) he shall be glad of the crummes, and reuersion of his good masters, the elders and deacons. To remedy this disorder, can the wisest platformer (for the simple sort stand like men amazed, when they heare these things, & vnderstand nothing) but can the wisest of them shew vs, how, Cathedrall churches being dissolued, and parsonages and tithes taken away, so many pastours and doctours as they would haue, and are requisite to furnish all or most churches in England, can be found?

nay,

nay, can they shewe howe so many may be mainteined, as nowe are, the state thus standing? if a hundred pounde bee allotted to one man, that to fiue hundred amounteth to fifty thousande pounde: cast then all the liuings of Cathedrall Churches and bishops, which (the Q. dueties discharged) amount not to fiftie thousand pounde, how then shall ten thousand parishes be supplied? or howe can they mainteine more then nowe, when by Cathedrall Churches and bishops so many learned men are maintained alreadie?

I heare say there is a certaine fellow, that in tender consideration of the desperate case of the Aldermen of the Church, hath deuised a meanes, howe all this feate shall be wrought: his deuice he calleth a motion with submission. he woulde haue all bishops and Cathedrall churches landes solde, and all appropriations redeemed with the money, and restored to the Church: this he sendeth vs as farre as from *Scotland:* from whence I wonder if hee can fetch any example of mainteining the ministerie, seeing the ministerie of that Church is vtterly ruinated and impouerished. but seeing he taketh such paines to worke some mischiefe to the state, this let him receiue for answere. If all were solde that he would haue solde, yet woulde not halfe the appropriations be redeemed: and if all were redeemed, yet would it not serue to mainteine the charge. the sale by computation commeth not to one million: the purchase of all appropriations would not be made with fiue millions. and now where there are mainteined many learned men, and three or foure thousand others to doe her Maiestie seruice; all this reckoning would bee lost, and the reuenues deuided, and no one man thereby mainteined to do the Prince and Countrey seruice: and therefore for motion he might better haue put commotion, and for submission subuersion. for therein the malitious patch seeketh nothing but to stirre vp the commons, & subuert this church and state. sufficeth that all men may see that his vaine deuice is rather the ouerthrowe of the learned men that are alreadie, then a meanes to mainteine either learning or learned men. Further, can any of them assure the pastors of their liuings, that (as in other places) they daunce not attendance vpon other mens pleasures, & spend the one half ere they can get the other, or how they may recouer their pention, being not payd then? can they all of them declare, how beside two pastors and one doctor, a fraternitie of elders and deacons may be mainteined in euery parish?

If the Pastor be charged with many children, how shall he mainteine them at schoole and vniuersitie, hauing but 40. 60. or at the vttermoſt 100.li.yeerely?how ſhall he mainteine his wiſe? what will he leaue his wife & children?howe ſhall he mainteine his owne ſtate and his ſeruants?theſe things by them are not ſo much as thought of. for notwithſtanding this penſion, his wife and children may begge, himſelgoe on foot, and all be diſcouraged to vndertake the calling, ſeeing a Cobler ſhall liue in more eaſe and reputation, & keepe more ſeruants, and leaue more behinde him then a miniſter. and a ſtrange fancie it is to thinke that men will not receiue humane affections.

The Paſtor not being able to ſerue, how he ſhalbe mainteined, and how his widow & orphans when he dieth, ſhall liue, they know not. which matters though ſmall in ſhewe, yet if they be not thought vpon, and prouided for, wee ſhall haue a thinne miniſterie, vnleſſe they will allowe men to leape from the ſhopboard to the pulpit, or as *Serranus* & *Cincinnatus* among the *Romanes*, would haue them remoued from the plowe & the fielde, to the helme of gouernment. For men liue not on winde: and the ſpoyles of the Church in other countreys may teach men that they are like to feede on winde, or faire wordes. If *T. Cartw.* could perſwade the Church of England to that communitie, which was vſed in the Apoſtles time, when all that had poſſeſſions ſold them, & brought the price before the feete of the Apoſtles, which communitie (ſaith he) ſhould now be obſerued: he might doe much for relieuing the neceſſitie of his elders. but the nobilitie, gentrie and lawes of England will neuer ſuffer this diuiſion. If they be wiſe, they will not begin with diuiſion of Church lands. Cõmunitie and diuiſion of landes, be plauſible matters in the eares of the multitude. If then the miniſters that haue ſo many textes to warrant their liuings, cannot defend themſelues from ſpoyles; what wil become of the nobilitie and gentrie, and their liuings, if they may come vnto the ſcanning of the multitude? the platformers may do well therefore to ſhewe vs out of ſcriptures, how all theſe matters may be ſetled, leaſt that the faithfulneſſe of Chriſt ſerue them nothing for theſe their ſtrange deuiſes.

After orders ſet downe for the paſtors maintenance, they ought to haue declared, what degree they will haue him to liue in; whether in the degree of an artificer, marchant, gentleman or what? lords we perceiue they will not haue the miniſters to be, for auoyding tyranny. but they are afraid without cauſe, for they will be kept ſhort ynough, and in paſture leane ynough. they ought likewiſe to ſhewe by what titles they may be called, what not? and what is *non reſidence*, and how long a paſtor may be abſent and not be reputed *non reſident*? and who

ſhall

ſhall giue leaue of abſence,and whether his leaue be not a diſpenſation for *non reſidence*? likewiſe whether going to Synodes,he is to be reputed *non reſident*,and who ſhall ſerue in his place being abſent?

Concerning the election of the paſtor, they ſay not whether the people may preſent and chuſe a paſtor if the Conſiſtorie agree not, nor why the people may not chuſe their paſtor & elders alwayes, as well as at the firſt? and why more then halfe the people diſſenting, a paſtor may be put vpon them, if none alledge cauſe againſt him and prooue it? If the Synode chuſe a paſtor, they tell vs not whether the pariſh may diſſent; nor whether the controuerſie hanging vndecided two or three yeeres,the pariſh ſhall all that while ſtand without paſtor, or be ſupplied by a hireling: nor whether the paſtor entring without ordination,he is to be reputed a ſufficient paſtor:nor whether the paſtor may leaue his charge,not receiuing his penſion.

Greater doubtes are theſe, which alſo remaine vndecided. firſt, whether a paſtor can exhort without experience, or confute without logike, or vnderſtand the ſcriptures without knowledge of diuers tongues:& *per conſequens*, whether a deacon or alderman that hath a great meaſure of zeale,but vnderſtandeth no tongues,nor artes,may be choſen paſtor. Secondly, whether a youth of 18. or 19. yeeres being choſen paſtor, hath as full authoritie in the gouernment of the Church,as the moſt ancient father of the Church? Thirdly, whether he may alledge Councels and fathers, and prophane writers in his ſermon? Fourthly,whether he may reade a lecture in another pariſh? Fiftly, whether he may nominate or deſcribe any particular perſon in his ſermons? Sixtly,whether he may examine any man publikely or priuately,and refuſe thoſe that come to the Lordes ſupper which he thinketh not to be wel inſtructed?Seuenthly,whether a paſtor falling into frenſie or ſickeneſſe, is to looſe his place, or to haue a *coadiutor* ioyned with him? and laſtly,what authoritie he hath in the conſiſtorie,what in the Synod,and for what cauſes hee may be ſuſpended,or depoſed,and by whom?

If I ſhould particularly recite al thoſe queſtiōs,that may be moued concerning the paſtors examination,election,ordination,age,liuing, autoritie,office,dignitie,diet,apparel,houſhold,which theſe new deuiſers neuer thought vpon, I ſhould but weary thee & tire my ſelfe: and I haue alreadie bene long ynough. theſe fewe doubtes may ſhewe howe confuſed their matters are like to proue,when nothing almoſt of that is required in their future paſtor, is determined. wherfore,ſeeing their opinions concerning the miniſter of the word,

 (wherein

(wherein they passe the orders of our Church) are new and strange, and repugnant to scriptures, and ancient practise, and that their fourme of discipline which doth concerne him is imperfect, and confused: let vs not refuse that order which we knowe to be according to scriptures, and long experience doth teach vs to bee good, to trie strange nouelties, which many sufficient reasons may make vs to suspect.

Of the Consistoriall Elders, and their vsurpation.

Chap. 4. Sect. 1.

The office of Church-aldermen is declared to be by them vsurped, by the example of the Iewes *gouernment, wherein it is made euident that there neuer were any such Church gouernours: First, by the lawe: then, by the practise of that gouernment. Thirdly, for that such authoritie as the Elders claime was practised by others, and neuer by any Elders. Fourthly, for that the Synagogues of the* Iewes *were brought in by humane deuise and resemble the Presbyteries in nothing. Fiftly, for that the* Iewish *Elders resemble not the newe Church-aldermen. And lastly, for that there is no probabilitie that the* Iewish *Elders should be translated into the Church of Christ.*

S in the rest of this discourse (I feare mee) I shall not winne any fauour at the disciplinarians handes; so in this part concerning the Eldership, I am assured, I shall spill fauour, if I moue their affections no further. for here I dispute against no one position or opinion of theirs, but against a chiefe pillar, and almost the groundworke of their newe discipline, I meane the sacred Aldermen; which ouerthrowne, the high commendation of their discipline doth threaten present ruine.

Aldermen I call them, for that themselues will not haue them called priestes: and elders is a word of doubtfull signification in our language. whereas Aldermen is both an office, and may signifie a man elder in yeeres, and may best fit these elders, that will be officers of the Church, and yet no Priests.

Thomas Cartw. doth not sticke to intitle them Christes vicars, and Gods prelats. for it pleaseth him to cal them contrary to al Grammer *Antistites*; (which is a terme not to be giuen to those that meddle not with priesthood, nor with word nor sacraments) and Christes vicars contrary to sence and reason. in the eldership he placeth the maiestie of his newe gouernment. You that desire to vnderstand the trueth, reade this treatise with indifferencie: you that are contrary minded, condemne not that you neuer read, nor striue not for that which you are not able by scriptures or reasons to mainteine. and generally, let

euery

euery man take heed how he beleeue glorious wordes without effect or performance.

Concerning the Eldership, and the Elders office, diuers particuler questions are moued: but I trust the whole controuersie may bee discussed, if I proue these three pointes. First, that there were neuer anie Elders onelie censours of manners, and moderators of discipline, which meddled not with the word nor sacraments. Secondly, that such lay Elders (for so I call them, to distinguish them from the Ministers of the word) without right, or institution from Christ, in those places where of late they haue bene receaued, intrude into the gouernement of the Church. Thirdly, that the same Eldership ought not to be placed in euerie parish or particular congregation; nor cannot be receaued, for many inconueniences and imperfections accompanying the same. Wherefore laying aside all other bymatters, let vs beginne to examine these three poynts. of which, that commeth first to be handeled which we first propounded; to wit, that there were neuer anie such Elders, which neither medling with the worde, nor sacraments, nor publike seruice of God, were notwithstanding, censors of manners, or moderators of discipline, and gouernors of the Church, in all matters pertaining to conscience.

For resolution wherof, let vs consider first the times of the Church before Christ: Secondlie, the time wherein Christ and his Apostles liued: lastlie, the times of the Church that followed foure or fiue hundred yeeres after, which I call the ancient Christian Church, after the Apostles times. And if in all this time we finde no Elders; wee may then conclude, that this order, or office of Church aldermen, hath neither testimonie from Christ, nor his Apostles, nor is to bee founde in scriptures, or councels, or fathers. What the order and gouernement of the Church was before Christ, where are we to finde or to seeke, but in the holy scriptures written by the prophets, and men of God before Christ? And vainelie doe they pretend the lawe of God, that can not finde the same in the lawes of *Moses*. Wherefore, if neither in the lawe of *Moses*, nor anie cannon of scripture, the institution of the Church aldermen is to be founde; in vaine doe they boast, that they haue authoritie or commission from God.

The Church aldermen were not instituted by Moses lawe.

That they haue no erection or institution from God it appeareth, for that the patrons of the Eldership haue bene long seeking for it, and yet haue not founde it. some imagine that it is to be founde in one place, some in another: but their vncertaintie and wauering, sheweth that themselues are not yet resolued and assured that they haue it. Three places are founde in scriptures, where (as by authori-

1. Reason.

tie of lawe) iudges and gouernors are appointed. if they can shewe any other places, where other colledges of iudges and gouernors are erected, let them not conceale it frō vs. the places are *Exo.18. Numb.11.* & *Deut. 17.* But the officers mentioned *Exo.18.* were ciuill. for they determined all small causes, and as yet the priesthoode was not appointed to seuerall persons. The Elders mentioned *Numb.11.* were of *Moses* counsell that bare the burthen with him, & holp him in deciding matters of difficultie which others could not order, and in gouernement of the state, which before that, rested most in *Moses*. The Iudges *Deut.17.* did onely heare matters that could not be decided of inferior Iudges. they had cognition of all criminall causes betwixt blood & blood, & ciuil causes of pleas & quarels, which came before them frō other. Such Iudges as these were, were but in one place, either assistant to the chiefe gouernor, or in the head citie. The Iudges & Elders named *Deu.1.* and *Deu. 16.* are those which were appointed *Exo. 18.* Of these three colledges of Elders, or iudges, let them chuse which they will, there is none of thē that resembleth their Elders, eyther in the causes they handled, or the places were they were placed: & therefore these places proue not the erection of their Elders. Wherefore, vnlesse they can name some other lawe, where their Ecclesiasticall aldermen haue commission giuen vnto them, they are lyke to proue Iudges without commission.

The rabbins make both these, and those iudges. Numb.11. and *Petr. Galat. lib.4.c.5.*

To omit lawe (which they must shew, or else acknowledge their Elders to be Apocryphal) can they shew any custome or Cabalisticall tradition that alloweth them? Nay, can they shew in all the storie of the Bible anie one Ecclesiastical alderman that dealt onely in Ecclesiastical causes? *Th. Cartw.* laboreth & sweateth to proue this point: but like *Sisyphus* stone it rouleth downe vpon him, & litle doth he profite. He alledgeth a place out of *Exod.4.* where Elders (I confesse) are mentioned; but if he make them his Ecclesiasticall Elders, these inconueniences will insue: First that they tooke vpon them authoritie without commission from God (for as yet there was no lawe giuen but the lawe of nature.) Secondlie, that Elders may doe all without priests or pastors. for as yet *Aaron* was not nominated to the priesthood. Lastly, that the same may dispose matters of the Church, and matters ciuill, for they had no other ciuill gouernors of their nation at this time. But if *Th. Cartw.* vnderstood anie matter of state, and could distinguish betwixt domesticall & publike ciuil gouernement; he would not fall into these absurdities, mistaking gouernors of houses for gouernors of the Church, & conceiuing that there was a com-

There is no practise found of them. which is proued first by enumeration of particulars, secondly, for that no action of theirs is mentioned.

monwealth

monwealth, before they had certaine lawes, or certaine gouernors appointed for the common vse,& wealth of the nation.anie one may see that considereth the state of the *Israelites* at this time, that they had no commonwealth,but were gouerned by domesticall gouernement of the heads of families. Which gouernement, as it goeth before ciuill gouernement,so ciuil and publike gouernement being dissolued, the same returned, for it is by instinct of nature and custome of all people, that children should obey their parents, and Elders. This answere will auoyde all his reasons drawen from the name of Elders, which still he conceiueth to be Ecclesiasticall Elders, if there be not plaine marks, that shewe them to bee ciuill gouernors. The Elders mentioned *Numb.11*.doe nothing releeue his cause:both because they were ciuill gouernors, and because that iudges, or rather councellors, were onelie in one place,& were about the prince: whither I beleeue our Elders would perch if they could, but their warrant will not serue them.Wherefore let *Th.Cartw.* and his fellowes shewe vs some institution or practise of Church; elders,& name vs some one of that sorte:or else we must tell them,that in the Iewish Church there were none such, and they themselues must confesse it. For if almightie God prescribed most,nay(as some of thē say) all particular orders for gouernement of the Church then must it follow,that eyther these Elders are somewhere appointed, or that they they had nothing to doe in the gouernement of the Church. and it were not reasonable, that pinnes, & bolts,& such small implements should bee described in the erection of the tabernable, & these Elders omitted,whom they make pillors of their discipline,which they gloriously entitle the Tēple & the tabernacle. Wherefore it is most apparant,that the Church of the *Iewes* had no Elders, distinct gouernors of the Church. For if histories doe describe the actions of the gouernors of the Church; seeing the actions of these Elders are no where described in holie scriptures, it followeth that the scriptures acknowledge none such, for gouernors of the Church.

Nay,which is the ouerthrowe of their Church-aldermen, that iurisdiction which they claime, we see it assigned ouer vnto others. so that if they deale therein,they doe not onelie vsurpe,but preiudice others. the iudgemēt betwene holy things and prophane, betweene cleane & vncleane (which they ascribe to the proper function of Elders)God gaue to ỷ priests. Wherfore, vnlesse they can shew like cōmission for their Elders in like case; let thē not thinke that ỷ Eders in the ancient Church did intrude vpon the Priests office. Ecclesiastical

The authoritie which Elders claime practised by others.

Leuiti.10.

 iurisdiction

iurisdiction, it was in the chiefe magistrate first principallie, as in *Moses*, *Iosua*, *Heli*, *Samuel*, *David*, *Iehosaphat*, and other chiefe princes: then in inferior iudges, appointed by the soueraigne magistrate, as in those appointed *Exod. 18.* in *Samuels* sonnes, in the iudges appointed by *David*, *Iehosaphat*, *Ezra*, is apparant. Which least anie man might conceiue to haue bene merelie Ecclesiastical; the appointment by the ciuill magistrate, the causes which they handeled being considered, declare to haue bene ciuill iudges. Lastlie it was in the priests

1 Chron 20. alone. I graunt the causes of God, & causes of the king are distingui-

2. Chron. 14. shed: but not so, but that ÿ same iudges did handle both. and were it not so, that ÿ same iudges dealt in both causes, which is most apparant; yet cãnot the places be so interpreted, that the causes of God shoulde signifie Church gouernement: for so the execution of the morall lawe should not belong to God, nor the kings gouernement be authorised by God, being deuided one against another. But by the causes of the king, is vnderstoode the kings priuate busines, belonging to the maintenance of his housholde, as is euident, where *Salomons* houshold gouernement is described. The wordes are plaine. for some are apointed for the publike gouernement of the realme, others are apointed for the busines & maintenance of the king and his house (as these words declare.) VEKILKELV ET HAMELEK BEET BETO.

3. Reg. c. 4. wherein the busines of the kings house is made a seuerall charge. Likewise the princes of *Israel*, and the princes of tribes, in *Dauids*

1. Paral. 28. gouernement are distinguished from the gouernors of the kings proper substance and possessions: and the kings treasures from the publike treasures. *1. Chro. 27. 25.* So that by the kings busines, we are to vnderstand not all ciuill causes, but the causes that belonged to the kings house, or eschequer: & by the causes of God, all iudgements &

Deut. 1. proceedings according to the lawes of God, as is manifest by the word *Deut. 1.* wherein the iudgementes of God are taken for all iudgements according to Gods worde. To saye that the power to prescribe lawes, to commaund, to consult, to chuse officers, was in any Ecclesiastical aldermen, is absurd: seeing ÿ same by continual course

Philo. de vit. Mos. lib. 2. of storie, is giuen to the chiefe gouernours of the Iewish nation. *Diuina & humana administret*: Let the prince administer things diuine and humane. So that to make Ecclesiasticall aldermen gouernours of the Church of God, before, or after the lawe, is to deny all scriptures, and to forge new commissions. For in scriptures we finde no commission for them; and the authoritie they would haue, we finde it wholie practised by the princes, priestes and prophets. If anie order

was

was to be setled, the prophets of God came to the princes & gouernours,not to the Ecclesiastical aldermen: if any disorder fell out in the gouernement of the Church, the same was imputed to the princes & priestes, not to these aldermen, which wee finde not once named.

Finallie, if there were anie Ecclesiastical aldermen, such as are surmised in that gouernement; euill did they acquite themselues of their charge, that suffered the people so often to fall to idolatrie in time of the Iudges, that neuer admonished them, nor censured the kings, nor either prescribed good order, or forbad confusion. The idoles of the gentiles, as it should seeme, were not more mute and senceles then the aldermen of the *Iewes* Church were, if any such were. But it is a vaine imagination. For who can imagine that such a famous colledge of aldermen should be in the Iewish Church, when there is neither lawe found to authorise them, nor practise to proue them, and all that authoritie they claime is deriued another way, to the princes and priestes, and such silence is made of them,as if they had slept from the time of their first entrance, vntill the time of Christ?

The aldermen of the Church did nothing in those causes vnder the lawe,wherein their iurisdiction now supposed to consist.

That which some alledge of Synagogues, that are surmised to haue had some iurisdiction, and authoritie of gouernement, eyther hurteth the cause of Elders,or helpeth them litle. For if Synagogues came in by deuise of man, contrarie to Gods lawe,that appointed his worship in the temple at *Ierusalem*: then if Elders be contained in the Synagogue, they will proue a humane deuise. That is apparant. for in the canonicall scriptures of the olde Testament, there is no mention of Synagogues,which moued *Caluin* to deriue the originall of his synedrion from the *Iewes* returne out of captiuitie. But admit there were Synagogues, and that they had a lawfull beginning: yet is it nothing to the cause of the aldermen. for if we take Synagogue for a place; in that place there cannot be proued to haue bene anie such Ecclesiasticall iurisdiction as is pretended, of Ciuill we reade; of Ecclesiasticall we reade not, nor by whome it should be executed. if it be taken for a companie; yet that Elders Ecclesiastical gouernors were therein comprised, none of them can make profe that striue to haue them. nay, it appeareth that they that vsed iurisdiction in the Synagogues, were ciuill officers, that punished with stripes, and other ciuill punishments. Of Priestes, Elders, Doctors, that iudged in Synagogues, there is not the least suspicion. *Peter Galatine* and *Iosephus* mention no other gouernors of Synagogues beside Rabbines and Doctors. But suppose the Church of the *Iewes* had Ecclesiasticall aldermen: what is that to the Church of the Christians, vnlesse

Synagogue a humane deuise.

*In Mat.*18.

*Math.*10.

*Ibidem & Math.*23.

*Adu. Appi.li.*2. *Philo. in lib. quod omnis probus liber. &c.*

lesse they can proue, that ẏ same Elders are trãslated into our church? which they haue often talked of, but neuer haue proued, nor neuer shalbe able, whatsoeuer some affirme: for ẏ trueth of God is against it. The Iewish Elders did many things, which agree not with their new discipline: and the late Ecclesiastical aldermen doe manie things which the Iewish Elders did neuer, and in the forme of the office of these two Elderships there is great difference.

The Iewish Elders differ much from Ecclesiastical aldermen, now vsed.

The Elders of the *Iewes*, whether we vnderstand those that are mẽtioned *Exo.18.* or *Numb.11.* or *Deu.17.* did determine ciuill causes as hath bin shewed. These last did not onely deale in matters of title and propertie, but also of life & death. Those which are mentioned *Num. 11.* were neere to ẏ prince and chiefe magistrate, & with him did beare the burthen of gouernement. such Elders as these were, onely were in one place, and no more of thẽ, but one societie & companie: they dealt not in iudgement of matters cleane nor vncleane, for that belonged to the priestes office; nor in excommunication; neither had they authoritie to set downe, or disanull orders, nor to choose, or depose officers and Iudges. For vntill such time as the Sanedrin were the soueraigne magistrates, we reade of none chosen by them, or deposed by them. But by the prince, we reade both to haue bene executed, as appeareth in the displacing of *Abiathar*, and substituting of *Zadok*, and in the appointment of Iudges and officers by *Dauid, Salomon, Iehosaphat*, and *Ezra*.

In the new church-aldermen, all things are turned cõtrarie. They deale not (as they say) in ciuill causes. as for criminal and capital causes, they thinke it abominable to touch them. they say as sayde the hie priests, that by their law it is not lawful to put any man to death. although they presume verie hie, yet doe they not thinke it lawfull for their Elders to deale in matters of warre, and peace, & such things as belong to the state; and of such as these Elders are, there are fraternities, and colledges in diuers places, our disciplinarians would haue them in euery parish. the argument which they handle, they pretend to be the discipline of the Church: they take vpon them to iudge of all matters concerning faith, and manners, and to throwe out & take in, and chalenge authoritie to set orders, to make lawes, and disanull them, and doe this without controlment of anie superior presbytery, vnlesse they will change their Synodes into presbyteries. Finallie, they take vpon them as princes, to nominate and chuse all officers of the Church, and to displace them whom they dislike. So that I wonder how they can call these new aldermen, the children of the Iewish

Iewish Elders, that are so vnlike their fathers. And what reason haue they, to say it is translated, that is so strangely transformed, rather thẽ transported? Neither matter, nor authoritie, nor forme of proceeding is alike in either. to make thẽ seeme like, *Th. Cartw.* and others, forme them & fashion thẽ at their pleasure. they take away, & they adde, as best serueth their turne. Where we say, that the Iewish Elders did deale in ciuill causes, that they take away, and say they did it *de facto*, and without authoritie, & that the same was part of the reliques of Babylonish confusion. Where we denie that they had authoritie to excommunicate, to make lawes, or disanull them, or to choose officers, or depose thẽ, they adde that authoritie vnto thẽ: but both these things we wil proue them to haue deuised. For both true it is, that the Iewish Elders had authoritie to deale in ciuil, & capital causes, and also ẏ they dealt not in excõmunication, making of lawes, & choyse of officers, vnlesse the Sanedrin were also the soueueraigne magistrat.

When *Moses* gaue instructions concerning the decision of most difficult matters to be heard before ẏ hyest iudges, it is manifest that he did furnish them with authoritie to heare, not onelie ciuill causes, but criminall also, and of blood. Which order of iudges taking notice of such causes as could not be decided before inferior iudges, it is also euident, that seeing the inferior iudges heard matters of controuersie, both of cõtracts ciuill, & criminal; that the other order of iudges must haue like authoritie too, otherwise could they not haue autoritie to decide such causes as were brought before thẽ. that inferior iudges did decide matters ciuill and criminal, it is apparant, for that all causes were committed vnto them, matters difficult excepted. the practise of the Iewish gouernement doth declare the same. for whẽ *Iehosaphat*, of the priestes, leuites, & princes had apointed iudges in *Ierusalem*, he gaue thẽ in charge that they should iudge vprightly, not in Ecclesiasticall causes, but in causes of blood, and betweene cõtrouersies about lawes & precepts. of which iudgemẽt of the priests to be restored after the captiuitie, *Ezekiel* doth prophesie saying, that the priestes shall stand to iudge in controuersies. And so *Ezra* in his time iudged not Ecclesiastically, but punished with death, banishmẽt, confiscation of goods, or imprisonment. Which course, seeing it was appointed by God; who can say it is vnlawful? Seeing he did foretel it, as a thing ẏ should be, who can say he disallowed it? & seeing ẏ Elders & priests had this power by erectiõ of their office, who can say it is vsurped, or rather ẏ it cõmeth in by cõfusion, then right? whẽ ẏ elders cõdemned *Christ*, *Stephen*, *Paul*, & the saints of God, none of thẽ did

Vide Vatablum in Deut. 17. & 2. *Chron.* 19. & *rabbinos.*

Cap. 44.

Ezra. 7.

charge them with doing things beyond lawe, or their commiſſion; which if they had done, it had bene a good exception: which our Sauiour Chriſt & the Apoſtle *Paul* that reprehẽdeth ſo manie things *Aduerſ. Apppi. lib.2.* in them, would not haue omitted. *Ioſephus* doth vtterlie ouerthrow this pretended Eccleſiaſtical iurisdiction. for he ſaith that all impietie was puniſhed by death. His wordes are ἀθεῦς ἀπόλλυται.

For anſwere whereof, the diſciplinarians ſay, that the *Iewes* had two ſortes of Elders: one Eccleſiaſticall, the other ciuill; and that the Eccleſiaſticall Elders iudged of lawe, the other of fact; matters both falſe (for it is a meere fiction) and abſurde. For what can be more abſurd, thẽ that iudges ſhould be appointed without knowledge of lawe? or that there ſhould be two ſentences giuen in euerie difficult cauſe, the one of the lawe, the other of fact? All proceeding of lawe, requireth that the fact be firſt agreed vpon, and that the ſentence ſhould conteine what is lawe concerning that fact. and moſt ſtrange it were, if princes ſhoulde not haue power to doe anie thing, before the Eccleſiaſticall Elders ſhould haue pronounced.

They doe alſo affirme, that the Eccleſiaſticall Elders dealt in the cauſes of God, and the others in the cauſes of the king. but the words *1.Chron.26.* of Scriptures teſtifie, that the ſame iudges dealt both in the cauſes of *2.Chron.17.* God, and the king: which is the ouerthrowe of the double ſorte of Elders, and a plaine proofe that the Elders of the *Iewes* dealt in ciuill and capitall cauſes. ſo that if by the cauſes of God we vnderſtood Eccleſiaſticall cauſes, yet no vantage will redound to their cauſe. But *1.Paral.28.* the cauſes of the king being expounded, the cauſes of the kings houſholde, and the cauſes of God, all tranſgreſſions, or cauſes concerning the lawe of God, which muſt needes be, or els they are not conſidered at all, nor cared for; then the aduantage will be much leſſe.

They ſay further, that the Iewiſh Elders did not condemne our Sa- *Math.26.66. He is worthie to dye.* uiour to die, which is contrarie to the text of ſcripture. Likewiſe, that *Stephen* was ſlaine by tumult, which is vntrue. for he was brought before the counſel and Elders, examined, heard, condemned, executed *Act.6.&c.* with all formalitie of lawe, the witneſſes laying their hand firſt vpon *Deut.17.7.* him, and ſo ſtoning him, according to *Moſes* lawe, being condemned (though wrongfullie) of blaſphemie. neither can it bee denyed, *Act.26.* but that authoritie which the Elders gaue to *Paul* to imprison, and to *Act.22.* bring bound to *Ieruſalem*, which they exerciſed, whẽ they cauſed the *Act.5.* Apoſtles to be apprehended and beaten, and practiſed in their counſels, was deriued from the lawe of *Moſes*, ſeeing the ſame was neuer reprehended nor found fault withall.

Now,

Now, where the Iewish Elders did excommunicate, no place can be shewed. The priests iudged of things cleane and vncleane, & not the Elders; and the shutting out of the Synagogue can be no elder then the Synagogue, and was practised by doctors, not by Elders, and was a ciuill punishment, for that they that were so shut out, were not shut out of the Temple, nor banished from the sacrifices. but whatsoeuer this was, it came not by authoritie from the Lawe of *Moses*, but by latter vse and tradition. where Elders of the *Iewes* made lawes and disannulled them, they can shew nothing; and as litle for their autoritie which they giue them in election and deposing of Ecclesiasticall officers: all which seeing the newe aldermen doe challenge more then euer the *Iewish* Elders had, they must needes be sore pinched & wrung in their translation, that are so strangely altered and changed.

Petr. gal. de rabbi Iehosua.

The conceit of the translating of the *Iewish* Elders into the church (which the disciplinarians do often alledge, and so much stand vpon) is a deuice very improbable. for in the place so commonly alledged *Matth.* 18. there is not the least inkling of Elders; of any commission giuen to them much lesse. if *Matth.* 5 where our Sauiour speaketh of the Sanedrin, no translation is made thereof, much lesse is it probable, that it should be here translated, where it is not named.

The *Iewish* Elders were not translated into the Church.

Caluin (whom some take to be the first autor of this translation) doth not say that the Elders are translated, but that the right of the Eldership is translated into the Church: that as the *Iewes* had an order to punish the obstinate, so there might bee the like in the Church of Christ. All which being graunted, yet would it not followe that the Elders are translated. neither doeth that argument helpe which they bring, that because complaint cannot bee made to the Church, therefore it must be made to the Elders: for complaint may be made to a whole multitude, as where the *Leuite* brought his cause before the whole congregation; and as infinite actions, pleas and defences made before the people of *Rome*, *Athens*, and other popular states declare. but be it that the complaint must bee made to the gouernours: are there no gouernours but Elders? what do they then accompt of bishops and pastors? & why were matters of controuersie of things cleane and vncleane, brought before the priestes? and who euer heard of such Elders (as these are) to bee gouernours? but if it were supposed that these newe aldermen were gouernours, and were ment here: yet is their authoritie nothing, that is here graunted. for vnlesse the order that is here prescribed be obserued, the Church doth nothing, so that first some priuate man must be offended:

in Math. 18.

Iudg. 20.

Neither *Phil.* nor *Iosephus* knew any such.

fended: then the partie that giueth the offence must persist obstinate: thirdly, the Church hath no power here giuen but to admonish: lastly, the sentence is to bee pronounced by the partie offended. for the wordes are, *Let him be to thee*, not let him be to the Church. and if so be we interpret it of publike offences, that are not brought to the Church by complaint, but reformed of the officers by vertue of their charge; then must it fall out that the Church should be partie complainant, and iudge also, and that the Church shoulde tell the Church, which is an absurd forme of speaking. but that this is but a weake reason to prooue the translation of the *Iewish* elders into the Church of Christ, it shall thē manifestly appeare, when we haue shewed that neither Christ translated from the *Iewes*, nor instituted in his Church any such Church aldermen, as the disciplinarians contend for. which discourse nowe followeth.

Of the Consistoriall Elders, and their vsurpation.

CHAP. 4. SECT. 2.

Therein diuers reasons are produced out of the newe Testament, and from our Sauiour Christs, and his Apostles practise, to shewe that there neuer were any Church aldermen by them instituted, or practised. First, for that the commission they claime, was giuen to others. Secondly, for that they are left out of the number of the ministers of the Church. Ephe.4. *Thirdly, for that neither the title of their office, nor their office is found in Scriptures. Fourthly, for that the Apostles did not appoynt them in any Church. Fiftly, for that they omitted the description of their office. Sixtly, for that the commission which they challenge cannot be prooued by one word of scripture. Seuenthly, for that their authoritie which they claime, is due to the magistrate and to bishops. Eightly, for that nothing can be more repugnant to Christes wisedome, nor to his proceedings, then to commit the Church to men ignorant. both antiquitie and the historie of the Church maketh against them. The reasons to the contrary are answered.*

WHen Christ Iesus did leaue his Church concerning his bodily presence, yet did hee not leaue the same without guides and gouernours. for he committed it to his Apostles to be fedde and to bee gouerned. Wherefore, vnlesse the Elders can shewe euidence, and proue their succession from the Apostles, they may not meddle with that which is committed to others gouernment. wherein this is no small preiudice against them, that claiming to be gouernours of the Church, they disclaime the ministerie of the word, both being committed to the Apostles in one word of feeding. Let them therefore shewe by what title they take vpon them the Apostles right, seeing they cannot shewe any succession from them, nor ioyne with them in their ministerie.

Ministers of the word made gouernours of the Church. *Iohn* 21.

They

They are not comprised among those ministeries, which our Sauiour appoynted for the perfiting of the saintes, and edification of his body. wherefore, to vse their wordes against them, what presumption is it to adde vnto those ministeries, whereby Christ coulde make vp the bodie of saintes, and to thinke to edifie the Church by other meanes then those which Christ hath appoynted? & what dishonour, if not plaine blasphemie, to say that Christ hath not appointed meanes sufficient for the edification of his Church? To auoyde this reason, *T. Cartw.* saith that Christ reckoneth vp those officers which are conuersant in the word: but neither saith hee truely (for Apostles and Pastors are conuersant in gouernment and edifie also by mainteining of order by their gouernment) nor is his saying any answere to our reason. for if these officers are sufficient for the gathering together of the saintes, and edification of Christes bodie; then are elders more then sufficient and supernumerarie. and if they be not sufficient, then hath not Christ appoynted meanes sufficient to atteine vnto the ende of gathering the saintes, and edification of his bodie.

καταρτισμὸν. This is their common reason against Archbishops.

3 And if Elders bee (as is pretended) officers appoynted by Christ for the gouernment of his Church; why are they not named in the place aboue mentioned, or in the *1.Cor.12.* where the Apostle reckoneth vp the ministers of the Church? or at least in the 12. of the Epistle to the Romanes, where (they say) the Apostle maketh a full rehearsall of the diuers functions of Church officers, and setteth out all the partes of the body of the Church? If Elders be as necessarie for gouernment as pastors, why are they not named as well as pastors? admit there were somewhat that sounded to the honour of Elders: yet that we finde no name of theirs in the rolle of Church officers, it is a foule presumption against them. for Christ doth not leaue his Church to be gouerned by namelesse persons, nor doth hee leaue his flocke in suspence, by whom it should be gouerned. but if neither the name of elders, nor office be found there, it is a plaine euidence against them. In the place out of the 4. to the *Ephesians* there is no steppe of them. in the 12. to the *Romanes*, albeit their name bee not, yet they beleeue their elders to be comprised vnder rulers: which cannot be. for if by rulers they vnderstand elders; and by exhorters, pastors; then can the pastor no more gouerne, then the elder can exhort, which they count absurd, and so iustly may, seeing true pastors are the Apostles successors. Secondly, it is absurd by rulers to vnderstand Elders, seeing they can shewe no one iote of Scripture,

Neither name nor office of the newe Elders found in Scriptures.

Elders not meant by rulers. *Romanes 12.*

where they are rulers, nor in what things their rule consisteth, and therefore ought not to take the helme out of the hand of other gouernours, whom scriptures acknowledge for gouernors and leaders.

*Hebr.*13. Thirdly, where they interpret *Presbyteros* elders, onely gouernours, they erre. for the scriptures knowe no Priestes or Elders of the Church, but ministers of the word. Fourthly, it were absurd to interprete rulers elders, seing they are put after distributors, whome they interpret deacons: which is as much as if the master shoulde be put behinde the seruant, rulers after subiects. Fiftly, they cannot shewe by any one example, that euer any Church alderman of theirs did gouerne the church in any one place in the Apostles time. Lastly, the Apostles meaning was to set out diuers functions & gifts of ministers, not diuers orders distinct. diuers giftes I say, but not in diuers persons, seeing the pastor ought to exhort, to teach, to rule, to minister, which he might not, if these seuerall giftes might not concurre in one person. neither did any one of the ancient fathers interpret it otherwise, nor would the latter, but to giue colour to their owne deuices.

1.*Cor.*12.

That the place 1.*Cor.*12. doth not help the newe Aldermen.

Their hold of the place out of the first epistle to the *Corinthians* 12. *Chapter* is slender and slipperie: for if by gouernances we vnderstand their Church aldermen, then might neither Apostles nor Pastors meddle with Church gouernment. for they make these offices and their functions distinct, & say that an eye might be placed aswell in the elbow, and a foote where the hand shoulde be, as these offices confounded or mingled. Secondly, ἀντιλήψεις or helpers which they interpret deacons, should very presumptuously step before gouernances, whom they construe Elders. Thirdly, the tenour of the Apostles words maketh against them. for after hee had distinguished apostles, prophets, & teachers, by first, second, third; he ioyneth power of miracles, gifts of healing, helpes, gouernances, & diuersitie of tongues in one tenour and sequell of wordes, which diuers kinde of speech may shewe a diuersitie betwixt those that are ioyned, and the other that are disioyned. Fourthly, if the Apostle had meant to distinguish these giftes in the persons that shoulde haue them; hee would haue said gouernors, not gouernances. Fiftly, these gifts that are disioyned, as power of miracles, gifts of healing, helps, gouernances, and diuersity of tongues, should not haue bene in one person: the contrary whereof is true. for most of those, if not all, were in the apostles. and *S. Paul* exhorteth not the *Corinthians* to desire euery one seuerall gifts, but euery one the best gifts. Ζηλοῦτε δὲ τὰ χαρίσματα τὰ κρείττονα. that is, Desire not one, but all, especially, the best of these graces.

graces. Sixtly, seeing diuersity of tongues, and power of miracles, and gifts of healing are distinguished alike; what reason is there to make gouernances a distinct person, seeing the other betoken neither distinct person, nor are distinguished in persons? If they were not peruerse, the aduersaries would neuer striue against the generall interpretation of fathers, and so many reasons.

That our Sauiour *Christ* appointed no church aldermen gouernours of the church, it may further appeare in this, that the apostles obseruing diligently his precepts & commandements, did no where appoint such elders. if they did appoint them, let the place of Scripture be produced, where they are mentioned. let the church be named, where they were placed. They produce the *14.* of the *Acts*, and the *1.* of *Titus*: but the places do witnesse against them that alledge them, that there are no other but ministers of the word, as shalbe shewed, when we answere their obiections. 4

4 No church aldermen appointed by the apostles.

Nay, the apostle *Paul* sheweth plainely, that there were none at *Philippi* (where the bishops and deacons onely are saluted as officers of the church) nor that any such ought to be in the church. for declaring the offices and qualities of bishops and deacons, in his epistles to *Timothie* and *Titus*, it is not probable that he would haue omitted Church aldermen, if any such had bene; especially so particularly setting downe the office of deacons, which in the disciplinarian policie come behinde Elders. that which some obiect that vnder the name of deacons, the elders duetie is described, is contrary to the course of the lawes, that vse not to prescribe the duetie of one office, by the name of an other: and contrary to the order of distinct teaching, that doth neuer confound diuers kindes vnder one name: and repugnant to common vse of speech, that calleth elders no more by the name of deacons, then an oke by the name of an ash, or one kinde by the name of another. but with the disciplinarians it is no woonder if words be confounded, for in their whole course they seeke to confound the Church and Commonwealth. 5

5 Elder would not haue bene omitted in *S. Pauls* description of the ministers office, if any such had bene.

But if that lay elders be (as they say) officers appointed by *Christ*, let them shew wherein this office consisteth, let them lay downe the particulars of their commission out of the word of God. for to haue the bare name of an officer, is nothing, vnlesse they shew the authority and function of the officer. They say it belongeth to the office of elders, to make and abrogate church lawes, to iudge in causes of controuersie, to suspend, excommunicate, and absolue, and to chuse, correct, and depose officers. Let them therefore prooue it out of the 6

6 The commission of elders forged without Scripture.

 word

word of God, and if they can bring no proofe nor coniecture, that euer these great matters were committed to the discretion of their aldermen, let them confesse that as the commission, so the name of the church aldermen is a matter newly forged.

7 The apostles, they gaue all that authority, for the most part, which the elders claime, to godly bishops and pastours, as appeareth by the instructions that the apostle gaue to *Timothie* and *Titus*. what presumption then is it, vnder colour of apostolicall orders, to take it from those to whom it is due, and to attribute it vnto them that haue no proofe of their name nor title, much lesse of that infinite power which they chalenge?

The authority of ministers inuaded by elders.

8 Nothing is more repugnant to *Christes* diuine wisdome, then that he should commit his church to the gouernment of men ignorant; for such they are, as experience teacheth. and if they should be otherwise, why do they not teach also, which is more excellent? In times past, the priests lips preserued knowledge; now the priests must receiue order of profane and vnlettered aldermen.

Absurd to cōmit ỹ church to men ignorant.

9 Neither can any thing be more repugnant to the proceedings of *Christ* and his apostles, then that men vnlearned should gouerne the Church, seeing gouernment and wisdome proceedeth of knowledge and doctrine. and to make elders gouernours (which do learne of their pastours) is to make scholars gouernours of their maisters, and maisters subiect to the checke and controlement of their scholars. In a popular state the people are gouerned by magistrates: how much more in the Church of God ought the common sort to hearken to their pastours? Neither is it likely, that all should be commanded to be subiect to the prince and higher powers, if the prince and pastours were enioyned to be subiect to the elders, which by the disciplinarians grant, ouer-rule all by plurality of voices.

Tit.3.1.

10 Further, seeing all antiquity is ignorant of this function of church aldermen, and that there is no mention of them in stories, councels, nor fathers (as shall be prooued, when we come vnto it) what probability is there, that *Christ* should haue appointed, or the apostles receiued any such office of these aldermen? Suppose that this should be a piece of *Antichristes* worke, to ouerthrow the presbyterie; yet did he not worke all at one instant, but by litle and litle: and therefore not likely, that *Christes* order shoulde be generally neglected euery where at one instant, but first in one place, then in another. Wherefore let them shew any one place, where this order of elders was established, or else know, that it is not like to haue

haue any discent or succession, or allowance, from *Christ*, or his apostles.

Finally, let vs adde heereunto, that when any thing was prescri- 11
bed to the Churches, order was giuen either to the whole Church, or to the pastours and ministers of the word. that appeareth by the whole tenour of the apostolicall writings: this in the examples of *Epist.ad Rom. ad Gal.Eph.&c.* *Timothie*, *Titus*, and the angels of the seuen Churches. where any thing was prescribed to any of these new Church aldermen, there is no proofe nor coniecture found. Againe, before the time of Christian magistrates, where any thing was amisse, either the pastours were reprehended and taxed, as in the epistles of *Iohn* to the Churches; *Apoc.2.et 3.* or the whole Church, as in the fact of the incestuous *Corinthian*. where Church aldermen were taxed for neglecting their duty, we finde not. nay, we finde not where they did any part of that duety which is said to belong to their charge. In the Church of *Rome* there were some that caused diuision and dissension. *Rom.16.* In the Church of *Corinth* there were schismes, errours, and disorders in the Lords supper. *1.Cor.1.et 11.* In the Church of *Philippi*, carnall epicures. *Philip.3.* At *Thessalonica*, idle and busie bodies: *2.Thess.3.* yet doe we not reade that any one of these offences was touched by the eldership, or they for neglecting to reforme them. So that one of these two things must needs folow; either that the elders did nothing, and serued for nothing but idols, or els that there were none: which is more true, and the reasons which they bring to the contrary, weake and friuolous.

That place of which they make greatest account, and place, as it were in the formost ranks of their authorities brought to proue their elders, bringeth forth a most weake conclusion. The elders that rule well (saith the apostle) are woorthy double honour, especially those that labor in the word & doctrine. *1.Tim.5.17.* therefore (say they) there are one sort of elders that gouerne onely, another that gouerne and labour in the word. Their reason is grounded vpon the word μάλιστα, that is, especially, for that it maketh a difference (as they weene) betweene elders gouerning and teaching. but of this their supposall, they allege no reason: for the difference is not betweene elders teaching and gouerning, but betweene elders gouerning, and vehemently, and earnestly labouring. For the word μάλιστα ioyned with κοπιῶντες, doth shew where the distinction and the emphasis is. Secondly, the word κοπιῶντες it selfe, betokening a wearisome labour, doth shew that the distinction is betweene such as labour most earnestly, and such as looke not so throughly to teaching as others doe.

Thirdly, the reason brought in the 18 verse, doth shew that the apostle speaketh heere of the ministers of the word onely; for that the words alleged out of the *25* of *Deuteronomy, Thou shalt not muzzell the mouth of the oxe that treadeth out the corne*; *1.Cor. 9.9.* are applied to the ministers of the word, that are to haue mainteinance of the churches to which they preach. and the intention of the apostle is to speake for the honour and interteinment of ministers. Fourthly, the Scriptures know no elders of the church, but ministers of the word. let them name them if they can. Lastly, both *Ierome* and *Chrysostome* make the emphasis in the word κοπιῶντες, and not so much as one father speaketh of elders, not teaching: no not *Ambrose*, who complaining that the counsell of elders was no more vsed in his time by bishops, doth not say that these elders were others then such as taught. neither is it likely that he would haue the bishops vse the counsell of others then wise and learned. If we expound the place of church aldermen, such as are crept into some churches of late; these inconueniences will follow, that these elders deserue double honour and wages, of which they are depriued. Secondly, that they ought to be, during their liues, gouernours: for so were the elders, spoken of in the apostles writings; and these are not. Thirdly, there must be an order of elders heere instituted, which neither the Scriptures knew, nor the apostle thought necessary: for he giueth no instructions concerning this elder; and the Scriptures acknowledge no elders of the church, but ministers of the word. Fourthly, the apostle must take elder heere, otherwise then he taketh it in other places, whereof there is no manifest distinction, or cause of distinction. Fiftly, the reason, verse 18, which is spoken of the ministers of the word, should not fitly agree with the proposition, if elders onely gouernours were vnderstood. Sixtly, we should digresse from the apostles interpretation, who exhorting the *Thessalonians* εἰδέναι τοὺς κοπιῶντας καὶ προϊσταμένους, that is, to know those that labour and gouerne in the Lords causes, doth shew that the difference is betweene κοπιῶντας καὶ μὴ κοπιῶντας, for that labourers and gouernours, are both to signifie the ministers of the word, that is, *re, non subiecto* distinguished. Lastly, we should digresse from all antiquity, that knoweth no church elders, but ministers of the word; nor expound this place of others then ministers of the word. no not *Ambrose* himselfe (as I said) who (as they thinke) speaketh for their elders. True it is, he speaketh of elders that were of counsell with the bishop, but there is no colourable coniecture that he meaneth mere lay men: for he doth not say, that

Where they expound the place.

The new elders cõmonly haue no wages nor interteinment.

the

the office is growen out of vse, but the action of consenting with them, by bishops was discontinued.

But were it granted, about which they striue so earnestly, that in this place the apostle distinguished teachers from gouerning elders, which is not true, nor can be prooued: yet would they want much of their conclusion, that there are such officers in the church. for there are magistrates, gouernours of houses, and such like, of whom the words are more likely to be spoken, then of such elders as were neuer. neither maketh it any thing against this interpretation, that there were then no magistrates of the church. for to proue a speciall point, the generall word must be affirmed; and so the apostle might doe without mentioning their aldermen, if he should affirme that all gouernours in Church and Common wealth are woorthy honour, especially such as labour in the word. and if they will not admit that the apostle speaketh of gouernours out of the Church; yet the heads of houses, and chiefe of families, may be vnderstood, which the apostle calleth gouernours, where he requireth in deacons, that they be καλῶς προϊστάμενοι τῶν ἰδίων οἴκων, gouerning well their owne houses. which interpretation might agree well with this place. for after that the apostle had declared the honour due to olde age; in this place repeating the same, he amplifieth that honour in the ministers of the word. But I do not willingly digresse from all antiquitie, which by elders in *1.Tim.c.5.* vnderstand none but ministers of the word. *1.Tim.3.*

That which I said in a word in passing, that the Scriptures call none elders, but such as were either elders by yeeres, or magistrates of the *Iewes*, or ministers of the word (for that it conteineth answere to most of their obiectiõs) is here more at large to be discoursed. this I say therefore, and purpose (God willing) to shew, that all Church elders, spoken of in the word of God, are ministers of the word of God, and that their obiections to the contrary prooue nothing. First, we allege against them the consent of all antiquity, that interpreteth the word *Presbyteros* priests. I name not any, for that no instance can be giuen, as shall be shewed, when we come to speake of the iudgement of fathers concerning elders. Secondly, the very words of Scripture do shew that all church elders are ministers of the word. their exceptions to the contrary are of no value.

The scriptures called none *presbyteros ecclesiæ*, but ministers of the word.

To prooue elders not teaching, *Daneau* allegeth two singular places: the first out of the first epistle to *S. Peter, c.5.* the second out of the twentieth of the *Acts.* but his allegation is not onely without testimony of antiquity, but also direct against the text. *Peter* na-

S meth

meth certaine elders : but that these were ministers of the word, it appeareth : First, for that he exhorteth them to feede the flocke, which can not be done without doctrine; and vseth that word ποιμαίνειν, which our Sauiour vsed when he committed his flocke to *Peter* and the rest of the apostles. Secondly, for that the flocke hath relation to the word pastour, which being committed to the elders in this place, they must needs be pastours. Thirdly, for that the word ἐπισκοποῦντες is giuen to them, to declare them to be bishops. Fourthly, for that the apostle ioyneth himselfe here in felowship with these elders: but the aduersaries themselues do not frame their consistory of apostles & elders, nor are elders to ioyne in felowship with the apostles. Fiftly, for that the elders here mentioned receiued wages, as may appeare, in that the apostle admonisheth them, not to respect filthy lucre : but the new aldermen in all churches where they reigne, liue vpon interest of their owne mony or goods, and receiue no salary of the Churches. Lastly, all antiquity repugneth against this interpretation, yea, *Caluin* himselfe, that by elders there vnderstandeth pastors.

Iohn 21.

In 1.*Pet*.5.

The elders *Act*.20. were ministers of the word.

The text, *Act*.20. is yet more pregnant, and direct against dumbe aldermen of the Church : for the apostle calleth them bishops, who ought not to resemble these dumbe idoles, but to exhort and teach. Secondly, he declareth that certaine of them should speake peruerse things to draw disciples after them, which argueth them to be teachers. Thirdly, in plaine termes he giueth them the charge of the flocke, which can not be committed but to pastours, speaking properly. Fourthly, the apostle proposeth vnto them his owne example in teaching, which would not well fit lay elders. Fiftly, *S.Paul* in that place speaketh nothing of gouernment, which is the proper duety (they say) of these aldermen : so that whosoeuer will say, the apostle addressed his speech vnto them, must confesse that he spoke from the purpose. Lastly, all interpretors, as they vnderstand the place of the ministers of the word, so they giue no signification of lay elders. most of their owne frends forsake them in the misconstruing of this place.

To helpe the matter, others bring more places out of the 15 and 21 of the *Acts*, for a new supply : but who would imagine dumbe elders to be meant in either? In the fifteenth of the *Acts*, the elders tried and discussed the matter of doctrine concerning the law of *Moses*, which fitteth not dumbe elders to do. and because some of them haue beene too saucy in that point; by an expresse article, they are in some Churches debarred from deciding matters of doctrine or faith. Secondly, if by elders, others besides ministers of the word

Disc .de Fr. Tit.du consist. art.10.

were

were vnderſtood, then were paſtours quite excluded out of the Synode, and matters referred to the voices of the ignorant: for heere is no mention of other paſtours then elders. Thirdly, theſe elders were ioyned with the Chnrch, as leaders and gouernours, but we know none at that time but apoſtles, prophets, euangeliſts, & paſtors. Laſtly, ancient writers repugne againſt thoſe that expound elders to be their Church aldermen, and fauour the contrary interpretation. And *Caluin* driuen by force of truth, expoundeth elders, teachers. *In ver.22.*

We reade, *Act. 21*, how (when *Paul* was to giue account of his *Act.20.* trauelles in the Goſpell) all the elders came to *Iames* the apoſtle; which as it ſheweth him to be biſhop there, and the elders to be vnder his charge, as ancient fathers affirme, and practiſe of the firſt Church confirmeth: ſo it hath nothing that any way ſauoureth of the proceeding of the Church aldermen. Firſt, the people were aſſembled, and the matter referred to the multitude. the words of the text are πάντως δεῖ πλῆθος συνελθεῖν, &c. in any caſe the multitude muſt come together. Contrariwiſe, in this new diſcipline, the eldership doth firſt heare and determine, and afterward make the multitude acquainted, if ſo they thinke meet. Secondly, the elders make a long diſcourſe of the law, which were not a matter likely, in the mouthes of ſuch Church aldermen, eſpecially the apoſtles being preſent; and very abſurd, if elders ſuppoſed to be mute as idols, ſhould fall in ſo long diſcourſe. Thirdly, the elders heere mentioned, were prolocutors; contrary to that courſe, which among the lay aldermen *French diſc.* is vſuall. for they may not moue matters, nor take vpon them to mo- *tit. du.conſ.* derate. Laſtly, all antiquity, by elders in this place, vnderſtandeth biſhops and prieſts. the aduerſaries are not agreed among themſelues who is vnderſtood. *Caluin* paſſeth from them to the enemy, & ſaith that doctours are meant by elders.

From hence driuen, they require ayde of the apoſtle S. *Iames*, who *Iames 5.14.* as he mentioneth elders, ſo he fauoureth nothing the conceit of the new elders. for theſe elders had power to worke miracles, which the Church aldermen haue not. Secondly, they ioyned publike prayer with their ointment, which is a part of the miniſters function. Thirdly, they viſited the ſicke, which is likewiſe a duty of the miniſters, and not of the Church aldermen. Laſtly, the ceremony of anoynting being a certaine ſigne, could not be ſeparated from the word, which is not committed to Church aldermen, but to paſtours.

Others, to finde out their aldermen, ſeeke in the 14 of the *Acts*, where *Paul* and *Barnabas* are ſaid to ordeine elders in euery Church.

but the maiesty of these aldermen is too great to be hidden in so nar-
row a roome : for it is litle enough for ministers of the word, and can
receiue no more company. All writers expound the place of ministers of the word : and if ministers were not appointed, then were
churches dressed and framed, without a guide and principall gouernour. To vnderstand the place of elders both teaching and vnteaching, both is contrary to the vse of speech, where that which is affirmed of another is particularly taken (as hath beene prooued) and
contrary to rules of teaching, to comprehend one office vnder another diuers office, and contrary to reason. for it is not credible, these
townes being newly conuerted, that there were men sufficient e-
nough to make such gouerning elders of, and new Christians are
not (but vpon triall) to be admitted to gouernment. Lastly, their
Calu.in Act. owne frends bewray and condemne their boldnesse in making this
place to serue for church aldermen, which all interpretours expound
of ministers of the word.

Thus, wheresoeuer they finde the name of elders, they imagine,
that they are the elders they dreame of : ὡς κυὼν μαντεύεται ἄρτως : so hun-
Theocrit. gry dogs dreame of bread : they as men inamored, dreame of many
Virg. goodly matters : *qui amant, vana sibi somnia fingunt.* nay, in diuers
places, where they doe not so much as finde the name of elders,
yet they note them diligently : as *Philip.4.8. 2.Tim.3.6. 1.Pet.3.3.
1.Cor.14.34.* as if these places did fauour them. If their boldnesse in
allegations, & forcing of Scripture, were not manifest, I would shew
it in this : but seeing that is manifest already, what should I answere
places brought for proofe of elders, where not so much as the word,
much lesse the office of elders, is mentioned?

These obiections answered, do affoord vs this firme conclusion a-
gainst Church aldermen. seeing there are no church elders mentioned in the New testament, but ministers of the word, as appeareth in
this, that they can neither name any that was such an elder, nor shew
where such elders are mentioned ; and for that also, their owne obiections proue the same : therfore they haue no confirmation of Scripture, or authenticall originall. This also is confirmed by the authority of *Ierome*, which they allege against the superiority of bishops;
and therefore can not refuse their owne witnesse, speaking against
In Tit.1. themselues. he saith that the name of bishop and elder signifieth
one thing by the text, and words of Scripture. out of which, who
can not conclude that there were no elders of the Church, but were
bishops ? Howsoeuer his authority is brought against vs, it is firme
against

againſt Church aldermen, that were no teachers nor biſhops.

Thus it may appeare what accompt we are to make of their diſcipline, when their Church aldermen which are pillars of their ſtate, are thus ruinated. but more clearely ſhall the ſame appeare, when returning backe to that we ſaid in paſſing, that the ancient fathers after the Apoſtles time neuer knewe any ſuch order of dumbe aldermen as they ſeeke, we ſhall particularly haue made profe thereof, and anſwered whatſoeuer can bee ſayde to the contrary, which commeth now to be accompliſhed.

Of the Conſiſtoriall aldermen, and their vſurpation.

Chap. 4. Sect. 3.

The Church aldermen are therein declared not to haue bene in the Church following the Apoſtles times: Firſt, for that no name or record is extant of any ſuch gouernours. Secondly, for that there is no ſuch praiſed or diſpraiſed for good or badde gouernement in ſtories. Thirdly, for that the gouernment of the Church in perſecution, was in biſhops: after perſecution, in the magiſtrate and biſhops. Fourthly, for that ancient fathers ſpeaking of the functions of the miniſterie, leaue them out. Fiftly, for that all antiquitie interpreteth Presbyteros Eccleſiæ, *miniſters of the word, or prieſtes. Sixtly, for that ſuch elders as were knowen to the fathers, had maintenance of their Churches. and Seuenthly, were not temporary. all which is contrary to the nature of the newe aldermen. The places which they force and wreſt from the fathers, are redeemed out of their fingers, and anſwered. Laſtly,* T.Cartw. *obiections are rebated, and driuen vpon him.*

THoſe that write hiſtories either of the Church or common wealth, howſoeuer they record other things, yet their principall care and vſe is to report the names, liues, and actions of the gouernours. the deſcription of times, and other matters they referre, and report moſt commonly to the times of the gouernours. if then theſe elders were the gouernours of the ancient Church (as *T.Cartw.* and his fellowes boldly auouch againſt all record of ſtorie) howe chance their names are not recorded? why is not their ſucceſſion noted?

1 Why doe we finde no mention of any action done by them? why is the memorie of ſo famous elders troden vnder foote and aboliſhed? why ſhould the proceedings of the elders of late churches be more famous nowe then in time paſt? wherefore, either let vs haue ſome record of their names, liues, and doings ſhewed, or els let the diſciplinarians acknowledge, that elders (though they haue their name of age) are but newe borne infants, and haue no ſucceſſion

 from

from the ancient fathers of the Church. that which some alledge, how litle it weyeth, shall be declared, when we come to the answere of their obiections out of the fathers.

2 Further, seeing neither the good gouernment, nor the disorders that fell out in ancient time in the church are ascribed to elders, what man that knoweth either matter of state, or practise of storie, wil take elders to be gouernours of the Church? if they were gouernours, as is pretended, where were they praised for good gouernment, or blamed for disorders? either the one or the other no question woulde haue bene imputed vnto them, if they had bene gouernours of the Church. for if matters succeede, the praise is ascribed to gouernors: if calamities fall vpon the state the burden is likewise layd vpon them.

3 Nay, in this we see plaine euidence of histories and fathers against the gouernment of elders; for that all that authoritie, which the disciplinarians doe attribute to their elders, they giue to godly princes and bishops. If the Church prospered or was afflicted, they assigne the cause thereof to godly or wicked princes. lawes and orders were made by bishops in Synodes authorised by princes after they were Christians: there were matters of faith and maners determined: there heretikes were condemned and remooued out of the Church, and others substituted in their places. which is so cleare by the actes of councels, report of histories, and witnesse of fathers, that I should but waste time in proouing that, which no man can denie.

Euseb. Eccl. hist. lib. 10. c. 3.

4 Seeing ancient fathers doe diligently report the functions of the ministerie, which had place in the Church in their times; it is not to be presumed, but if the newe Church aldermen had bene then, diuers of them (at least some one of them) would haue mentioned this braue order of gouerning elders: but we see the same omitted and passed ouer in great silence. They speake of bishops, priests, deacons with great consent: no one of them giueth out any one word of only gouerning elders. If *T. Cartw.* can shew, where beside ministers of the word and sacraments, any one father mentioneth the order of his aldermen or gouerning elders, let him shewe it: otherwise his deare friendes the elders stand in danger to haue sentence passed against them by all ancient councels, fathers, and stories.

5 The tenour of all ancient writings which speake of no priestes nor Church elders, but only ministers of the word and sacraments, maketh against these new Church aldermen. for what man can auow that the fathers allowed these newe aldermen, seeing in all their writings they take elders to be ministers of the word and sacraments,

and

and a degree vnder the bishops? *Ignatius* a most ancient writer oft times mentioneth elders: but who can gather out of his epistles ẏ he vnderstandeth other elders then priests, seeing he maketh thē successors of Christs Apostles, & calleth them σύνδεσμον ἀποστόλων χριστοῦ that is, a colledge of Christs Apostles, and nameth them ἱερεῖς καὶ ἀρχιερεῖς, that is, priests & chiefe priests, & speaking vnto them saith, οἱ πρεσβύτεροι ποιμάνατε τὸ ἐν ὑμῖν ποίμνιον. that is, elders, feede the flocke which is committed to your charge? *Dionisius* that ancient writer, distinguishing and declaring the diuers officers of the church, maketh bishops hiest, which hee calleth ἱεράρχας, priestes or pastorall elders next, which he calleth ἱερεῖς, the third place he giueth to deacons, whō he calleth λειτουργούς. to priests or elders he giueth the managing of the word & sacraments πῶς (saith he) ἐξαγγελοῦσι τῷ λαῷ τὰς θείας ἀρετὰς &c. πῶς φωτιοῦσιν οἱ ἐσκοτισμένοι; how shall they preach vnto the people the power of God? how shall they baptize, themselues not being enlightened? οἱ ἱερεῖς ἐκφάντορες εἰσὶ τοῦ θεοῦ. the elders or priests, they are ẏ preachers or messengers of God. where he nameth men of occupation elders, let them shew that make an occupation so boldly to affirme it. *Tertullian* deuiding the ministers of the church into bishops, priests, deacons; doth shew that these did baptize at the appoyntment of the bishop. and although it was not the custome of *African* churches, that priests should preach or baptize in ẏ presence of bishops; yet that custome is blamed by others, & *S. Austin* had that licence of *Valerius* the bishop to teach in his presence, when he was but priest. *Ireneus* knew no other elders of the church but ministers of the word. *adhærendum est his* (saith he) *qui Apostolorum doctrinam &c.* we are to adhere to those, which with their order of priesthood keepe sound doctrine, & liue ẇout offence, that others may by their examples be informed & corrected. and againe, *we ought to heare those elders or priests which haue succession from the Apostles, which with succession of their episcopall office, haue receiued the sure grace of trueth according to the fathers pleasure. Presbyteris* (saith he) *obaudire oportet &c.* so that (by *Ireneus* rule) seeing these Church aldermen haue no succession from the Apostles, we are not to heare them nor obey them. *Ireneus* further doth charge *Cerinthus* and *Basilides* with presumption, for reiecting the doctrine kept in the Church by succession of priests, & accompting themselues wiser then the apostles and priests. so ẏ he that would finde church aldermen in *Ireneus*, must haue not that of *Epictetus*, but *T.C.* his lanterne, whereby he can see *non existentia*, and finde out men ẏ neuer were. That elder that did not teach, the Canons decree to be excōmunicat, & if he persist to be deposed. *Can. Apost. 57.*

Ad Trallen.
Ad Smyrnen & Philadelph.
Ad Antioch.
Epistola ad Demophilum.
De Baptis.
Ierom ad Nepot.
Iren. lib. 4. c. 44. contr. Hæres.
Ibidem. c. 43.
Lib. 5. c. 7. contr. Hæres.

Lib.3.ep.13. & lib.4.ep.10. Lib.1.epist.3. *Cyprian* calleth those elders which he speaketh of, *Sacerdotes* or Priestes, and *Collegium Sacerdotum* a Colledge of Priestes; and reprehendeth them, that they ministred the Communion to those that had Ibidem. fallen, without his licence. and lest we might thinke he had some conceit of these Church aldermen, he deuideth the ministers of the Epist.4 lib.1. Church into *episcopos, sacerdotes, & diaconos*. that is, bishops, priestes, and deacons, for *Presbyteros* putting the word *Sacerdotes*. that his elders serued at the altar, and taught the word, it is euident by his 8. epistle of the first booke, and first of his second: & very absurd it were if *Presbyteri elders* should not be ministers of the word, seeing he ma- Lib.2.epist.5. Epist.22.lib.3. & epist.15.16. keth readers ministers of the word, and deacons, and subdeacons too, which were vnder them.

The ancient Canons of the Church do all testifie, that elders were Can.14. ministers of the word and sacraments. The *Nicene* counsell giueth a prerogatiue to priestes before deacons, in that they minister the communion. The Apostolicall Canons decree that elder to be depo- Can.3. sed, that offreth in stead of wine, milke, hony, or other licour. Those priests that leauing their bishop erect an altar apart, the same the ca- Can.32. nons pronounce worthy for his ambition to be deposed: which maketh not only against Church aldermen, but also against those schismatikes that refuse the communion of godly bishops, and erect conuenticles and presbyteries, and another gouernment in other places.

Can.32. That priests ministred the communion, the councel of *Eliberis* also doth witnesse. of other Church aldermen, neither that councell nor any other saith any thing.

Moral. reg.70. *Basil* describing the office and ornaments of elders, sheweth plainly, that it is the office of all elders to teach. that *Arrius* after the broching of his heresie, gaue cause that elders in some places were forbidden to preach, is reported as a matter rare, & is reprehended of *Ierom*.

Lib.3. *Epiphanius* (shewing that priestes or elders begat children to the church as bishops begate fathers) declareth, that none were accompted elders, but such as by preaching or teaching might beget sonnes to God, and were in respect of their teaching fathers. what neede I in Tit.1. alledge more authorities, seeing *Ierom* sheweth that bishops and elders were by the institution of Christ both one? which could not be, if there were an order of dumbe idoles called elders.

Apol 2 ad Antonin. *Iustin Martyr* acknowledgeth none for presidents but those that deliuered the word and sacraments. and that the fathers had no such elders as these newe vpstarts, these reasons may further declare.

6 The elders whereof the fathers make mention, had wages, and maintenance,

maintenance, and liued of the altar. *Omnium aliorum primitiæ Episcopo, & presbyteris domum mittuntur, non super altare.* The first fruits of all others are to be sent home to the Bishops, and priests (saye the ancient canons) and not to bee layde vpon the altar. *Cyprian* speaking of *Celerinus* and *Aurelius* sayeth, he had appointed vnto them the honor and wages of priesthoode. and by the wordes of the same father it appeareth, that not onelie Priestes, but all clerkes had wages. The same is confirmed by the wordes of the Epistle of *Cornelius* bishoppe of *Rome*, to *Fabius*. to whome hee signifieth, how the Byshop, the Priestes, Deacons and others, were mainteined: but these Church-aldermen receiuing honor without labour, content themselues, and of the Church receiue no wages, nor maintenance: and therefore farre vnlike to the Priestes of the ancient Church.

Can. Apost. 5. *Lib. 4. c. ep. 5.* *Lib. 1. ep. 9.* *Euseb. lib. 6. cap. 35. secund. Gr. 43.*

Further, the ancients and Priestes of the primitiue Church, were not chosen for a time, nor exercised their office for certaine yeeres, nor might they giue it ouer. *Tertullian* accused this lightnes in heretikes, that hee that was a Priest to day, to morowe (changing liuerie) became a laye man. Whereby hee sheweth, that it was not the vse of Christians, and ioyneth our disciplinarians with heretikes, which make no more a doe, but casting their cloake ouer their apron, runne into the Consistorie, and from thence returne to the marchants stall, or to some other occupation. The *Nicene* counsell decreeth; that those Priestes and Deacons which forsake their Church, shall not be receiued in anie other Church: and if they doe not returne, that they shall be excommunicate.

De prescript. *Can. 16.*

These Elders, as they are not desired to take on them the office, so they departe sometime at pleasure, alwayes at the ende of the terme: and doe not thinke the wordes of our sauiour, *Hee that setteth his hand to the plow, and looketh backe, is not worthie of the kingdome of heauen*, anie way to concerne them. these, they serue for terme of yeeres, one, two, or three; and not for life: and therefore are not like the Elders spoken of by the ancient fathers. if they doe not yet beleeue me, let them trye, if in all ancient fathers, they can finde anie temporarie Elders.

Wherefore, considering these reasons and authorities out of councels and fathers, hee must be verie dull sighted that will not see the trueth: and verie speculatiue that can see anie Elders: and verie obstinate, that will still defend that which cannot be founde, against so manie testimonies against it.

The obiections which with long studie & labour they haue found out of all writers to ouerthrowe this trueth, and to proue Church aldermen, are not manie, yet most of them to no purpose. in the Epistles of *Ignatius*, they finde Elders and Eldershippe: but it is impudencie to make them vnteaching Elders, whome *Ignatius* matcheth with the Apostles, whose preceptes hee exhorteth them of *Tralleis* to followe, and whome hee calleth Priestes, and chiefe priestes, and whome hee exhorteth to feede the flocke of Christ, which were neither temporarie nor yet without stipend, as hath bin proued.

Ad Trallen.

Next after him, commeth *Tertullian*, who in his Apologie mentioneth Elders, which he calleth presidents. but it appeareth in the same place, that the same presidents did exhort & nourish the faith of ẏ hearers with holie sayings. who these presidents were, he declareth more plainely; where he saith, that the Church receaued the Sacraments at the handes of their presidents. which word also *Iustine* vseth in effect, and both *Tertullian* by president, and *Iustine* by προεστὼς, meaneth the Byshop. which worde they both auoide, for that they write to the gentiles, which did not vnderstand the worde Bishop, proper to Christians.

Apolog. ad Antonin.2.

De corona milit.

Diuers places are alledged by *Th. Cartw.* out of *Cyprian* to this purpose: one singuler, where *Cyprian* hath *Spotulantes fratres*: which he (like a great and profounde gramarian) supposeth to *be basket carriers*, that caried the communion bread about in baskets and trayes: then which what can be more euident proofe of his pitiful igrorance, both of the worde *Sportula*, that doeth signifie wages, and of the custome of those times, that did not cary about the communion bread in baskets, for the communicants were not then so manie? good it had bene for him, that he that had furnished him with this braue text, had bene voyded away in a basket: or if she were one of his sisters, in some fine pretie casket, that both by this and other places, his ignorance had not bene made notorious. that *Cyprian* neuer knew other Elders then Ministers of the worde it may appeare; for that they are called *Sacerdotes* or Priestes, were attendant on ẏ altar, ministred the cōmunion, as hath bene shewed. that they were not like the newe aldermen, these arguments declare. First, for that *Cyprians* Elders had wages. Secondlie, for that they were not temporarie. Thirdlie, for that the same were subiect to the Bishop, which was none of the Eldershippe but aboue the Eldership. Lastlie, for that presbyterie and Deacons made one bodie of the clerkes.

Cartw. rest. 2. reply. pag. 42.
Cyp. lib. 1. Ep. 9.

Irenaus

Irenæus is also drawen into this quarrel, yet sayeth he nothing but which the newe aldermen wish vnsaide. for hee maketh all those Elders which he mentioneth, Ministers of the worde. he giueth vnto them succession of doctrine, and accounteth the Bishops of *Rome* among those Elders, which were not dumbe then as nowe they are. Where *Irenæus* testifieth in the cause of these Elders, that not medling with the worde nor sacraments, did notwistanding giue men to Satan, and were censors of manners; the place is not yet founde.

Basil, although hee doeth not so much as name Elders, yet is brought forth by *Daneau*, to giue some credite to the cause of Elders, because hee speaketh of eyes. *Daneau* imagineth that he speaketh of the curious eyes of his Elders, that are prying maliciouslie oft times into corners, where they ought least to looke. but how litle *Basil* fauoureth dumb Elders, it appeareth by his commentaries vpon the third of *Isai*. where, by Elder, hee vnderstandeth the Minister of the worde. and *Gregorie Nazianzen* doeth by the example of *Basil* declare, that priesthoode was a degree to the bishopricke, and an office of a teacher in the Church. *In ps. 34.* *In verb. presbyterum.* *In monod.*

When these saye nothing, gladlie would *Daneau* scrape a litle acquaintance with *Dionysius*. and albeit they speake of him otherwise dishonorablie, yet would they bee glad to haue anie credite by his commendation. but it will not bee: for he knoweth no Elders, but which were priestes, and by him called ἱερεῖς, and placed after the Bishop, called ἱεράρχεις.

Albeit neuer so base, they refuse no witnesse. therefore doe they bring a sentence out of the canon lawe drawen out of *Ierome*. but let them not trust too much to his deposition, least he proue the bane of the Church aldermens cause. For that which they would pull downe (that is an Eldershippe of Ministers in cathedrall Churches) that hee alloweth: the newe aldermen composed of artificers, laborers, marchantes, gentlemen, (which they woulde haue) he neuer knew. he maketh three principall degrees of the Ministerie; Bishops, Priestes, Deacons. whether hee make dumbe Elders gouernors, his bookes testifie, and his example being an Elder, and his wordes that make not onelie Priestes, but clerkes to feede by the worde. hee sayeth in the person of a monke: *Illi, (id est, Clerici) pascunt, ego pascor*. that is to say, the clerkes feede, wee monkes are fed. and finallie, his reproofe of the custome of *Alexandria*, that for the fault of *Arrius*, suffered not Priestes to teach, contrarie to the institution of the Apostles as he thought. *16. q. 1. c. Ecclesia.* *Ad rustic. Gal.* *Ad Heliod.* *Ad Nepotianũ.*

When trueth ſerueth not, *Cartw.* falleth to plaine forcing. For out of *Poſidonius*, hee would make vs beleeue that an Elder by the cuſtome of the *Affrican* Churches, might not preach. where hee ſayeth not ſo, but that in the preſence of a Byſhop, a prieſt might not teach. and where *Socrates* telleth vs, that there was a cuſtome at *Alexandria*, that Prieſtes ſhoulde not preach (which began as I ſayde vpon occaſion of *Arrius* hereſie) hee ſayeth that it was decreed that Prieſtes ſhoulde not preach: which is vntrue. And laſtlie, where *Ierome* ſayeth, that the Prieſt vpon the Byſhops commaundement did baptize, he maketh *Ierome* to ſay that which hee neuer thought, that Prieſtes might not by their office preach: which was onelie forbidden when the Biſhop was preſent. in which order, *Tertullian* and *Poſidonius* agrее with *Ierome*. But if the Prieſts might adminiſter the Sacramentes, either in the Byſhops preſence, or otherwiſe, then were they no laye aldermen, and *per conſequens*, *Th. Cartw.* hurt himſelfe with his owne weapon.

Lib.5.c.21.

Ad Luciferianum.

To carie away the matter, at length commeth forth *Ambroſe*, and yet (a great matter to conſider) he ſayeth not a worde for laye Elders. hee ſayeth that the Church had ſeniors or Elders: but hee denieth them not to bee Miniſters of the worde. nay, hee plainelie teſtifieth that the Elders ſpoken of by the Apoſtle, *1. Timo. 5. 17. & 19.* were Miniſters, for that he calleth them *Vicarios Chriſti*, and *Antiſtites dei*, that is to ſaye, Chriſtes lieutenants, and prælates of God. which *Cartw.* not onelie boldlie, but ignorantlie would applie to his aldermen. But ſeeing all that vnderſtand Latine, interprete *Antiſtites*, Prieſts that deale in the prieſthoode, ſeruice of God and Sacraments, he cannot change the vſe of wordes, nor make vs a newe grammer, nor make profane men to bee Prieſtes. beſides, that order and Miniſterie which *Ambroſe* ſpeaketh of, was not ceaſed; but the courſe of vſing their counſell, of which he complayneth.

De offic.lib.2. cap.24.

Ambroſe obſerueth the common diſtinction of the Miniſters of the Church into Biſhops, Prieſtes, Deacons: and giueth teaching both to Prieſtes, Deacons, and readers, which ouerthroweth mute Elders. neither is it to bee preſumed, that *Ambroſe* ſhoulde lament the decaye of an order of Church-aldermen out of the Church, ſeeing neither hee himſelfe, nor anie talketh of anie ſuch matter: nor is it likelie that hee would haue learned Biſhops to bee directed by vnlettered aldermen. but hee complaineth that Byſhops raſhlie did thinges of their owne head, and tooke not the aduiſe of their moſt

experi-

experimented learned clergie, as in times past was vsed. Lastlie, this counsell of seniors, it was assistant to Bishops, who were for the most parte in great cities onelie; but these men would haue aldermen not counsellers, but rulers in euerie village or congregation, and therefore let them no more tell vs of *Ambrose*, who in his booke of offices, and all his commentaries, doeth vtterlie condemne mute aldermen.

Manie places are alledged out of *Eusebius*, *Socrates*, and *Sozomen*. which as they shewe that Elders were Ministers of the worde and sacraments: so if *Th. Cartw.* proue by anie one place, but one laye Elder, such as hee would haue, *Phillida solus habeto.* Let him take the calfe with the white face alone for his labour. let him reade ouer *Socrates. lib.7. cap.36. Ruffin. lib. cap.1. Theodoret. eccle. hist. li.1. cap.2.* and *Sozomen. lib.1. cap.14.* and *Socr. lib.7. cap.2. & lib.7. cap. 21. & cap.26.* What shoulde I saye, reade these speciall places? nay let them reade the whole Ecclesiasticall histories, they shall finde continuall testimonies against such church aldermen, and no one testimonie for them.

Thus you see how that the authorities alledged both out of scriptures, and fathers faile them, and leaue the newe aldermen without defence. let vs nowe therefore proceede and consider how they are fenced with reasons, and arguments. it is necessarie, that there bee some to looke vnto the manners of men, and to haue an eye that offences and scandales be not suffered in the Church: therefore saith *Beza*, there must be an order of Elders in the Church. which is as much as if hee should haue argued thus: *Menalcas* had a bowe and arrowes, therefore he had a bowe of ygh, and arrowes of birch. the reason is all one. for as bowes & arrowes are framed of diuers kindes of timber beside vgh and birch, so there be diuers kindes of officers that haue these matters in charge, and would take order, although these Elders had neuer bene dreamed of. There are Christian magistrates, godlie Byshops and pastors, that are appointed to this watch; what these aldermen are, we knowe not, nor whither they will.

To strengthen the feeble knees of this discrasied reason, *Th. Cartw.* concludeth formally in this sorte. that office without which the principall offices of charitie cannot be exercised, is necessarie, and hath alwayes bene. but such are laye Elders. *Ergo, &c.* So *Th. Cartw.* would haue this office to be not onelie before pastors, but before Apostles, and that it hath originall with the lawe of nature, which is ridiculous, and contrarie to their practise. for if it come not in with Christ, it is no office of the Church. The assumption is false and not to bee prooued. God forbid, that the offices of charitie could not bee exercised without this office, or that others could not better exercise the offices of charitie, or that there were no other fruites of charitie, but admonition, & reprehension, and excommunication; wherein (as matters are vsed) there is seldome anie charitie. The workes of charitie are to feede the hungrie, releeue the oppressed, fatherles and widowe, to clothe the naked, with which these laye Elders doe not meddle. Finallie, it is an euill signe that this office wil bring forth anie fruites of charitie, the authors whereof haue troubled both Churche and common-wealth, and dissolued the bandes of charitie.

Further sayeth *Cartw.* that two eyes see more then one. I graunt, so three eyes more then two: yet where God hath placed two eyes, it is a deformititie to haue three. Now then, vnlesse hee can shewe where this office is ordeined by God, this similitude of two eyes is not worth two chippes, seeing with one eye, the weakenes of the aldermens cause may easilie be discouered, which neither in the example of the Iewish Consistories, nor in the institution of Christ or his Apostles, or the allowance of ancient times, or anie probabilitie of reason hath anie grounde, or support.

Of which this corollarie or conclusion ariseth: that whatsoeuer authoritie or iurisdiction the same aldermen doe claime or practise, the same is vsed and claimed without title, as shall appeare by the particulers of their commission. which as *Th. Cartw.* lorde great Master of discipline hath set them downe, are these.

First, the Elders shall haue authoritie to make all orders and decrees, and abrogate the same.

Secondlie, they shall haue power to chuse officers in the Church, and to depose them.

Thirdlie, they shall be iudges in all causes of faith, doctrine, and manners, so farre as appertaineth to conscience.

Lastlie, (that they want no meanes to bring vnder the rebellious) they shall haue authoritie to admonish, suspend, excommunicate, and absolue. and because somewhat is yet wanting vnto them; as for example, authoritie to prescribe, and commaunde, and to dispense against lawe, which is a matter to them odious: therefore doth *Th. Cartw.* and the authors of the admonition hide that vnder a generall clause, of gouerning all matters perteining to the Church.

Church. Wherein wee may note in generall: first, that they haue left no office, nor authoritie to the magistrate in Ecclesiasticall affaires: for they doe not so much as name him, or thinke vpon him, when they giue forth their commissions for Church gouernement. Secondlie, that they giue vnto the Elders such a large commission, that if the same be obserued, they may rule all in soueraintie without controlment.

This commission therefore,& euery clause thereof I shal(God willing)shewe, that it is forged: that you may see, that not onelie the name, but also the whole office of Elders is newlie coyned by platformers, without allowance or stampe of Gods worde. I knowe that their meaning is not, that the Elders shoulde doe these thinges by themselues simplie, and seuerallie, but in Consistorie, all being together. which I admonish before hand, because I woulde not wrangle about wordes. but it shall be shewed, that neither singlie, nor ioyntlie they haue authoritie in these matters.

Of the Consistoriall aldermen and *their vsurpation.*

CHAP. 4. SECT. 4.

Wherein the power of Church aldermen in making lawes, is proued to be vsurped. First, for that the Iewish inferior Sanedrin neither resemble them, nor had anie such power. Secondly, for that the same authoritie, both in the Iewish and first Christian Church belonged to princes, and to Bishops vnder princes, saue in time of persecution. Lastlie, for that this authoritie of aldermen in making lawes, is contrarie to the practise of other Churches, and preiudiciall to the prince, and commons.

THis graunted, that Church aldermen haue no approbation of lawe nor antiquitie, it is needelesse to dispute of their authoritie, and commission. For how can thinges that neuer were, haue cōfirmation of their authoritie? As there is no colour seene of thinges hidden in the earth; nor qualitie of things that neuer were: so what commission can bee deuised for them that neuer were? But least some might thinke them an office necessarie nowe: I will briefelie shewe, that the authoritie which they clayme in making lawes, is not onelie without worde of God, but that it is repugnant to the practise of the Church vnder the lawe, to the Apostolike Churches, and their owne rules and practise: and that it is priudiciall to the prince, dangerous and combersome to the subiectes.

That they haue no warrant of the worde of God for this point, their owne silence argueth: for they would not conceale it from vs, if they were able to saye anie thing. But they doe not so much as goe about to proue it. neither if they shoulde endeuour, could they. For admit that there were Elders, and had the name of gouernors, yet doth it not belong to all gouernors to make orders, but to those ỳ haue authoritie. That the Elders were present, when the synode at *Ierusalem* made decrees, concerning blood, fornication, and things sacrificed to Idoles, it maketh nothing for these laye Elders. and too too great presumption it were, if euerie odde conuenticle should take vpon them that which the Apostles of Christ, and the whole Churche did: which are no president for the Consistorie to followe.

Acts.15.

Authoritie of Elders to make lawes, is contrarie to the Iewish policie.

In the policie of the *Iewes*, whether we respect the gouernement of the Church, or common-wealth; the Elders had no authoritie to make or abrogate lawes. whatsoeuer was to be innouated, either in the Church or common-wealth, the same was done by the kings, and soueragine princes. to them God addressed his holy Prophets. *Moses* that was the first lawgiuer, was the chiefe gouernor of that state. king *Dauid* and *Salomon* that setled all thinges about the temple and seruice of God, had soueraine iurisdiction. where the Sanedrin had that power, vnlesse it were, when they did thinges by authoritie of the prince, & were the soueraigne gouernors of the state, we reade not. In the erection of that colledge, authoritie was giuen vnto it, to iudge according to lawe, not to make lawes, which proceede from a diuers power.

1.Chro.24.

Deut.17.

The same contrarie to the practise of the ancient Church.

During the Apostles time, the chiefe commaundement was in the Apostles. Saint *Paul* prescribed orders how *Timothie* shoulde conuerse and demeane himselfe in the Church of God. What hee thought conuenient, hee prescribed vnto the *Corinthians* and to the Churches of *Crete*. The Apostles set downe canons in their counsels. and after them, the authoritie was by succession deriued to their successors, which they practised in the time of the afflictions of the Church. When the Emperors became Christians, they continued that authoritie which God gaue vnto them, with their scepters, and which the godlie kings of *Israel* practised. Where anie laye aldermen concurred with the Apostes, or with princes in making lawes, there is not anie coniecture. where priestes or Elders had deciding voyces, no authoritie can be shewed, vnlesse they were bishops: much lesse Church aldermen, which wanted much of that

autho-

authoritie that was giuen to them. wherefore to make lay aldermen law makers, is contrary both to the practiſe of the *Iewiſh* and Chriſtian Church.

The ſame contrary to their owne rules.

Nay further it is repugnant to their owne rules. they make Chriſt
a king and lawgiuer, in reſpect of the outward policie of the Church,
and ſay that his faithfulneſſe conſiſted in making a perfect externall
Church gouernment: here they giue that authoritie to their Church
aldermen, and denie that he is ſo faithful, but that many things be left
to the diſpoſing of the elders. neither will it helpe that they diſtinguiſh circumſtances & ſubſtance: for neither do they ſo obſerue this 1
diſtinction, but that they both make lawes concerning their paſtors,
aldermen, deacons, which they make ſubſtance, and alſo leaue ſome
circumſtances vnchanged: nor if they did obſerue it, would it helpe.
for if Chriſt be a lawgiuer in reſpect of externall gouernment, then
may no man preſume to adde, take away, nor alter, nor ſet downe any
other gouernment. *T.Cartw.* full ſoberly telleth vs, that his diſcipline 2
is a part of the Goſpel, ſo that adding or altering their diſcipline, the
aldermen (by his reckoning) adde vnto and alter the Goſpel. Thirdly 3
(they ſay) whatſoeuer is done in the Church without the word, is
ſinne: but theſe aldermen haue no authoritie out of the word to make
lawes, *ergo &c*. Laſtly, they ſay that no man may take any authoritie 4
vpon him in the Church, but he that is thereunto lawfully called, and
hath warrant ſufficient: but theſe Church aldermen make & diſanull
lawes without calling and warrant. *ergo.* which be things ſo repugnant, that I am earneſtly to requeſt *T.Cartw.* to reconcile them. they
ſay he beginneth (like an olde decaied ſaint) to worke miracles. ſure
in doing this, he ſhall worke a miracle in mine eyes.

Ordon. de Gen. The ſame contrary to the practiſe of other churches.

The practiſe of the Churches is likewiſe contrary. at *Geneua* the power of making & altering lawes is in the magiſtrate & people. in the *French* Churches there is an expreſſe article, that no conſiſtorie, no nor conference of miniſters ſhal take vpon them to diſanul lawes, or to make other lawes then they ſhall haue appoynted them by a Synode prouinciall or nationall: that conuenticle that takes vpon them otherwiſe to doe, and ſeparate themſelues from the reſt of the body, they excōmunicate as ſchiſmatikes. which peremptorie dealing, if it had bene vſed alſo in England, their formes and ſchiſmaticall platformes, had long ere this bene buried in ſilence.

The princes prerogatiue preiudiced.

The princes prerogatiue and royall authoritie is tranſlated from the ſoueraigne prince and giuen to the elders, if they haue authoritie to make leaws. for who can call that prince ſupreme, that muſt receiue orders & lawes in church matters from other? or denie that the elders haue supreme power, if they haue power to make lawes? some there are that of modestie say, that the prince may set downe orders by the aduice of the elders: but it will not excuse the disciplinarians disloyaltie. for that the prince may with the aduice of such as she shal chuse make lawes, they denie. that the elders are not tied to haue her consent either to meet in Synods, or to prescribe orders, they affirme, that the prince is an officer of the Church, they will not graunt. of which it followeth that whatsoeuer the prince doth in the Church, it is without authoritie. Lastly, in making the prince subiect to their lawes and excommunications, they allowe him no further time to be actual prince, then it shal please the consistorie. for we may not come neere a person excommunicate and giuen vp to the deuill.

Def. against. Br. sland.

For they deny her Synodes, and giue the same to the President of the Synode. *French disc.*

The Church aldermens lawes preiudiciall to the commons.

The subiects likewise haue their part in this indignitie. (I will not call it tyrannie, vntil I haue made the rigour of their gouernment palpable.) for if the elders may prescribe what lawes they thinke fitting, and (as they teach) the magistrate is to punish and to compell those that disobey them; who can liue in safetie of landes & goods, & rest in his countrey, vnlesse he submit his necke to the yoke of their pleasures? If there had bene like practise in England against this faction, there had not many schismatikes bene nowe to be found amongst vs.

Wherefore, seeing this is a poynt of such sequele: they haue dealt very loosely to leaue it destitute of all proofe, & must proue the same substancially before they obteine it. hitherto they haue presumed too much of mens ignorance, and negligence: as also in that power which they giue to elders, in electing and deposing of Church officers, which I will now shew not to belong vnto them.

Of the Consistoriall aldermen, and their vsurpation.

CHAP. 4. SECT. 5.

Wherein that power which they challenge in election and deposing of Church officers, is confuted by the practise of the state both of Iewish, and first Christian Church, and declared to be vnreasonable, and preiudiciall to the state.

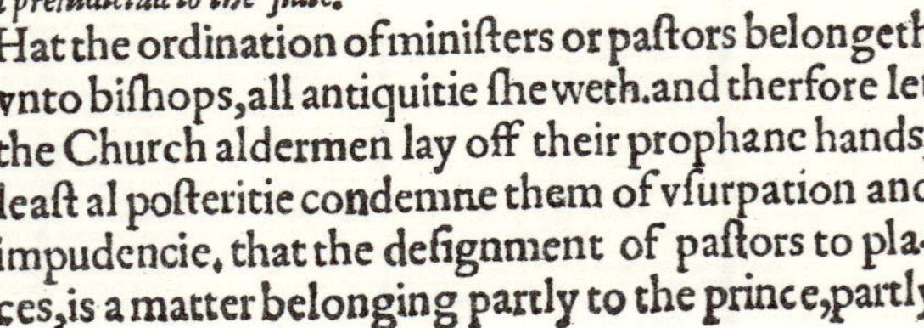

THat the ordination of ministers or pastors belongeth vnto bishops, all antiquitie sheweth. and therfore let the Church aldermen lay off their prophane hands, least al posteritie condemne them of vsurpation and impudencie, that the designment of pastors to places, is a matter belonging partly to the prince, partly

to

to those that giue the stipend, and both after the allowance of the parties sufficiencie by the bishop, cannot be disprooued nor misliked, and in part hath bene shewed. Likewise that the prince hath interest in nomination vnder her in externall Church gouernment: that the Church aldermen haue no authoritie either in the choise, or deposing of pastor or other Church officers, these reasons may ascerteine vs.

Wee finde not in the state of the ancient *Iewish* Church any such power belonging to the Colledges of Iudges. priestes were not chosen, but succeeded. Iudges and officers were chosen by the princes and chiefe gouernours. *Dauid* chose out of the *Leuites* those that he thought meete for seruice: and placed them iudges and gouernours beyond *Iordan*. *Iehosaphat* of the priestes and Leuites and chiefe fathers placed such as he thought fittest in *Ierusalem*, and all the Cities of *Iudah*. If any alteration was to be made in the priestes office, the prince was autor of it, as is euident, in that *Salomon* displaced *Abiathar* and substituted *Zadok* and that *Dauid* appoynted the courses of Priestes, Leuites and singers. The Sanedrin at *Ierusalem* did nominate the inferior Sanedrioth: but them did the same gouerne in soueraigntie. they that giue this power to certaine elders, speake as men palpably ignorant in that state.

Designation of the church officers belonged to princes in the state of the Iewes. These the disciplinarians suppose to bee Church aldermen.

Petr.gal.l.4.c.5.

In the gathering of the first Christian Churches we doe not finde any such aldermen, much lesse any such authoritie due vnto them. neither is it probable that Christ Iesus the wisedome of his father, would commit his church to be gouerned by those, which men vnlearned shoulde chuse, after extraordinarie giftes should cease. when the Emperours began to fauour religion, lesse probable it is, that the election and deposing of officers should be in three or foure of the vulgar sort in euery particular congregation of the world.

The same belonged to no Elders in the ancient Church.

Fourthly, in the Apostles time wee haue shewed that they had chiefe authoritie to appoynt pastors by the examples of *Saint Paul* and *Barnabas*, *Timothie* and *Titus*.

If others had any intrest in other offices (as that of deacons *Act.6.*) or some speciall seruice (as that of *Peter* and *Iohn Act.8.*) yet what is that to Church aldermen being no ministers of the word, nor hauing any gouernment ouer the people? In the ancient Church, bishops were not deposed but by Synodes or by the prince, as is euident by *Constantines* letters to the Councell of *Tyre*. Priests and other officers were chosen and deposed by bishops, as hath bene shewed heretofore. Howe absurd then is it to giue that to certaine Elders

Eccl.hist. Theod. l.1.c.29.

(whereof there is neither office nor authoritie founde in antiquitie) which both ſcriptures and ancient fathers giue to princes and godly biſhops? eſpecially ſeeing the ſame is preiudiciall to the princes prerogatiue, diſſolueth the right of diuers of the ſubiects, and repugneth to reaſon(for what more vnreaſonable then that they ſhould iudge that haue no ſkill) and contrarieth ſo many lawes of the land. He that deſireth to ſee more of this poynt, let him turne backe to the treatiſe of the election and ordination of paſtors.

Of the Conſiſtoriall aldermen, and their vſurpation.

Chap. 4. Sect. *6.*

Therein the preſumption of Church-aldermen is taxed, which contrary to the practiſe of the Church of the Iewes, *and firſt Chriſtians and other Churches, yea contrary to reaſon, challenge authoritie to iudge in matters of faith and doctrine.*

IF the qualities of theſe aldermen in other Churches were knowen , a man would eaſily thinke them to be ſimple iudges of maners , being themſelues in their affections and maners moſt diſordered , but be they ſuch as they ſhould be, yet multitude of popular iudges is troubleſome and dangerous, and therefore iudges are choſen of moſt wiſe and learned men, and ſuch as haue knowledge in lawe: and are placed not in euery village, but in conuenient diuiſions, and diſtances. where ſuch aldermen as theſe were iudges of maners, there is no example in the *Iewiſh* policie, no precedent of Apoſtolicall practiſe, no teſtimonie of ancient churches, and therefore inconuenient to make them iudges. and preiudiciall it muſt needes proue to the princes prerogatiue that hath the chiefe gouernment of externall maners, beſides the confuſion of this gouernment , and the ouerthrowe thereby of moſt of the lawes of this land.

But to make them iudges of faith, doctrine and religion, it is both abſurd and ridiculous. for who woulde not laugh to ſee marchants, artificers, and husbandmen ſitting to iudge of hie matters of the trinitie?

Tractent fabrilia fabri.

If religion were to be bought or ſolde, or if a Church were to be built, the marchants could tell what it were worth, and artificers could ſhewe how to worke.

*Leuit.*10 Farre was this abſurditie from the ancient Church where prieſtes iudged

iudged of things cleane & vncleane,and were interpretors of the difficulties of the law;far frō the apostolicall grauity of *Christs* disciples, whē the ministers of the word decided such controuersies as did arise; far from the proceeding of the ancient Catholike church,where matters of faith were handled by Synods of bishops; & far from reason: for what more vnreasonable, then that blinde men should appoynt the way, and ignorant men teach matters doubtfull? They themselues beginne now to condemne it. *Art.* of *Fr.disc.tit.du cons.art.10.* *Deut.17.*

The same likewise is preiudiciall to her Maiesties prerogatiue, whose authority to appoint high commissioners, and iudges of disorders, that as occasions rise, may compose matters, is deriued to ignorant aldermen, that take vpon them, without authority,not onely to iudge matters of faith, but (vnder colour of these two points, Doctrine and Maners) presume to call all matters before them, and to controll prince,and iudge,and whomsoeuer they allow not.

The same is likewise preiudiciall to the liberty of the subiects: which can neuer stand with the infinite number,and absolute authority of such iudges. But these things shall be declared more at large iu their proper places. Now let vs examine the aldermens authority, which they chalenge in the censures of the church.

Of the Consistoriall aldermen, and their vsurpation.

Chap. 4. Sect. 7.

Wherein the boldnesse of the Church aldermen, that take vpon them to execute the censures of the Church, is reprooued, and the same declared to be enterprised by them, contrary to our Sauiour Christes *direction, contrary to apostolike examples, contrary to practise of the Church both vnder the Law and the Gospell,and with no reason,authority,nor example, to be iustified. The obiections and excuses made for them,are answered.*

As about new statutes and lawes, so about new officers and opinions, many new questions arise. to seeke no further, the same may be verified in the case of the aldermen,and the present question concerning the censures of the Church, wherein they claime a singular prerogatiue and interest. it is a question, whether admonition and reprehension are fitly placed among the Church censures, especially seeing the same are practised sometime by priuate men, sometime by the minister, and sometime by those that are not of the Church. the disciplinarians make no doubt,whatsoeuer antiquity speaketh to the contrary. Secondly,it is doubted by whom the cenſures are to be executed; whether by the miniſter alone, or by the whole Church, or by certaine aldermen. And great doubts may be mooued concerning the effects of excommunication, which the diſciplinarians affirme boldly to be the ſentence of *Chriſt*, by his lieutenants the aldermen. to whom they imagine that he hath giuen power to deliuer men vp to Satan. but (whenſoeuer we ſhall haue occaſion or leiſure, to reſolue the reſt) in the meane while, we ſhall (God willing) ſhew that the aldermen haue no right to deale in excommunication. a matter contrary to Scriptures, apoſtolike practiſe, and formall gouernment.

Our Sauiour *Chriſt*, as he gaue his word to his apoſtles, ſo he gaue vnto them the power of the keyes, and authority to binde and looſe; as in the 16 and 18 of *Matth.* is declared. If he ſhould haue giuen the ſame power to others, which are not to deale in the miniſtery of the word, he ſhould haue ſeparated the efficacy from the word, and as it were depriued the ſame of force: which the wiſdome of *Chriſt* will not ſuffer vs to conceiue. Seeing then the aldermen deale not with the word, what doe they meddle with the keyes, that depend vpon the word? Secondly, ſeeing *Chriſt* gaue the ſame to his apoſtles, what reaſon haue they to vſurpe the keyes, that claime no ſucceſſion from the apoſtles? Thirdly, ſeeing godly biſhops are the ſucceſſors of the apoſtles, both in preaching, & vſe of the keyes, why do they without title inuade others poſſeſſion? *Claues regni cœlorum in beato Petro*
De dignit. ſacerdot. *apoſtolo* (ſaith *Ambroſe*) *cuncti ſuſcepimus ſacerdotes*. In the bleſſed apoſtle *S. Peter*, we that are miniſters of the word, haue receiued the keyes. Fourthly, why, ſeeing they pretend to follow the apoſtolicall church ſo nere, do they digreſſe in this materiall point ſo far? The a-
1.Cor.5. poſtle himſelfe determined to deliuer vp the inceſtuous *Corinthian* to Sathan. he ſaith κέκρικα, I haue, not We haue determined. he likewiſe
1.Tim.1. gaue vp *Hymeneus* & *Alexander* to Sathan, and gaue authority to *Timothy* & *Titus* in iudiciall cauſes. That which *Peter* did in the fact of *Ananias* and *Saphyra* (which *Beza* holdeth to be excommunication)
Adu.Eraſt. he did alone without other. The Holy ghoſt reprehendeth the biſhop of the church of *Pergama* for ſuffering the *Balaamits* & *Nicholaitans*, and no aldermen. If the power had bene in theſe, then might the biſhop haue had a lawfull excuſe that it lay not in him to root them out.

In the times following, the biſhops tracing the apoſtles, reteined and practiſed this authority. *Cyprian* therefore calleth excommuni-
Lib 1.ep.3. cation, *Sacerdotalem cenſuram*, the cenſure of prieſts. and in the ſame place *Sententiam epiſcoporum*, the ſentence of biſhops. to biſhops he giueth

giueth alſo the releaſe of excommunication. *Per epiſcopos* (ſaith he) *pax danda.* That biſhops only haue power to excommunicate, *Origen* is alſo witneſſe, *Qui habent* (ſaith he) *quod Petrus habuit, illi Petro ſuccedunt, & claues regni cœlorum à ſeruatore acceperunt.* They that haue that which *Peter* had, they are *Peters* ſucceſſours, and haue receiued the keyes of the kingdome of heauen from our Sauiour. he ſpeaketh this of biſhops. *Ierome* teſtifieth for the excõmunication of biſhops likewiſe, where he ſheweth how the *Origeniſts* were excõmunicated by *Theophilus. Auguſtine* giueth the cenſures to paſtors hands. *c.16.de cor.don.* Thoſe that exerciſed the cenſures, of whom *Tertullian* maketh mention, were biſhops. for, as is euident in that place, they ioyned the word & cenſures together. *Chryſoſtome* hauing long ſpoken againſt certaine faults vſuall in his church, doth in the end threaten the cenſures, if they would not reforme them, & that he would keepe them frõ the ſacraments. Neither was this cuſtome of late inuention.

Lib.4. ep.2. *Tract. 1. in Matth. & etiam 12.* *Ep.68.& 70.* *Apolog.c.39.* *Hom. 19. ad pop. Ant.*

In the time of the Law, the iudgement of things cleane and vncleane, holy and profane, apperteined to the prieſts alone. and moſt abſurd it were, if elders, that could not approch to the altar, ſhould exclude from the altar. That which ſome conceiue, that this cognition of cleane & vncleane, was done by a college of elders, with great ſolemnity, is ridiculous: the text ſpeaketh contrary. for any one prieſt was iudge ſufficient; and oft times the iudgement was tried without the campe. So that if the iudgement of things cleane and vncleane, was a figure or rule of excommunication; the ſame being done by prieſts, vtterly excludeth the aldermen. wherefore, vnleſſe *Th.Cartw.* can bring ſome good ſtrong reaſon, his aldermen ſtand charged, and almoſt conuicted of manifeſt intruſion.

Leuit.14.

Bezaes obiections are all too weake to ſupport the weight of this cauſe, and as decayed as the aldermen themſelues. The apoſtle (ſaith he) *1.Cor.5.* blameth & chideth the *Corinthians* that they had not deliuered vp the inceſtuous perſon to Satan. Firſt it is falſe, and contrary to the text. for he vſeth the power of deliuering to Satan himſelfe, and reprehendeth them, that they ſought not meanes to haue the inceſtuous perſon remooued, but priuately gaue him incouragement. Secondly, if all the *Corinthians* had any power, what is that to the presbytery, which was not now erected? for then the apoſtle would neuer haue ſaid, Is there not a wiſe man among you? Further, the apoſtle willeth them to refraine the company of falſe brethren, & telleth them that they had power to iudge of thoſe within. And *2.Theſ. 2.* he willeth the *Theſſalonians* to ſignifie or marke ſuch as were diſ-

Adu.Era.p.118 *1.Cor.6.*

ordered: whence *Beza* also would insinuate some authority giuen to his aldermen, but there is not the least step of them. Secondly, these words belong to all, for all the Church are to refraine leud company, and to discerne them and marke them: therefore can not these words be appropried to some. Thirdly, these words import no excommunication, and therefore are to no purpose. and better it were to haue said nothing, then to bring that which hurteth, or at least helpeth nothing. That the word Church, *Matth.18*, concerneth these elders nothing, otherwhere hath bene declared. Lastly, nothing can be more vnreasonable, then to giue the power of the ministery of the word into the hands of those that are not ministers; and make them iudges, whose lippes preserue no knowledg: and to giue them power to shut all out of the Church, that call none into the Church.

Of all this we conclude, that seeing the office of elders is a new inuention, & vsurpeth iurisdiction without commission; that the same ought not to be placed, nay, nor tolerated in any Church, much lesse in euery parish. But because *T.C.* hath taken on him to shew the contrary, we will also examine his reasons concerning that point.

Of the Consistoriall aldermen, and their vsurpation.

CHAP. 4. SECT. 8.

Wherein the obiections of Th. Cartw. *that would haue elders placed in euery Congregation, are answered, and the imperfections and absurdities of their deuises concerning their elders, noted.*

BVt were it granted, that such aldermen as they haue, were officers of the Church: yet is it not necessary they should be in euery parish. Apostles, prophets, & euangelists were appointed in the Church; yet were not apostles, prophets, nor euangelists in euery parish. There were at *Corinth* certaine iudges appointed for composing of priuate controuersies: yet doe we not reade that euery Church had the like, much lesse the diuisions or parishes of euery Church. In the olde Church of the *Iewes*, the Priests and Leuites were not diuided by parishes, which notwithstanding were more necessary then officers of gouernment: and therefore let this deuise of a college of elders to be in euery parish, be placed in another fancy of theirs, in the Calendar of discipline.

They were diuided by companies.

First, there is no commandement, nor rule, that they should be in euery parish or congregation. Secondly, there is no example, nor

practise

practise either of the apostles times, or first Churches, to prooue that it ought so to be. for albeit in the great Churches there were priests or ministers assistant to the bishop, yet euery Church had not a bishop, much lesse a company of priests and deacons. In the Church at *Ierusalem* there was a bishop and elders: but the villages had neither bishop nor elders; but the Church there was gathered by some minister comming out of the head city. Thirdly, it is a matter burthensome, to mainteine such a number of elders as they would haue. Lastly, so many wise gouernours can not be found in euery parish. such men are hardly found in a diocesse: how difficult then would it be to finde them in euery parish?

Cor. epist. ad Fabium. Euseb. lib. 6. et Cypr.

The reasons that are alleged to the contrary, are deuoid of sence and reason. The apostles (saith *Th. Cartw.*) appointed elders church by church; and *Titus* was commanded to appoint elders in euery city: *ergo* (saith he) Church aldermen were appointed in euery parish. which is to trifle rather then to dispute. for the elders that the apostle speaketh of, were ministers of the word. and were there any other elders of the Church; yet the forme of speech will not admit that the word pronounced of another affirmatiuely, should be taken generally, both of ministers and others. and as well may a man conclude out of this speech, God sent to them prophets, that God sent all sorts of prophets at one time. and whereas *Moses* commanded iudges to be placed in euery city, that they had all sorts of iudges there appointed, as this, that all elders were appointed in euery Church. Lastly, there is great difference betwixt church by church, and city by city, and euery parish; for that many parishes were vnder one city. But what a ridiculous thing is this, to say that elders were in euery city, when it can not be prooued that they were in any one city, no, not in the world?

Answere to *Cartwrights* reasons for the plurality of elderships.

But (saith he) gouernours are necessary for euery parish: so are princes and iudges; yet are not princes and iudges to be placed in euery parish. It is sufficient if euery parish be partaker of the effects of gouernment, although the gouernours be not personally present. Apostles were gouernors, yet were not in euery parish. But what doth this concerne lay elders, that neither were gouernours, nor euer were *in mundo*?

Further, he saith, that discipline administred by elders, is a part of the Gospell; which is a most blasphemous vntrueth: and yet granted, prooueth not that elders ought to be in euery parish. for discipline might be administred by those that be out of the parish, as at

Geneua, and in *Scotland*, where one consistory serueth for diuers parishes. but let him proue his assertion, and it shall suffice.

That pastours of villages are not more able to looke to all disorders, then pastors of cities; and that therefore an eldership must be assistant vnto him in euery village, is like this, that officers in villages are not more able to execute their charge, then those of cities; therefore there ought to be a mayor, shiriffes, a councell, and a recorder in euery village as in the city of *London*. There are those that ouersee the pastors of villages, and therefore this new policy of *Cartw.* is but a peeuish conceit of vndigested zeale.

Neither is it to any purpose that all churches are daughters and heires of one father and mother: for all heires haue not like & equall giftes and graces, nor portions. this reason resting vpon a similitude, is woorth nothing: for that the similitude holdeth not. for of coheires, some may haue their inheritance present, some lying farre away, some may be heires *ex quadrante*, some *ex triente*, some *ex semisse*; and yet all coheires.

Further, although bishops were in euery church, yet are they not in euery parish. The Church of *England*, as in time past, the Church of *Crete*, and *Macedonia*, had bishops; but not in euery parish. but suppose they were: yet had they not any one Church alderman in their churches or parishes. for these be gentlemen of late beginning.

Finally, that which he affirmeth of the practise of the *Iewish* and *Christian* church, that elders were in euery congregation, is a manifest vntruth, proceeding from the ignorance both of the *Iewish* state, that had no ecclesiastical elders at all, nor ciuill elders but in cities & great townes; and of the *Christian* church also, which neuer had any such elders as these dumbe censours. and such presbyteries of ministers of the word as they had, they were in no other places beside chiefe and head cities, as at *Ierusalem*, *Rome*, *Ephesus*, *Philippi*, and such like.

2.Chron.19. Peter Galat. lib.4. Ioseph.lib.4.c.7.

Reasons why the elders are to be refused.

Therefore do we refuse this eldership: First, for that it is an office newly deuised. Secondly, for that the authority they haue, is without colour vsurped. Thirdly, for that not onely in particular parishes, but in the whole realme, it would breed great trouble & confusion. They themselues can not yet tell by speculation, how things should be; much lesse do they know by practise, how to remedy the imperfections of their plats, when they shall come to execution.

Their conceits concerning elders, as yet are like a lumpe of flesh without forme: there appeareth scarse any delineation of parts. They are not yet resolued, whether the prince hath any interest in the election of elders : they can ſhew no reaſon why women and yoong men being Chriſtians ſhould not giue voyce in elections: they haue not determined whether women being princes, may be elders or not. neither can they euer ſhew how day labourers, and artificers, neglecting their trades, to execute the office of elders, ſhall become wealthy men, or wiſe gouernours. It is a very hard queſtion, whether a cloſe papiſt being choſen elder, be a member of *Chriſtes* body or no. for they holde that elders are members of *Chriſtes* body, and yet deny it to papiſts. And doubtfull it is, whether a magiſtrate or great lord ſhould relinquiſh his ciuill offices and lordſhips, for auoyding of confuſion of offices, and auoyding lofty titles in the officers of the Church. Likewiſe, whether a noble man (as he is a iuſtice in more then one place) may be an elder of two Churches.

Likewiſe, how a ciuill ſhoomaker, or thatcher, may be a ſufficient eccleſiaſticall officer. theſe matters, they are not yet determined. how long an elder may be abſent from his church about his worldly affaires, & who ſhal giue leaue of abſence, they haue not yet reſolued.

Certeine matters there remaine which can not be decided: as how an elder that neuer ſtudied diuinity, can iudge of controuerſies concerning the Trinity. Likewiſe, if three be againſt two, why the odde voyce ſhould make the determination of three to be the ſentence of the Church, eſpecially, if the greater part ouercommeth the better, which often falleth out. Likewiſe, where of foure elders two excommunicate the other two, how theſe two contrary ſentences can with any probability, be the ſentence of the Church. Againe, if the elders excommunicate the paſtour for teaching the truth (as for example, that there neuer were any elders in the Apoſtolike church) how wil this prooue *Chriſt* his ſentence?

There are alſo diuers other queſtions, which will trouble the ſerenity of their elders : as how elders can giue ouer their office at the yere or two yeres end with ſafe conſciences, ſeeing he that hath an office, is to attend on his office, and men that lay their hand on the plough, may not looke backe : and *Timothy* is willed to abide in his calling. Likewiſe, how one elder may admoniſh another, ſeeing equalles haue no iuriſdiction vpon equalles. Likewiſe, what intereſt elders haue in Synodes to ſet downe lawes for other pariſhes, ſeeing they will allow them no authority out of their precincts. How the Church of *Geneua* can be a perfect body, will be another queſtion, ſeeing they want elders and deacons in all the pariſhes of their territory saue one : and how those can be perfect Churches that want doctors, seeing our platformers call all churches maymed and deformed that want elders or doctours.

Can they shew vs for what causes elders are to be deposed, and what not, and what redresse they shall haue, being deposed wrongfully? If they can neither set downe the trueth concerning these matters, out of the word of God, nor haue resolued them in their discipline; these two things they must needs confesse. First, that their discipline can not be drawen from the word of God : secondly, that the same is not yet come to perfection. Wherefore, let them shew better proofes, and resolue more doubts ; or else, all that see it will refuse their discipline (concerning elders) as an absurd and imperfect deuise.

Of Deacons, and their office.

Chap. 5. Sect. 1.

Wherein is prooued that the deacons office is an holy ministery about the word and sacraments, and attendance of bishops : First, by the words of the apostle, that maketh it βαθμὸν, a degree, and indueth it with παῤῥησία, liberty of speech. Secondly, for that the same resembleth the Leuites office, which taught and ministred : which is confirmed by Ieromes *opinion. Thirdly, by the examples of* Stephen *and* Philip. *Fourthly, for that the deacons had the gifts of the Holy ghost, which to distribute almes were not so necessary. Lastly, for that the fathers with one consent make the same an holy ministery, conuersant about the things aforesaid, and neuer did profane it in meere collection of almes.* Th. Cartw. *his reasons to the contrary are answered.*

AS decayed merchants oft times make greatest shew of wealth: so the disciplinarians hauing confounded all orders, make greatest brags of order and discipline, and sticke not to chalenge all Churches that are not conformable vnto them. It is apparant in the principal grounds of their discipline: but in the deacons office especially. for as they giue out, that they haue restored the deacons office to his natiue purity; so they say we haue confounded and mingled the same, and turned it from the first institution. where in truth they haue not the office of deacons among them, and haue absurdly profaned the name of deacon, in giuing the same to certaine collectors, which they call proctors of the poore, so far different from ancient deacons, as vaine & wordly affaires from the holy ministery. these they make annuall, and place them in euery congregation. some of our platformers, contrary to the custome of the *French* churches, would haue them to deale in the gouernment of the church. The *French* articles of discipline make them equall to elders, and assistant to

Ler. disc. Th. Cartw. second reply.

Ordon. de Gene.

Tit. des ancient et deac. art. 5. et 6.

to the conſiſtory. againſt which conceites I am now to argue, beginning with the office of deacon, which wee make a miniſterie of the Church conuerſant about the word and ſacraments, and not onely in matters of collection for the poore.

The Apoſtle hath in plaine termes, that they that miniſter well (in the deaconſhip) procure themſelues a good degree, and a great libertie in the faith of Chriſt Ieſus. If a degree, then is it a ſteppe to prieſthood. if libertie in ſpeech, then are they to ſpeake: for παῤῥησία is libertie in wordes (to ſpeake properly) as θεἀσος is boldneſſe in courage. and ſo *Ambroſe* expoundeth degree, & the ancient fathers euer vſed the deaconſhip. *Caluin* I know interpreteth βαθμὸν Honor. But neither will the word permit it, nor will the words παῤῥησίαν ἐν πιστεῖ admit the office of deaconſhip to be mere collectors: and ſmall honour it is ſeruilely to collect almes. βαθμὸς is a ſteppe, and ſignifieth an aſcending. Honour may be without ſtepping hier, and therefore I muſt craue pardon of *T.Cartw.* to beleeue antiquitie with reaſon rather then the *Geneuians*, that ſpeake what they can for their prophane proctors, although without reaſon. *1.Tim.3.* See all the fathers on that place.

The deacons (ſaith *Ierom* to whom the reſt of the fathers conſent) anſwere the Leuites in the proportion of their miniſterie: but *Leuites* did teach the lawe, and were conuerſant in the ſeruice of the Church and helping of the prieſtes: and none of them dealt in collections for the poore, and fewe about the treaſurie. What is then the reaſon that the Chriſtian *Leuite*, the deacon, ſhould be abridged of the moſt neceſſarie part of his office? howe can they that drawe the forme of their Conſiſtorie from the *Iewiſh* gouernment, refuſe to yeeld to this office of teaching in the deacon? manifeſt it is that it came from the inſtitution of God. *Ad Euagr. epiſt.85.*

But who can abſolutely ſay the office of teaching may not be giuen to deacons, that conſidereth the apologie of *S.Stephen*, his diſputation againſt the *Libertines*, his great graces being full of the holy Ghoſt? the preaching of *Phillip* to the eunuch & to them of *Samaria*? this the diſciplinarians thinke to auoyde by ſaying he was an euangeliſt: but howe he became an euangeliſt, and when, they can ſay nothing. that he was a deacon we know: that he paſſed not ẏ bonds of his vocation, it is not to be ſuſpected: that he was not then an euangeliſt as a ſeuerall officer, the ſhort time betwixt his preaching and office of deacon, is an euident ſigne. that he was afterward an euangeliſt alſo, doth take away the nice diſtinction of their offices. the argument of *Stephen* remaineth vnanſwered. for they haue nothing to *Act.6.* *Act.8.*

ſay, but that he preached not;as if thoſe giftes he had,and that diſputation and diſcourſe he made, could be made of him that hand-
In Encom. Stephani. led not the worde. *Gregorie* of *Nizza* calleth him κήρυκα τῆς πίστεως a
preacher of faith; and ioyneth his deaconſhip & preaching together.
that other deacons did the like wee may coniecture by theſe two,
whoſe actions are examples what the reſt did: as in the Apoſtles
it is apparant likewiſe what the reſt did, by the diſcourſe of the liues
of them, whoſe actions are ſet downe.

4 And to what purpoſe ſerued thoſe giftes which they had of
wiſedome and the holy ghoſt, if they did nothing but collect and diſtribute almes, which the pooreſt Artiſan in *Geneua* thinketh himſelfe
ſufficiently able to performe? Why doth the apoſtle require that they
1.Tim.3. ſhould haue the myſterie of faith in a pure conſcience, if they did not
teach it to others? for the Goſpel is not a myſterie to be concealed
like the *Iewiſh Cabala*, but to be preached.

5 The practiſe of all antiquitie, that made deacons a degree of the
miniſterie, & employed them in the ſeruice of the church, doth make
for the practiſe of our Church againſt the prophanation of the deacons office. τύπος γίνου τῶν πιστῶν ἐν λόγῳ, ἐν ἀναστροφῇ. be thou an example (ſaith
Ad Heron. Diaconum. *Ignatius* to a certein deacon) of the faithfull in word & conuerſation.
lectorem. τῇ ἀναγνώσει πρόσεχε, ἵνα μὴ μόνον αὐτὸς εἰδῇς, ἀλλὰ καὶ ἄλλοις αὐτὰ ἐξηγῇ ὡς θεοῦ ἀθλήτης .i. vſe
diligence in reading that thou maieſt not only know things thy ſelfe,
but teach the ſame vnto others as a valiant champion of God. and of
Ad Philadelph. *Philo* a deacon he ſaith, ὃς ἐν λόγῳ ὑπηρετεῖ μοι. which doth miniſter to me
Ad Smirnen. in the word. and in another place, εἰς λόγον θεοῦ διάκονοι χριστοῦ ὄντες. being
Chriſtes deacons in the word of God.

Cyprian witneſſeth that prieſtes and deacons did inſtruct in the
lawe of the Goſpell. *lib.3.epiſt.15.lib.3.epiſt,16* of deacons he affir-
Lib.1.epiſt.8. meth, that with daily exhortations they ſtrengthened the weake.
Lib.3.Epiſt.22. neither is it to be doubted of deacons, ſeeing ſubdeacons and readers
& lib.4.epiſt.5. did teach the word, which were inferiour degrees in the externall
miniſtration.

The miniſter did miniſter the ſacraments of baptiſme vpon the
biſhops commandement. *Tertullian de baptiſ.*

Iuſtin Martyr ſheweth that deacons holpe to baptize and miniſter the Communion. *Apol.2.ad Antonin.*

Of the practiſe of the Church of *Alexandria*, *Athanaſius* is a
witneſſe, who being a deacon and ſingularly learned, did greatly
aſſiſt *Alexander* the biſhop in diſputation.

In

In the Councell of *Nice. Hierom* in *1. Tim. 3. multam fiduciam acquirent apud Dominum petendi, apud homines docendi.* Deacons saith *Ierom* got vnto themselues boldnesse in praying to God, and teaching men. of *Valens* deacon of *Aelia Eusebius* reporteth, that he was most expert in the scriptures. *eccl. hist. libr.6.c.8.* τῶν θείων γραφῶν εἰ καί τις ἄλλος ἐπιστήμων.

I neede not alledge the later writers which are cleare for the teaching of deacons. neither vnlesse they of *Geneua* speake for their prophane proctors, will the aduersarie put their cause to their arbitrement.

T. Cartw. striueth what he can to shadowe the trueth. but his reasons are so full of holes, that they keepe out no light, nor beare off any force. That deacons are excluded from teaching the word in the *1. Cor. 12.* is vntrue. for deacons are not there named. and were they vnderstoode by helpers, yet are not those things so contrediuided, but that they concurre in one person. for the Apostle did teach, and the pastor doth gouerne, doth helpe, and in those times had diuersitie of tongues and other graces.

But where the Apostle maketh a full diuision of ministers of the word (saith he) there deacons are not named: as if in a generall signification all that teach the word, are not comprised vnder pastors and teachers. but if the Apostle make a full enumeration or perfite diuision of all offices necessary for building of the Church, where will the Church Aldermen shroude themselues that haue no shadowe vnder any of these offices? and howe coulde the Apostles bee pastors and teachers and Euangelistes, as the fathers affirme? *Ob.2.*

That the Apostle required not aptnesse to teach in a Deacon, doth not exclude him from teaching, for he requireth not aptnesse to gouerne in the pastor. yet that it is incident to a deacon to teach, it appeareth that he requireth that they haue the mysterie of faith and a libertie of speech: and that the first deacons were full of the holy Ghost, and chosen to serue at Cōmunion which was ministred after the loue feastes ended. *Ob.3.* *Act.6.*

He obiecteth further, that the Apostles gaue ouer the office of deaconship, as not agreeing well with their ministerie of the word. which is not true. for then they would neuer at first haue taken the office vpon them. *Ob.4.*

But they ioyned others with themselues because of rhe multitude of loue feastes and seruing at them, and great trouble about the money which came of the sale of possessions. which ceasing now is no hinderance for our deacons, that haue not that troublesome office that they had as is supposed. and if the newe deacons can notwithstanding their deaconship attend an occupation most of the weeke, why is *T.Cartw.* so rigorous that he will not suffer deacons to doe seruice to the church any one houre?let him therefore shew where they are excluded from handling the word or peace babbling against all antiquitie wrthout reason or authoritie.

Of Deacons and their office.

CHAP. 5. SECT. 2.

The temporary Deacons of the platformers are declared to haue come into the Church, contrary to the practise of the Leuites vnder the lawe, of the Apostles and the ancient fathers which knewe none such : and that the same ought not to abandon their ministerie in the Church at a time prefixed, no more then the pastor may renounce his calling, if we follow either the Apostles, or antiquitie.

AS men that affect noueltie and hate ancient customes, the disciplinarians haue left the ancient nature of deacons, and deuised newe fancies of their owne. for beside that they thinke any marchant, artificer or husbandman sufficient for the deaconship: they further (because they will not anoy vs too long with things of euill sauour) make their deacons annuall. wherein they dissent not only from antiquitie, but from all reason.

1 The *Leuites* into whose ministration the deacons haue succeeded, were not chosen for yeeres, nor departed as tenants doe from their fermes at the ende of a certaine terme: but they continued *Leuits* vntill death, vnlesse for their offences they were sequestred from the altar, or that after 50. they were spared from the toilesome seruice about the sacrifices.

Act.6. *1.Tim.3.* 2 This custome did continue in the time of the Apostles. they chose no souldiers, that after a certaine time woulde abandon their leaders, but such as continued in their ministerie.

Can.Ap. *Cyprian.* *Tertull.* 3 Nothing is more notorius both by course of histories, and acts of councels, then the continuance of deacons in their office. and a most grieuous punishment it was for the deacons to be deposed. if the charge had bene such as is in the newe discipline: deposition had bene a fauour, rather then punishment, seeing the terme is short, the place so base.

4 Neither

Neither can anie thing be more repugnant to the office of the Miniſterie, then for Deacons leauing the ſeruice of God, to followe the cares of the worlde. which is, as if a ſouldior ſhould forſake the warres, and a watchman abandon his watch, contrarie to the Apoſtles commandement, which chargeth him that hath an office, to attend on his office. *Tertullian* noted this lightnes in heretikes, verie *De preſcript.*
vnſeemelie therefore is it for Chriſtians.

5 Finallie, if a Deacon be an officer of the Church as well as a paſtor, as the diſciplinarians tell vs, when they iumble about the partes and members of their diſcipline: then may the Deacon no more forſake his ſtation, then the paſtor, vnleſſe it be when hee is called to higher degree, in which caſe the Churches profite is his warrant.

Of Deacons and their office.

Chap. 5 Sect. 3.

That Deacons are not neceſſarie for euerie pariſh, is proued firſt by the ſimilitude betwixt them and the Leuites, acknowledged by the aduerſarie. Secondlie, by the Apoſtles practiſe. Thirdlie, by the cuſtome of the Churches ſucceeding the Apoſtles, and authoritie of fathers. And laſtlie by the example of Geneua. the places that make ſhewe of the contrarie, are anſwered.

Will ſaye nothing how in their new diſcipline contrarie to antiquitie, they allowe their Deacons no wages, vnleſſe they can of themſelues gripe ſomewhat of the poore mens almes: for going ſo ſoone out of their office they deſerue no fauour: and did they, yet their terme would bee ended before the ſute were obtained. but this noueltie, contrarie to antiquitie likewiſe, that Deacons ſhould bee in euerie pariſh, maye not be ouer paſſed.

1 For it is repugnant to the ancient practiſe of the Leuites, who *1.Paral.23.*
ſerued firſt in the tabernacle, then in the temple, and were employed chiefelie about the ſacrifices and ſeruice of God, which was in one place. who although they had cities throughout *Iſrael* and *Iuda*; yet by turnes they ſerued in one place. If of the Leuites ſome were appointed Iudges through the cities; yet was it not by reaſon of their Leuiticall office (for then ſhould all haue bene Iudges) but by the princes deſignement: neither was it in villages, but in cities. for

there was the seate of Iustice. those that borowe a patterne of their presbyteries from the *Iewes*, may not refuse this argument for good, if the Leuites were not placed in villages, that Deacons ought not likewise to be placed in euery parishes.

In the Apostles times, Deacons were onelie in chiefe cities, as those
Act.6. seuen ẏ were appointed at *Ierusalem*: yet may it be doubted, whether they deserue to be called Deacons in that forme of speach, that the disciplinarians doe vse. Of which doubt these are the reasons: that they are not called Deacons there, nor else-where; that their seruice was about tables at loue feastes, and the ministration of the communion. It is sayde in another place, *who was one of the seuen*, which sheweth there were but seuen. but because antiquitie calleth them Deacons: be it they were Deacons seruing tables; yet were they onelie, at that time appointed at *Ierusalem* the mother Church, and serued the whole Church of *Iewrie*, yea, and of the gentiles too that was gathered at that time. who then is so simple as to conceiue, that euerie litle portion of the Church had Deacons as the Church of *Ierusalem*? likewise at *Ephesus* and *Philippi*, it is manifest there were Deacons: for else the Apostle would not haue declared the dueties of Deacons so particularlie to *Timothie* then resident at *Ephesus*, nor would hee haue saluted the Deacons at *Philippi*. but that they were not in euerie inferior countrie village appointed, the proceedings of the Church, which had not all offices at one time, declareth, and that the Apostles made a difference betwixt great Churches and villages.

That all Churches had like officers and gouernement, is but a vaine surmise of doting platformers, confuted by the Actes of the Apostles, and stories of the Church.

After the death of the Apostles, Deacons were appointed not in villages, but in chiefe cities, where Byshops had a clergie: (so it is euident by *Ignatius*, who maketh mention of Deacons that serued
Euseb.6.Sect. 43.Gr. him) and in other great Churches. at *Rome* in the time of *Cornelius*, there were seuen Deacons which had the ouersight of the Churches of the suburbes, and territorie there about. The Deacons of *Carthage* had charge in the whole Church of the territorie vnder *Cyprian* that was Byshop. Those that imagine Deacons to be in euerie village where a priest was, are abused, not knowing that Byshops were commonlie in great cities or townes, hauing large territories about them, and of all antiquitie were distinguished from Priestes,

or

or inferior Ministers of the worde. Wherefore vnlesse they can shewe that Byshop and Priest were all one in the time of the fathers, or that Deacons were in other places, then where there were Byshops: let them leaue off to thinke, that Deacons were in euerie village or parish in ancient times.

If they will not ascend higher, but lye still sucking of their deuises out of the naked commentaries of them of *Geneua*; yet they might vnderstand, that they haue no proctors of the hospitall, which they call Deacons, in the countrie parishes, but onelie in the head citie. which being obserued in our cathedrall Churches, what cause haue they to accuse our Church, that excuse and honor the Church of *Geneua*? especiallie seeing they haue as I saye, no Deacons at all, but certaine base almoners, or proctors of the hospitall, entitled Deacons, but in nothing resembling the Deacons of the ancient Church. But I perceiue, by the whole course & byasse of these mens platformes, wherein they striue against the orders and gouernement of our Church, that they had no regarde, nor consideration to couer themselues, or their friendes imperfections; and cared not how farre they hazarded themselues, so that they may saye somewhat to hurt others.

Ordon. de Gen Art. 157.

Now seeing they commend vnto vs discipline, which they bragge before the multitude to bee drawen out of the worde of God; why doe they not shewe vs a commaundement or rule, whereby Deacons as they would haue them, are commaunded to bee in euery congregation? the place out of the twelfth of the *Romans* helpeth them not. for neither are Deacons mentioned: nor if they were, is there anie assignation of places to them. If it were graunted, that the similitude betwixt the bodie of the Church and naturall bodie, did holde so farre as to prooue the Church ought to haue all the partes (which notwithstanding passeth the termes of Scripture) yet may wee not thinke, that the partes of the Church are compared to a naturall bodie, but the whole Church to a whole bodie. If so be in euerie part of the Church generallie, there ought to bee all the partes; it were as much as if in the foote, a man shoulde haue eyes, and heart in the heele, and euerie parte of the bodie in that parte.

The allegation of the 1. *Cor.* 12. doeth helpe them lesse. for neither are Deacons mentioned, nor were they vnderstoode. is it more necessarie that they should bee in all villages, then Apostles, Euangelistes, power of miracles, diuersitie of tongues? for all these come in by one title, and in one frame of sentence.

Lastlie, seeing there is not the same reason of pastors and Deacons, for that the Church is alwayes to bee fedde with doctrine, but hath not alwayes like necessitie of prouiding for the poore; seeing in some parishes there are no poore; it is absurde to thinke that Deacons are as necessarie as pastors: especiallie, seeing one mans care may looke vnto the poore of a great circuit, which cannot be done so easilie by one pastors preaching. but this assertion may seeme tollerable, in respect of that which foloweth, concerning the gouernement of the Church by Deacons, which now commeth in sequele to be refuted.

Of Deacons and their office.

Chap. 5. Sect. 4.

Wherein the opinion of those that make Deacons, either partes of the Consistorie or assistants, is refelled by the practise of the Church of the Iewes. 2. By the signification of their name, being called Deacons, or seruantes, and no where gouernors. 3. By the testimonie of fathers, that make them to attend the Bishop, and to serue about the word & sacraments. 4. For that they haue no commission of gouernement. 5 No giftes. Lastly, for that it is absurde to laye so weightie a burthen vpon Deacons shoulders, and therefore now at length layde vpon others. In the ende of this section, the imperfections of their platformes in the office of Deacon, are also touched.

Lthough the French Church (from which as tender infantes, our disciplinarians doe sucke their discipline) excludeth Deacons out of their Consistorie: yet diuers of them that take vpon them the restoring of our Church (for diuers causes to them alone knowen) doe make them necessarie partes of it. because the Deacons in the new reformation doe carie the bagge; it may bee that some of the authors of it woulde currie fauour with them. this I affirme to be contrarie, both to ancient gouernement, and sound reason either of scripture or policie.

The Church of the *Iewes* was gouerned by the soueraigne magistrate, and the priests. the Leuites were vnder the charge and commaundement of priestes. and although some of them were by certaine princes, as *Dauid*, and *Iehosaphat*, chosen iudges and gouernors; yet their gouernement was not in respect of the Church, but in respect of the ciuill estate. For they were appointed by princes: they had

had charge to execute the lawe of God and the king; they sate in the gates of cities where ciuill causes were determined, and not in the Temple, which was destinated to the seruice of God. and finallie, were not chosen by vertue of the office of Leuits (for then all should haue bene chosen) but either for speciall sufficiencie, or speciall liking of the prince.

Hee that will saye, that the Deacons had the gouernement of the Church in the Apostles time, doeth but wilfullie (shutting his eyes) striue against the trueth. for where soeuer gouernors are named, Deacons are excluded. Our Sauiour Christ maketh Deacons seruantes, and opposeth them to those that are in gouernement. *Luk.22.* ὁ ἡγούμενος ὡς ὁ διακονῶν. Hee that gouerneth, let him be as a Minister, or seruant. the platformers themselues, when they talke of gouernors and rulers, leaue Deacons out of their Consistorie, though afterwarde by a newe deuise, they aduaunce them into the Consistorie.

After that the gouernement of the Church was committed to the Apostles successors, deacõs were Ministers vnto Bishops, attended on them. If they dealt in oblations, or goodes of the Church, or reliefe of the poore, it was vnder the Bishop, and at his commaundement. the oblations were brought to the Bishop: τὸ συλλεγόμενον παρὰ τῷ προεστῶτι *Apol.2. ad Anton.* ἀποτίθεται, καὶ αὐτὸς ἐπικουρεῖ ὀρφανοῖς τε καὶ χήραις καὶ τοῖς διὰ νόσον ἢ δι' ἄλλην αἰτίαν λειπομένοις: That which is gathered, sayeth *Iustine martyr*, is brought to the gouernor (that is to saye, Bishop) and there layde vp, and hee relieueth orphants, widowes, sicke, and those that want. Bishoppes, as hath bene shewed out of councels and fathers, had the whole gouernement of the Church. οἱ διάκονοι πειθαρχείτωσαν τοῖς πρεσβυτέροις, ἀρχιερεῦσι καὶ *Ad Philadelph.* πάντες τῷ ἐπισκόπῳ. Deacons sayeth *Ignatius*, let them obey their Elders, which are principall priestes, and all (let them bee subiect) to the Bishop. *Cyprian* euerie where sheweth the ministerie of Deacons *Lib.1.Ep.3.* to bee at his appointment, by so manie charges and commaundements as hee gaue them. the whole brotherhoode was subiect to the Bishoppe. Deacons, they were ordained and appointed by the *Can.Apost.33.* Bishop. Can. Apost. 2. Deacons were subiect to the Bishops censures and correction. Alexander deposed diuers Deacons that tooke parte with *Arrius*. I neede not vse manie authorities, for there is not the least presumption of the Deacons gouernement in the ancient Church.

And verie absurde it were, if the Apostle describing the speciall dueties of Deacons, and not mentioning anie matter of gouernement, neither there, nor in anie other place, should notwithstanding

ding make Deacons gouernors of the Church.

They themſelues that talke (I knowe not what) of giftes may ſee, that the Deacons haue no gifts for gouernement. if thoſe that diſtribute, were Deacons, *Rom.* 12. yet haue they no gift, but ſimplicitie, which is not agreeing with gouernement. the Apoſtle 1.*Cor.*12. doeth contradiuide helpers, which they expounde Deacons, from gouernances: and they themſelues calling their Conſiſtorie Eldershippe, can no where ſhewe where ſuch Deacons are called Elders. Wherefore, ſeeing they ſaye that no man is to take vpon him an office, but hee that is called; why doe they giue gouernement to Deacons, that are no where called to gouerne? why doe they not remoue them themſelues, ſeeing the Deacons breake through ſo manie rules of diſcipline made againſt them?

To ſhut vp this treatiſe of Deacons, what is more abſurde, then to giue Deacons authoritie to make and abrogate lawes, to iudge of faith and maners, to elect, ordeine, and depoſe the officers of the Church, and to execute the cenſures, ſeeing they can neither ſhewe one worde of commiſſion out of ſcriptures, nor ancient counſels, nor are fit for ſuch matters, being in the reformed Churches baſe fellowes, ſome of them crept out of the bordell, or other backe houſes, and by the poſterne entred into the Church?

I neede not vſe anie long diſpute againſt this noueltie in the Deacons office: ſeeing not onelie the French Churches haue ſhut them out of office, but the late plats abrenounce their maſters of the admonition, and *Th.Cartw.* their good patrone. and not ſo much as the vnlearned diſcourſe, but ſayeth, that the Deacons (which abſurdlie hee would haue to bee choſen of the moſt worſhipfull gentlemen of the countrie) muſt hearken to their learned paſtors.

To theſe Deacons, the platformers giue beſide their iuriſdiction, the diſpoſing of the Church goods. they except not anie tenthes, firſt fruites, ſubſidies, or contributions dewe from the clergie to the prince. Nay, they leaue neither tithes, nor glebe, houſe, nor land, to their thred bare, and bare legged paſtor, whom as it ſhould ſeeme, they will turne vp into a megre and leane paſture: which would bee the confuſion of the Miniſterie, which they ſeeme to honour. this plat therefore, for manie diſorders that are brought in by the Deacons office, is to bee refuſed, and not onelie for want of authoritie.

Aricles of French diſci.

What

What more absurde, then that Church-aldermen and Deacons, men of occupation, and voyde of learning, shoulde ouerrule the Ministers in matters of faith, and doctrine? What more senceles, then to see Bishops and pastors pleade their cause before Masons, Carpenters, and Tylers, intitled Deacons? How vnseemelie is it for motley iackets to throwe out the Church censures? The prince is in danger to loose a great parte of her reuenues consisting in tenthes, subsidies, and other contributions and commodities shee enioyeth by the liuings of the clergie: certeine harpyes and rauinours shoulde bee enriched by the spoyles of the Church: for when the Deacons had not so much committed to their handes as these would haue, yet they grew riche, and therefore prefererd themselues before priests. What then would they doe, if all the liuings of the Church should passe through their fingers? The poore that now manie wayes are relieued by the Church, should want all that helpe, and reliefe; and while some pretend care of the poore, the true poore shall be spoyled. and who should gaine? who but my masters the Elders, and Deacons, who meane in the ruines of the Church, to build themselues great houses?

Absurdities in their conceites concerning Deacons.

Hierom. August.

Which inconueniences, as they are hardlie remedied: so I see not how the imperfections of their plats concerning the Deacons offices can bee supplied. they haue not yet tolde vs of what age and occupation Deacons shall bee: nor whether they ought to giue ouer their occupation for that yeere, being chosen Deacon: they cannot tell what meanes to vse, that worshipfull gentlemen shall take vpon them the Deacons charge: nor what allowance the Deacons shall haue trauailing in the Churches busines: if men will not be moued of charitie to relieue the poore, they can not tell how the Deacons shall prouide for them: concerning their absence, and the causes thereof, and who shall giue Deacons leaue of absence, they say nothing. for what causes Deacons shalbe deposed, and in what case and by what meanes they shalbe restored, they are not yet resolued. in sūme, pretending to speake of the restoring the office of Deacons; they turne it from the institution: and seeming to relieue the poore, they take away the reliefe of the poore: and pretending to set orders, they bring all out of order. for if now, when rates and taxations are made by iustices, by warrant of law, & vpon paine of imprisonmēt, money notwithstanding is hardlie leuied, & the poore hardlie maintained; what do we think, 3 or 4 poore odde compagnions wil be able to do, whē they haue neither help of prince, nor law, nor autoritie in themselues?

Imperfections of platformes.

 for

For I thinke they meane not to excommunieate all that refuse to giue as the Consistore shall set downe a rate. if they doe, perhaps a man shall be excommunicate, for not paying that which hee hath not to paye. Thus ye see as in the rest, how in the Deacons office pretending reformation, they bring all to confusion.

Of widowes and their office.

CHAP. 6.

Wherein widowes are proued to be no officers of the Church: that is to saye, by the nature of publike officers, this being a domesticall state of life: 2. For that it is absurde to saye, we may no more want widowes, then pastors: 3. For that there is no commandement for their charge or continuance: 4 For that the practise of all antiquitie speaketh against them. 5 For they are not reckoned among Church officers by the Apostle: nor lastlie thought necessarie in Churches that receiue the new discipline. The same are declared to be a state of life not necessarie for euerie congregation, both by rules of the Apostle, and practise of all olde and latter Churches. Last of all, the imperfections of their new deuises are set downe, wherein is declared, that themselues knowe not what to make of their widowes.

Clem. Alex.

AS truth is alwayes one, so error hath many changes & turnings. the diuers opinions of the disciplinarians about their officers, doe shew it to be true. some thinke pastors and Elders sufficient for gouernement: others adde Deacons: a thirde sorte haue deuised a new kinde of Doctors. and yet not content herewith; there is a fourth sorte risen vp, which vnlesse they may haue Deaconesses, they exclaime that the Church is maimed and deformed, and sticke not in their zeale of reformation to condemne all Churches, that themselues may seeme to say somewhat. their error springeth as it should seeme, of a false exposition of a place in the twesth chapter of the Epistle to the *Romans*. for there they conceiue that the partes of euerie seuerall congregation or Church, are compared to the partes of a bodie, and that widowes are a parte of the Church, and vnderstoode by the wordes: *Hee that sheweth mercie, with cheerefulnes.* the furious women did neuer so teare the partes of *Pentheus*, as these men haue torne and racked this place, to make it yeelde to their purpose. against whose opinions, I purpose here (God willing) to shew, that widowes are no officers of Christs Church.

Fruitful sermon. Rom. 12.

Secondlie, that whatsoeuer we make of them, that they are not necessarie for euerie congregation.

Officers

Officers we call those that haue some publike charge by lawfull authoritie: but we see no publike charge in the Church committed vnto widoes: for the attendance on the sicke is a priuate & domestical charge, and is not in respect only of Christianitie, but of common humanitie bestowed on the poore and sicke. and therfore vnlesse somewhat be found out, wherein this publike charge consisted, they can haue no office.

2 Further, if so be the widowes or deaconesses be an office appoynted by Christ to remaine in the Church; then may wee no more want widoes then pastors: then no man may dispence with Christes commandement: then are the Churches of *Geneua* & other churches in *France* and other places deformed that want widoes. but this them selues or their fellowes at least will accompt absurd.

3 Of the placing of widoes in the Church there is no commandement, nor rule, neither can they produce any example. that which the Apostle saith to *Timothie* of chusing of widoes, is not of chusing of widoes to beare office, which deceiued the platformers: but of appoynting which widoes should be respected in receiuing the almes of the Church. for of widowes there is mention *Acts.6.* which were of the same sort that these were, of which the Apostle to *Timothie* maketh mention: but they were poore widowes receiuing almes, not widowes bearing office. which if it had bene otherwise, then had widowes bene the principall officers of the Church, erected before deacons and pastors. those which the Apostle speaketh of *Rom.12.* that shewe mercie with cheerefulnesse, are not widowes. for then no man by the rule of the platformers might shewe mercie, but they, forasmuch as no officer might encroch vpon anothers office, as they hold.

4 The practise of ancient Churches is against the office of widowes. they had in diuers Churches widowes, so they had virgins, but no officers: but such as in that state of life serued God as they thought. but of any charge that widowes had in the Church, wee reade not.

Such if they were restored would resemble Nunnes.

5 In the 12. to the *Romanes*, the 4. to the *Ephesians*, and *1.Cor.12.* where the platformers make reckoning of all the officers of the Church, yet are there no widowes found, and to make such widowes as then were to continue, were to returne vs things forepast, & gone. widowes were chosen thē, that had washed the saints feete, & lodged strangers: which customes now if they should be recalled, we should then return to the *Iewish* customs, & the times of the first persecution.

Admonit. Eccles. discipl.

6 Last of all, if widowes be an office appoynted by Christ, why are not widowes appoynted in the Churches of *France* and *Geneua*? why doe not they of the admonition and most of our platformers thinke them necessarie?

Widowes are a state of life as the state of yong men, maried men, olde men. and although they be in the church, yet you may not make yong men, maried men, and wiues, an office. no more reason haue you to make widowes an office. such we acknowledge, that there are but too many in euery parish which neede reliefe: that they are officers of the church to be placed in euery congregation, we thinke it most absurd. we haue no commandement for it: and therefore by their owne rules they ought not to require it in euery church. In ẏ ancient church this order was a state of life rather burdensome, then an office profitable for the Church.

Widowes not necessarie for euery congregation.

1

2 That of the 12. to the *Romanes* maketh not widowes necessarie for euery parish. although we should grant ẏ the Apostle ment widoes by those that shew mercie: yet is not mercie to be restreined to those only that be of one church or parish: that is one of the lenten dreames of discipline. for if the Apostle had ment to make widowes necessarie officers, he would not haue communicated the workes of mercie and charitie to all, nor left out widowes out of the enumeration of offices *1. Cor. 12.* and other places.

Wherefore seeing widowes are thrust vpon the Church without autoritie, what reason hath the same being oppressed alreadie to take vpon it an vnnecessarie, and insupportable burden? shall wee haue Nunnes brought into our Church a fresh?

The imperfection of their plats concerning widowes.

The platformers themselues cannot tell yet what to make of this office of widoes, as they call it. they haue not yet resolued what number should be in euery Church, nor how they shalbe chosen, nor whether they shal haue impositiõ of hands as other officers: but least of al are they able to shew how they shalbe mainteined. they knowe not what it is, nor wherein their office shall consist. for if all sicke persons shalbe laide vpon the Church, there will be a stirre indeede, but they know not how this stirre will be composed. they cannot distinguish betweene the dueties required of housholders in looking to their sicke, and the publike dueties of the Church. they shew not whether these widowes shall be annuall, or for their liues, nor howe they shall be gouerned, nor for what causes deposed. wherefore desiring them to leaue vnto vs our hospitals and almeshouses, we leaue vnto them their widowes, vntill such time as they are resolued what to desire,

and

and can shewe more sufficient proofes and reasons of their desires. If *T.Cartw.* will take them into his hospitall, there you shall haue one hospitall, if not one Church furnished with widowes.

Of the Consistories and their vsurpation.

CHAP. 7. SECT. 1.

Wherein is declared that the forme of the newe Consistorie was neuer vsed in the Iewish *Church: for that their* Sanedrin *or Colledges of Iudges dealt by vertue of their office in ciuill causes, and were of another forme and nature. Secondly, for that the authoritie supposed to be in the Ecclesiasticall Sanedrin of the* Iewes,*belonged by right to princes and priestes. Thirdly, for that we finde no mere Ecclesiasticall Consistorie in that gouernment to haue bene erected or vsed, which is prooued for that there is no lawe founde of the erection of it, or practise or mention of it. and Lastly, because the Consistories that were in the* Iewish *Church, had no such authoritie as is surmised, but the same belonged to princes and priestes.*

WHen I was come to the ende of the widowes office, I had well hoped that I had bene at an ende of my labours. for the disciplinarians seeme to desire nothing, but that they may haue their officers, and offices: which they accompt the summe & substance of their discipline, against which I haue said sufficient alreadie. and therefore as trauailers that haue passed vnpleasant wayes I began to take new breath, and looke behinde me. but I had not long rested, before I perceiued that although I was come to the ende of their discourses spent for the most part in the description of of these officers and their functions, yet was I not arriued to the middest of their desires. for beside the single dueties of pastors and others, they require first a Consistorie in euery parish: then, certaine conferences and Synodes, and those both prouinciall & nationall: and lastly they claime a certaine preheminence due as they say to the people. which although passed ouer and couered in the treatise of elder and pastors, and lightly touched, yet are they the principall poyntes of their newe deuised discipline, which I may not leaue vntouched. for although the elders and doctors gouernment refuted, the Consistorie falleth to the ground: yet there be diuers speciall reasons against their Consistories and Synodes, which deserue a speciall treatise apart. If the matter bee not pleasant and delightfull, it is their fault, whose strange deuises haue drawen me into this vnpleaſant argument. and ſuch is the force and loue of trueth, that it moueth any man that is not caried away with preiudice to reade things, though vnpleaſant.

Not content with paſtors and doctors, elders and deacons, which they ſeeme to craue, they deſire (as I ſayd) a Councel or Colledge compoſed of all theſe. ſome exclude deacons. and to this Colledge (which they call the Conſiſtory) they giue that power ioyntly, which before they gaue to elders ſingly: which they giue out likewiſe, that it is the inſtitution of Chriſt & his Apoſtles. but as they began in the elders, ſo they continue in the conſiſtory to ſpeake vainely, for neither was the *Iewiſh* Church gouerned by any ſuch Conſiſtorie, nor did Chriſt inſtitute it, or his Apoſtles vſe it, nor euer did the ancient fathers acknowledge it. whatſoeuer autoritie of gouernment the ſame practiſeth, it is vſurped without law or example, and for many inconueniences that thereof redound to the Prince, the Realme, and diuers particulars, is to be reſiſted and repelled.

In the policie of the *Iewes* we finde Colledges of Iudges, that determined all matters ciuill & criminall, which the later *Iewes* call *Sanedrin*, or rather *Sanedrioth*: for that terme, vnleſſe better reaſons moue mee then yet I ſee, perteined κατ' ἐξοχὴν to the chiefe Colledge of Iudges that ſate at Ieruſalem in *Gazith*. Of other Eccleſiaſtical conſiſtories appoynted for diſcuſſing of Eccleſiaſtical cauſes ſpecially, I finde no ſtep why they ſhould be inſtituted. thoſe Iudges that were erected *Exodus 18.* were not of them: for they heard all cauſes (matters of great difficultie excepted) and were appointed before the ſeparation of the *Leuites*, and prieſthood of *Aaron*. ſuch a Colledge of Iudges as thoſe, were mentioned *Deut. 17.* or *Numb. 11.* was but in one place, and dealt in matters of ſtate, and matters criminall. other Colledges of Iudges I find none. for thoſe mentioned *Deut. 1.* & *16.* are ſuch as were firſt appoynted *Exod. 18.* but theſe apperteine nothing to the Eccleſiaſticall Colledges of Iudges which the diſciplinarians ſuppoſe to haue bene placed in euery citie, and almoſt village, for deciding of eccleſiaſticall cauſes. Wherefore vnleſſe they can ſhewe vs ſome lawe, of the erection of this Eccleſiaſticall *Synedrion*, the ſame will proue an earthly inuention, nothing ſauouring of God, or heauen.

Petr. Galat.

The Iewes had no Conſiſtorie, like to that is newly erected.

Which is confirmed in this, that the ſame authoritie which the Eccleſiaſticall presbyterie is preſumed to haue in the Church of the *Iewes*, is giuen either to the chiefe magiſtrate that preſcribed lawes and orders, and appoynted gouernours, or to prieſtes that iudged betwixt

All authoritie ſuppoſed to be in the Iewiſh conſiſtorie, was in the prince or prieſtes.

betwixt cleane and vncleane, as they who had the knowledge of the law, or ciuill iudges, that decided controuersies.

Of ecclesiasticall iudges that determined ecclesiasticall causes, there is no practise nor example found. the Leuites that king *David* appoynted to iudge in the causes of God and the king, were of another nature: for they were ciuill iudges, they had no elders nor priests adioyned to them as colleagues; they were appoynted by the prince, not by the priests and people. which answere may serue to that obiection, which is made out of the *2.Chr.19.* where *Iehosaphat* appointed priests, Leuites, and of the chiefe of the families, for iudges: for they were ciuill, and were appointed by the prince. And this further, that those iudges that are mentioned in the eight verse of that chapter, were onely appointed at Ierusalem: and that seeing these godly kings did nothing but according to the law of *Moses*; it is not to be surmised that they appoynted other iudges then such as were commanded in the law of *Moses:* which I haue shewed to be ciuill. Neither is the place alleged out of *Ieremy* the prophet, more pregnant then the other, to prooue an ecclesiasticall presbytery: for that the priests, prophets, and people, giue sentence of *Ieremy* that he should die the death, it is not to be imagined that they gaue it iudicially. Secondly, albeit they did, yet ecclesiasticall iudges pronounce not sentence of death. Thirdly, the prophets, and people, were no parts of that presbytery that is imagined. Lastly, if these had giuen the sentence of the law, then the ciuill iudges ought not to haue digressed from it, as themselues say. for he that obeyeth not the priest, ought to die.

No practise nor example of a mere ecclesiasticall presbytery among the *Iewes.*

Ierem.26.

Deut.17.

That there was no vse of the ecclesiasticall presbytery, so long as the *Iewish* state stood, these reasons may further assure vs: that we finde not where the same appointed orders or disanulled orders; nor where they appointed iudges or officers; nor where they excommunicated any one person, or decided any one ecclesiasticall controuersie in ecclesiasticall maner: matters which ordinarily fall out in the gouernment of the Church. but all these matters we finde executed either by princes, priests, or ciuill iudges.

The authority practised by the new consistory, not vsed by the *Iewish* iudges.

Secondly, we do not see where the prophets of God were sent to the ecclesiasticall consistories, either to set order, or to reforme disorders, but they were addressed of God to the princes, priests, & chiefe ciuill gouernours.

Thirdly, we finde no apparance of any good the ecclesiasticall consistory did in reclaiming the people from their idolatry; nor

No practise of the ecclesiasticall consistories authority among the *Iewes*.

harme in confirming them, or tolerating them in their leud behauiour. Lastly, we see not either where the ecclesiasticall presbytery is reprehended for transgressing the lawes, or their misgouernment; or where they are commended for their vertues, and good gouernment. Wherefore, seeing there is no mention of any ecclesiasticall presbytery in the whole discourse of that state, it is absurd to thinke that the gouernment of the Church belonged to the same.

Of Consistories, and their vsurpation.

CHAP. 7. SECT. 2.

That Christ did not translate the Iewish *presbyteries or sanedrins into his Church, is prooued: First, for that the words of the Gospell, where the translation is conceiued to be made, argue no such matter, but the contrary rather. Secondly, for that the* Iewish *consistory did that which the new consistory may not doe: and the new consistories doe things which the* Iewish *presbyteries neuer practised. Lastly, for that the Holy scriptures make no mention of two distinct presbyteries, whereof one is supposed to be ecclesiasticall. and that the same hath hitherto bene sought for in vaine.*

BVt had the *Iewes* any such consistory, or college of ecclesiasticall iudges; what is that to vs, that are not obliged to obserue their gouernment? To helpe this inconuenience, they say that *Christ* translated the same into his Church: but neuer are they able to prooue it. The words whereby the translation is supposed to be made, the nature of the *Iewish* presbytery, the trueth and euidence of story repugne against it.

The words, *Dic ecclesiæ*, proue no consistory translated into the Church.

The words, *Dic ecclesiæ*, though neuer so framed and forced, will neuer signifie, *Let there be a cousistory*; much lesse, *Let there be a consistory consisting of pastours, doctours, elders, and deacons.* for our Sauiour speaketh of a Church then present: else how could his disciples, or others complaine, if there were none present to heare their complaint? Secondly, he giueth this Church here spoken of, power but in one case: that is, where the order heere prescribed is obserued; which is nothing to the iurisdiction which the new consistory claimeth. Thirdly, he doth not so much as name or speake of a presbytery: and therefore strange it were, if he should institute one according to the patterne of another, and name neither. Fourthly, power of correction is not giuen by these words to the Church: for then he would not haue said, If he heare not the Church: for if he be bound to abide the sentence of the Church, it is not in the parties power to heare or not to heare. and if by the Church be vnderstood the gouernours

uernours of the Church then present, why should not *Christ* and his apostles be vnderstood? if the gouernours that were to succeed in the Church, why are not godly bishops to be vnderstood (as *Chrysostome* interpreted) but I know not what consistoriall elders? seeing we know that BB. are the apostles successours and gouernours of the Church (as hath bene prooued) these are neither the successours of the apostles, nor ought to haue any gouernment, that we know of. In summe, *Caluin* that is made the authour of this translation, doth not say, that *the consistory*, but the *right of the consistory*, that is, *a proceeding against* such as giue offence, is translated into the Church.

Caluin doth not plainely holde the translation of the consistory.

The nature of the *Iewish* presbytery, doth plainely declare that the deuise of the translation of it into the Church, is but a fantasie. for it is euident that the same had ciuill iurisdiction. The high priests and councell sent foorth their seruants armed, to apprehend *Christ*, they examined witnesses against him. *Caiphas* gaue sentence against him, that one must die. *Pilat* that knew the orders of the *Romanes*, being their lieutenant, and the iurisdiction of the *Iewes*, being their gouernour, acknowledged their authority to put men to death, when he said, Take him, and iudge him according to your law. They condemned *Stephen*, though wrongfully, yet orderly, to death, and caused him to be stoned. They apprehended the apostles, put them in prison, and whipped them. they gaue commission to *Paul* to bring Christians out of other cities, bound, to *Ierusalem*, that they might there be punished. they apprehended *Paul*, and would haue iudged him according to their law, if they had not bene hindered; as appeareth in the oration of *Tertullus*.

The nature of the *Iewish* consistory doth argue the same.

Iohn 18.

*Act.*4.*et* 5.

*Act.*22.

*Act.*24.

All this they make account to auoyd in one word, saying that this authority was not lawfull, and that it was part of the reliques of the confusion brought with them from Babylon: which hath small colour of reason. for looke to the first institution of it, *Deuteron.*17, there is manifest authority giuen to the colleges of iudges to proceed in ciuill causes, and to iudge in causes of bloud, and ciuill controuersies: which was confirmed by practise. and if this authority had not beene lawfull, then would our Sauiour *Christ* and his apostles, that reprehend so many little things in the priests and *Iewish* gouernment, not haue passed this notorious disorder. and the apostle *Paul* would not haue omitted this notable exception. Nay, the apostle sheweth plainely, that it was lawfull: for speaking to the high priest, he saith, Thou that sittest to iudge according to the

Vatablus ex Rabbinis.

law: which he would not haue said, nor could haue said, if he could not iudge in matters of life and death.

That the Romanes had taken from the Iewes the power of the sword, is vntrue: for *Gallio* driuing the Iewes from his seate, confesseth that they had power in questions of their law. And *Iosephus* testifieth that the *Iewes* had their liberty, or αὐτονομίαν in matters of religion. and it was not the vse of the *Romanes* to deny their religion to any nation. but admit at this time the *Romanes* had taken away the power of the sword from the *Iewes:* yet doth not that hinder, but that they had it by the lawes of God, which is the question.

Act.18. Ioseph. antiq. 14.c.12.et 16.

That the iudgements of *Stephen* and the apostles were not executed onely tumultuously, it may appeare by the examination of witnesses, the apology of *Stephen*, the execution according to the law, the witnesses first laying hands on him: and in that the apostles were apprehended by officers, heard and iudged by the councell. so that if they will haue this consistory that then was in the *Iewish* state translated into the Church, they borrow a patterne of their gouernours from those that put *Christ* to death; and are like to be no good president of gouernment in *Christes* church. Secondly, they translate ciuill iurisdiction into their consistories: for the *Iewish* Synedrion by right of institution did exercise such iurisdiction. Thirdly, they must haue but one consistory in the Church. for such a councell (as this was at *Ierusalem)* there was but one in that Church, and in that not one elder beside princes, priests or Leuites.

Deut.17.

Deut.17.

If they will borrow an example of their gouernment from the colleges of iudges, that sate in euery city, they must likewise bring ciuill iurisdiction into their consistory: for they were ciuill iudges, as is euident by their institution, *Exod.18*, and by their practise. for they sate in the gates of cities, to iudge of matters of inheritance, and matters criminall: and although they had the authority of those iudges, yet should they not haue power to prescribe lawes or orders, nor to chuse officers of the Church, nor to exercise ecclesiasticall censures, nor to determine matters of doctrine and faith. for looke all the stories of the bible, yet we shall not finde any proofe, where these inferiour colleges of iudges did either make lawes, or disanull them, or appoint priests and Leuites their offices & charges, or did determine matters of religion, or excommunicate any person.

The iudges *Exod.18, deut. 16*, not translated into the church. *Ruth. Deut.17.*

The whole history of the gouernment of the *Iewish* church, doth testifie against the presbytery; insomuch that *Bertram* (that indeuoured what he could, to proue this authority to be in the *Iewish* presbyteries)

teries) hath brought nothing to purpose, but his owne conceit; which is no more to be esteemed then one mans opinion, without reason, and against so many reasons as before are alleged. But this deuise of translation shall then appeare a plaine fiction, when we haue shewed that the new consistory hath neither authority from *Christ*, nor testimony of *Christ* his apostles: which discourse now foloweth in course.

Of Consistories, and their vsurpation.

Chap. 7. Sect. 3.

Therein is declared that the new consistory hath neither authority from Christ, *nor testimonie from the writings or practise of his apostles: First, for that* Christ *neuer gaue name, nor commission to any such gouernours. Secondly, for that the words,* Matth. 18, *are contrary to the proceedings of the consistory. Thirdly, because in the apostles writings there is no steppe, nor practise of it: for the apostles neither commended the same, nor reprehended it, nor mentioned it. Fourthly, for that the consistory is no where reckoned among the ministeries of the Church. Lastly, for that the authority which the consistory claimeth was by commission of* Christ *and his apostles, practised by others, and otherwise. The obiection of the word* πρεσβυτέριον, 1. Tim. 4. *is answered.*

C*Hrist Iesus* sending his ambassadors into the world, 1
gaue them the title of apostles, and furnished them with power and authority. If then it had beene his pleasure likewise to institute another office to gouerne his Church, beside that of his apostles, why did he not name it? why did he not tell vs what maner of consistory it should be? why did he not furnish the same with a sufficient commission, and authority? That our Sauiour *Christ* did not so much as name this presbytery, nor declare of what parts it consisted, nor in what matters it was to exercise iurisdiction, nor what power or authority it had; be plaine arguments that *Christ* did neuer appoint any such office.

That *Christ* neither gaue name nor commision to the consistory.

Adde heereunto that the words and law whereupon the consi- 2
story should be built, are no where to be found. The words, *Tell the Church*, that commonly are alleged, are neither proper to the consistory, nor sufficient for the authority which it claimeth, as in part hath beene shewed, and may further appeare by this. First, for that our Sauiour maketh no distinction of ciuill and ecclesiasticall iniuries, but in all causes of offence and iniury, would haue this proceeding vsed, which he there prescribeth: but the consistory pretendeth onely to deale in ecclesiasticall causes.

The words whereby the consistory is pretended to be erected, proue no such matter.

Secondly, the authority which is heere deliuered to the Church, is to proceed vpon complaint onely; for here are degrees mentioned, which who ſo contemneth, obſerueth not *Chriſtes* rule : and therfore where the conſiſtory proceedeth without denũtiation, or cõplaint of others,& admonitiõ before witneſſes,it proceedeth without warrant.

Thirdly, all the iuriſdiction, which by this rule the conſiſtory can claime,is to proceed in priuate offences. for the words are not, If thy brother offend againſt the church : but if he offend againſt thee. and the Church and priuate men are manifeſtly diſtinguiſhed, for the Church is iudge : he that is offended, is party, which who ſo confoundeth, he maketh the ſame perſon iudge and party.

Fourthly, the words of our Sauiour, are not, if a man offend the church,let one of the conſiſtory admoniſh him; & in caſe he reforme not himſelfe, let him be brought to the conſiſtory, & ſo to be excommunicate if he heare not the conſiſtory, as they moſt ſhamefully and abſurdly wreſt the words of our Sauior : But,if thy brother offend againſt *thee*, then tell *thou* him betweene him and *thee*, and ſo before witneſſes,and then before the church,and laſt of all,account *thou* him as a publicane and heathen.

Fiftly,the words are not,if a man offend againſt the church:but if a man offend or do iniury to *thee* : and therefore thoſe that reaſon *à maiore*, that if in priuate offences matters come before the church, much more in publike ſcandals;they make a conſiſtory of their owne reaſon,and not of *Chriſtes* inſtitution.

6 If we expoũd the words, if thy brother offend thee γενικῶς,or generally,if a brother offend the church;thẽ wil it folow that the church muſt complaine before another church, & ſo at laſt bring the matter to a third church, which is an abſurd interpretation and proceeding.

7 Of this expoſition it will folow,that publike ſcandals are not to be brought before the church. for if he that offendeth repent,then is the church to proceed no further. for the church is only to take notice where the partie contemneth admonition,before two or three.

8 Whoſoeuer by the church vnderſtandeth others then the Apoſtles, doth take power of exommunication from them,which our ſauiour giueth to them in the words,Whatſoeuer ye ſhall binde,&c.

9 Our ſauior *Chriſt* doth ſpeake of ſuch offences wherin the party may refuſe to heare the church without penalty inflicted by the church : but no man may contemne the conſiſtory in ſuch cauſes wherein they deale, and therfore the conſiſtory can claime no power by theſe words ; firſt for that the church hath here no authority ; ſecondly,for that the conſiſtory is not the church.

10 The

10 The ſentence is not pronounced by the church,in theſe words of our Sauiour : but by ſome other diſtinguiſhed from the church. and therfore if the conſiſtory claime by theſe words,they ſhut themſelues out from power to giue ſentence.

11 Laſtly,if the conſiſtory doth claime to be the church, and that their ſentence is *Chriſts* ſentence,then doth there lie no appeale from the conſiſtory : and whatſoeuer they ſay, that muſt ſtand as if *Chriſt* had ſaid it; which is moſt abſurd : and they themſelues will not chalenge (I hope) that authority, ſeeing they permit ſometime an appeale from the conſiſtory to the ſynode,and ſo forward.

But who can beleue that *Chriſt* meant to inſtitute a conſiſtory,whē 3
in all his precepts there is no mention of it, nor in all his doings any example of it?no not in the apoſtles time is there found either mention or practiſe of it. The apoſtle *Paul* doth mention πρεσβυτέριον or eldership; but the ſame is of another forme & quality then the presbytery they ſeeke for. the ſame doth ſignify either the function of prieſthood, or a number of miniſters of the word, not by law bound together,but vpon occaſion meeting; conſiſting of apoſtles,& (as may be coniectured) their felow helpers that had power to do extraordinary & miraculous works. The new presbytery admitteth no apoſtles,nor ſuperior degree of miniſters of the word into ẏ conſiſtory: the makers of the conſiſtory adde elders, and ſome of them adde deacons ; theſe they ioyne in one college,& giue thē authority not to do matters extraordinarily, but to deale in the outward gouernment of the church, & that with ordinary power. If the preſent presbyteries do claime to be of that making,they muſt firſt work miracles: for *Timothy* had the power of the holy ghoſt giuē him by impoſition of that presbyteries hands. ſecōdly they muſt only admit biſhops to be of their conſiſtories,and exclude elders : for the holy ſcriptures call none elders of the church,but miniſters of the word; and therfore *Chryſoſtome* interpreteth the elderſhip biſhops. laſtly, they muſt haue no ſet nor ſtanding conſiſtories, but all miniſters of the word (meeting together) muſt execute matters belonging to gouernment. The euangeliſt likewiſe, *Act.22*,vſeth the word πρεσβυτέριον,but it ſignifieth the elders or gouernors of the *Iewiſh* ſtate. wherfore,ſeeing they can not ſhew any college of elders ioined by *Chriſts* order,no not of miniſters of the word; it is ſimplicity to imagine (as they do) a presbytery,or college of miniſters, doctors, elders,and deacons in euery pariſh.

1.*Tim.*4.

That *presbyterium* 1.*Tim.*4. is not meant of their conſiſtory.

That there was none in the apoſtles time,theſe reaſons declare:firſt that the apoſtles did preſcribe no orders vnto thē, nor giue them any

No conſiſtory in the apoſtles times.

instructions: which they would haue done, if any had bene, and not haue directed their epistles to particular men, for the gouernment of the whole Church. Secondly, if matters had bene amisse, as in the Church of the *Corinthians* and *Galathians*, they would haue reprehended the consistory. Thirdly, they would haue commended them for obseruing their orders. Lastly, they would at the least haue made mention of this society of elders. for who euer writ the story of the Church, or made report of the proceedings of a state, that neuer named nor mentioned the assemblies of the gouernours?

4 Nay, where the roll of the ministers names is set downe, the consistory is not once mentioned. In the epistle to the *Ephesians* we finde apostles, prophets, euagelists, pastours and doctours. In the epistle to the *Corinthians*, apostles, prophets, teachers, power of miracles, gifts of healing, helpes, gouernances, and diuersity of tongues are mentioned; yet in neither place is there any appearance of a consistorie. if they suppose that it is contained vnder pastours, they abuse themselues. Things which are giuen (as the Lawyers say) distributiuely, can not be exercised of all collectiuely. Both the magistrate and ministery is of God: yet that magistrates and ministers should gouerne together in a college, is not commanded. They can not holde that consistory is one office with pastours, without great confusion: so the consistory should teach and minister the sacraments: so one man might haue iurisdiction ouer himselfe, as the consistorie hath ouer the pastor: then need not we to haue elders. That gouernances, and the word doctours helpe not to maintaine the consistorie, hath bene shewed.

Where the ministery of the Church is reckoned vp, no consistory is mentioned.

5 Finally, seeing *Christ* gaue all that authority which the consistory claimeth, to his disciples, when he gaue the keyes vnto them and their successours, and committed his flocke vnto them to be fed and gouerned; it is a most sencelesse imagination, to thinke that in the apostles times the eldership consisting of pastours, doctours and elders, did gouerne the Church. The apostles prescribed lawes and orders, which they thought conuenient to be obserued. by their authority lawes were likewise disanulled, as is euident in the decree concerning the ceremoniall lawes. The apostles and fellow helpers and bishops, appoynted pastours; as is euident in *Paul*, *Barnabas*, *Timothie*, and *Titus*. The apostles exercised the censures, as appeareth in the excommunication of the incestuous *Corinthian*, of *Alexander*, and *Hymeneus*, and in the authority giuen to *Titus*. they likewise determined matters of controuersie, as appeareth in the iudiciall

All that power which the consistory claimeth, exercised by others in the apostles times.

1.*Cor.*5.
1.*Tim.*1.

iudiciall cognition of *Timothie* in hearing of accusations without parcialitie or preiudice. although they dare say much more then they can proue: yet I thinke the disciplinarians will not say that the Consistorie did practise this authoritie in the time of the Apostles. If they say it, they haue the whole course of the holy stories against them, and not one witnesse for them.

Of the Consistories and their vsurpation.

Chap. 7. Sect. 4.

That the Consistorie hath no testimonie of antiquitie, is shewed. First, for that there is no record found of the names or actes of Consistoriall gouernours. Secondly, for that wee finde no Consistorie, either commended for good gouernment or discommended for the contrary. Thirdly, for that the name πρεσβυτέριον, or Eldership, among the fathers did onely signifie the ministers of the word, and no where is taken for a Colledge of pastors, Church aldermen, or deacons. Lastly, for that the iurisdiction supposed to be in Elders, was in those times practised by the godly magistrates or bishops. the places that make shewe for the Eldership, are answered.

That there is no rule nor practise of the Consistorie found in scriptures, maketh a presumption sufficient to proue, that the same is not to be found in the ancient Church following the Apostles times. for it is not likely, that the voyce of the Apostles yet sounding in the eares of the fathers, that they would presently so generally digresse from the precepts of so diuine teachers.

The Consistorie hath no testimonie of antiquitie.

1 That it was not afterward vsed, these reasons may perswade vs, First, for that in Ecclesiasticall stories wee finde no mention of their names, no record of their actes, no report of their liues: which is a thing incredible, if the presbyteries (as the disciplinarians giue out) had bene gouernours of the Church,

2 For those stirres & contentions that happened in the Church, we finde them not blamed, as those that either suffred them or mooued them: we finde not any eldership commended for any gouernment. if any thing happened contrary, it was imputed to the misgouernment of princes and bishops: if by good gouernment the Church florished, the same was ascribed to the bountie of princes, and godlinesse, and wisedome of bishops.

3 The name which they giue vnto their Consistorie, is otherwise vsed of ancient writers then they vse it. the presbyterie mentioned by *Ignatius*, signifieth the whole companie of inferiour pa-

ſtors, ſubiect to the biſhop. τί δὲ πρεσβυτέριον, ἀλλ' ἢ σύστημα ἱερὸν σύμβουλοι καὶ συνεδρευ-
Ad Trallen. ταὶ τοῦ ἐπισκόπου: what is the presbyterie but a holy companie of councellors and aſſiſtants to the biſhop? *Cyprian* likewiſe taketh it for the number of prieſtes ſubiect to the biſhop. but neither of them (as the diſciplinarians) doe accompt the biſhop one of the number, as is eui-
Lib.3.epiſt.11. ter epiſt.Cypr. dent by the place of *Cornelius* his epiſtles. *placuit contrahi Presbyterium* (ſaith *Cornelius*) *Affuerunt etiam epiſcopi quinque*. I thought it good to call the prieſtes together, there were alſo fiue biſhops preſent. neither doe they accompt any of the presbyterie, but thoſe that had the order of prieſthood, and both taught and miniſtred the ſacraments.
Lib.1.epiſt.3. *Cyprian* calleth the presbyterie *Sacerdotum Collegium*, that is, a Colledge of prieſtes. *Ignatius* calleth them ἱερεῖς and ἀρχιερεῖς that is, prieſtes and chiefe prieſtes. they make them ſubiect, not fellowes with the bi-
Can.Apoſt. ſhop. they were both choſen and depoſed by biſhops. Afterward *presbyterium* was taken not for the perſons, but for the order of prieſthood. ſo *Irenæus* taketh it, and ſo *Cyprian*. If they can ſhew me where in all the ancient fathers *presbyterium* is taken for a companie of lay Elders, doctors & deacons, or vnteaching elders onely ioyned to the biſhop; I will acknowledge their presbyterie to be ancient. If they cannot, let them frankely confeſſe that their presbyterie hath his antiquitie from *Geneua* vnder a popular ſtate: and approbation from men deſirous of nouelties.

4 For who can accompt that more ancient, of which we doe not finde any mention or iuriſdiction before that time? nay, al that power and iuriſdiction which they giue to their Conſiſtorie, we ſee that hiſtories doe giue, either to princes or to godly biſhops. the emperors called councels, confirmed and authoriſed the actes. biſhops they in councels ſet downe orders & made conſtitutions, and diſſolued ſuch as they thought not conuenient. in matters of controuerſie the emperours either iudged themſelues, as in *Athanaſius* cauſe *Conſtantine*, or committed the ſame to others, as the ſame emperour did in *Cecili-*
Can.Apoſtolor. *ans* cauſe. the biſhops ordeined prieſtes, the ſame depoſed them:
Conc.Nicen. they iudged of matters of faith and hereſie. *præpoſiti ſingula diſpone-*
Lib.3.epiſt.5. *bant* (ſaith *Cyprian*) that is, the biſhops or gouernours diſpoſed all matters, they executed the cenſures againſt heretikes, & ſchiſmatikes.
Lib.1.epiſt.3. Excommunication is called by *Cyprian* the cenſure of prieſtes, *ſacerdotalis cenſura*. If ſo be the diſciplinarians will haue the teſtimonie of antiquitie, let them leaue babbling about matters from the purpoſe, and proue that their Conſiſtorie of paſtors, doctors, elders & deacons, did make lawes and diſanull them, ordeine miniſters, or depoſe them,

iudge

iudge of matters,of maners,and of religion,and vse the censures. otherwise we must thinke that all these conceites are some obscure dreame, that hath of late passed through the iuorie dore, through which (as *Homer* saith) no trueth passeth. Let them(I say)proue that either in the Apostles times, or in the times following, there was in euery,nay in any congregation a Colledge of pastors, doctors, elders not teaching, and deacons, or any two of these, and that they had that power which they assigne vnto them in making lawes, iurisdiction, censures, election and deposition; or els they must knowe that all antiquitie deposeth against them.

They alledge diuers authours mentioning Elders. but if they will prooue any thing to their purpose, they must shewe, First that these elders were not priestes and ministers of the word: Secondly, that they were conioyned in a Colledge, and did things *tanquan vniuersi,non tanquam singuli.* that is,as a Colledge,not seuerally. Thirdly, that pastors, doctors, elders,deacons made one Colledge. Fourthly, that this Colledge gouerned the Church with supreme authoritie: and then we will imbrace their presbyteries with heartie affection, otherwise, the same doth bring such a sequele of inconueniences with it, that he deserueth not the name of a good subiect that will seeke it or desire it. Some of which inconueniences in this place, I haue thought good to gather into one summe: for the infinite particulars cannot be conceiued nor gathered, but by too late lamentable experience, and set downe in great bookes.

Of the Consistories and their vsurpation.

Chap. 7. Sect. 5.

Wherein is declared, that the Consistoriall gouernment ouerthroweth her Maiesties supreme authoritie, and prerogatiue in causes Ecclesiasticall: First, in denying her to be aboue all persons within her realme, and making her subiect to their excommunication and lawes: Secondly, in taking away her right of calling Synodes, so that none is called but by her commandement, and right to make Ecclesiasticall lawes or orders. Thirdly, in denying her right to appoynt Ecclesiasticall commissioners. Fourthly, in denying her the last appeale in Ecclesiasticall causes. Fiftly, in taking away her right of patronage paramont, and nomination of bishoppes. Sixtly, in taking away tenthes, and first fruites, and subsidies, and custodie of bishops temporalities. Lastly, denying her right to moderate rigour of Ecclesiasticall lawes: all which they giue to their Consistories. their excuses and gloses are taken away. Further, the Consistoriall gouernment is declared to be preiudiciall to her Maiesties reuenues. Secondly, to the Parliament. Thirdly, to the liberties of her subiects. Fourthly, to the statutes and lawes of the land. Fiftly, to the Queenes courtes of iustice. Sixtly, tw the Vniuersities. Seuenthly, to the whole commons.

The Consistorie ouerthroweth the Queenes supremacie in Ecclesiasticall causes.

FIrst it ouerthroweth her maiesties supreme and royall gouernment in Ecclesiasticall causes by Gods lawe due, and by act of Parliament vnited to the crowne, and by generall consent of the realme (vnlesse the disciplinarians repine & repugne) giuen to her royall Maiestie. for all those poyntes wherein the same supreme autority consisteth, by the disciplinariās are denied to ỳ prince, and giuen for ỳ most part to the Consistorie or some limmes of their Consistorie or new congregations, or to their Classies and Synodes.

*Eliz.*1.

The statutes that set downe her supremacie in Ecclesiasticall gouernment, first giueth her authoritie ouer all persons, and declare her not to be subiect to the controlment or iurisdiction either of foreiner or subiect. The disciplinarians denie that she hath authoritie ouer the Consistorie in Ecclesiasticall causes, and declare her to be subiect to their Elders iurisdiction, and excommunication.

Eccl. discip. W. Tr. T. C.

This of late was practised in Northamptonshire, whence the late Synodicall decrees proceeded.

Secondly, the statutes giue vnto her Maiestie authoritie to call Synodes, so that none can assemble but by her appoyntment: and to confirme Ecclesiasticall lawes made by Synodes, so that none shall haue autoritie of lawe without her confirmation and allowance. they giue power to their pastors and elders to assemble when they thinke good, and thinke that without iniurie they may not be restrained. and whatsoeuer lawes Ecclesiasticall the prince maketh, they accompt them voyde and of no force. but their owne lawes made by their Synodes, or Consistories, they say binde all men, yea, the soueraigne magistrate to whom they giue no power but to execute their lawes, as long as they proceede according to Gods word, of which they make themselues Iudges.

Thirdly, the lawes and statutes giue vnto the prince authoritie to appoynt Ecclesiasticall commissioners for reformation of Ecclesiasticall disorders: they denie that any may be appoynted Iudges, but their Synodes, Conferences, Consistories, and exclaime against her commissioners.

Fourthly, the statutes giue vnto her Maiestie right of last appeale, or right to redresse all wrōngs offred to her subiects in Ecclesiasticall courtes, and to appoynt delegates to doe the same: the disciplinarians denie that there lyeth any appeale from their Synodes or Consistories to any prince in the world. for they take themselues to sit in Christes tribunall seate.

Fiftly, the lawes giue vnto her Maiestie the nomination of bishops, and some other dignities electiue in the Church : the custodie of

bishops

Bishops temporalties during the vacation: and patronage paramont, or right to present by last lapse. the platformers giue away the election of all Church officers to their Consistories, and people: they take away all patronages, and would (if they could bring in their lawe *Agraria*) deuide the liuings among their Elders and Deacons, whom they appoint the paymasters of their pastors.

The lawes giue vnto her maiestie first fruites, and tenths, out of the Ecclesiasticall liuings: and subsidies, and contributions of Ecclesiasticall persons: these account them to be sacrilege and robberie, take them from her handes, and assigne them to the disposition of their politike Consistorie. *Ecclesiasticall discipl.*

Lastlie, the statutes giue vnto her maiestie, power to release the rigour of some generall Ecclesiasticall lawe, for some speciall consideration: these disciplinarians doe condemne all dispensations, and licences, and account the same Antichristian in others, howsoeuer they fauour it in themselues.

The penaltie of the lawe they respect not, that it is high treason: and because the state of supremacie was made (as they conceiue) against papistes; they thinke it concerneth not them, although they offend together with papistes in equall degree. but let them not abuse themselues any longer, and recall their opinions in time, for they impugne as ye see, the princes supremacie directlie, and deserue not to be accounted (as they terme themselues) simple minded traytors, but simple witted, and peruerslie conceited feytors, for dissoluing the sinewes of her maiesties gouernement, most happie and quiet, if their importune, and blundring stirres had not troubled, and steined the same.

To cleare themselues of this accusation, they turne and transforme themselues and their wordes into diuers shapes, and deuise diuers excuses. yet the wisest of thẽ haue thought best to let the matter alone, least the more it is stirred, the more it would anoy them. one of the most simple of the companie (though in his owne conceite no small doctor) he standeth vp, and forsooth would smoothe all the matter with a fewe faire wordes. but his defence is most naked and simple, and sheweth him (beside his dangerous opinions of the supremacie) to haue no great iudgement in diuinitie. first, he alledgeth the opinions of others, as if companie rather then iustice should cleare them. these men he nameth, were nouseled vp in a popular state, and therefore no maruel, if they neither knew, nor acknowledged the right of kings, and princes. what is that to these men that are subiectes Defence against Br. slanders.

to a prince, whose authoritie they disclaime with more vehemencie then the other?

Secondlie he alledgeth certaine glauering speaches of their owne, which reach no further then to giue her maiestie power in ciuill causes. their new communion booke giueth the Queene authoritie ouer all causes: but in all Ecclesiastical causes, he wil not say. By *Dud.Fen.* diuinitie, allowed and commended by *Th.Cartw.* it is lawfull for certaine *Ephori* or inferiour magistrats to depose the prince. and all that knowe the controuersie betwixt vs and the disciplinarians, doe vnderstand, that they deny those poynts of the princes supremacie that I haue set downe. I haue not wrested (I doe protest) their sayings, neither will they (I thinke) denie their opinions. iudge then I praye you, when these are their opinions and sayings, what wise men they are that thinke, that their owne deposition can cleare them in their owne case.

Lib.5.

Thirdlie, they alledge the wordes of the statute most ridiculously, and make themselues iudge, what is lawfull, what vnlawfull. because the statute giueth to her maiestie no authoritie but lawfull: for that they in their owne opinion, thinke the poyntes of her supreme authoritie to be vnlawful, they suppose, that it is sufficient, to excuse them. but they are not aware, that the statutes account all that which they giue to her maiestie lawfull. and to take away all colour, when they will defend the contrarie, we will God willing proue, that the same is lawfull by the word of God: and that most vnlawfullie (to set vp a popular gouernement neuer heard of,) they impugne that lawfull authoritie, which the lawes of God and the realme giue to princes.

4 Like wise men, they alledge certeine speaches out of Bishop *Iewel* of reuerend memorie his booke, and somewhat out of maister *Bilsons booke*, who learnedlie defend the princes authoritie against the Pope: as if it were like that they should colour the disloyaltie of those that impugne the princes authoritie. but they can haue no defence in those mens writings. for all those poyntes of the princes supremacie, which the disciplinarians doe denie, they mainteine. a man may see what wisdome was in the author of that defence; who, because he saw seene and allowed, imagined that the same was to be holden for the publike faith of the Church of England, seeing many trifling bookes, as *Raynold the foxe*, and such like, haue the same, which signifie nothing, but that there is nothing against the state in those bookes, and that they may lawfullie be sold without forfeite, and that they are no libels, such as most of the platformers are, which are therefore iustlie condemned

condemned and disallowed.

Wherefore so long as they make the prince subiect to their Consistoriall gouernement: Secondly, to their excommunications, and say that they haue power to giue the prince to Satan : and thirdlie, giue power to their consistories and Synodes to make lawes, without anie calling or authoritie from the prince: and fourthlie to decide all matters of manners and faith, and denie her power to appoint graue godlie & wise men, iudges & reformers of Ecclesiastical disorders, and to receaue appeales frō all Ecclesiastical courtes within her realme: and fiftlie, take away her right of patronage paramont, and to nominate Bishops: and sixtlie, to enioy first fruites, tenthes, and subsidies: and lastlie, to dispense in certaine cases of lawe: so long these excuses are friuolous and ridiculous. let them yet denie these opinions wherewith I charge them, and I will for my part, hold them for reasonable loyall subiects.

In taking away first fruits, tenths, & subsidies, & contributiōs of the Ecclesiasticall state from the prince, howsoeuer they meane to mainteine more Ministers, it is apparant that they meane to abate a good third part of the princes reuenues. which they doe with that boldnes, that they go not about to excuse it. nay, proudelie they say, that the prince ought to lay off her hands of that sacriledge. and *Th.Cart.* would haue the stipend of Ministers without charge. the disposing of the Church goods, they giue without question to Deacons, a kinde of birdes as yet vnfledge: but if once they might couer themselues with the fethers of the Church, they would soare aboue Elders, as experience of former times may teach vs. therefore let them hereafter blush to commend their plats to the prince, whose reuenues they dissolue, and leaue her open to the enemie in these dangerous times: or to the parliament, seeing they take away one of the estates of parliament, and refuse the iudgement of the parliament, which they giue to a conuenticle of marchants, artificers, and husband-men, guided by a youth oft times, without wisdome, learning, or experience. and let all indifferent men iudge, what subiects these are, that challenge immunitie of their goods, as did the papists, and take away so notable reuenues from the crowne.

The Consistoriall gouernement abateth her maiesties reuenues.

W.Tr.

2.reply.

The gouernemēnt of the Consistorie it taketh away the authoritie from the parliament in making Ecclesiasticall lawes; it dissolueth the three estates, and taketh away bishops. finallie, it maketh their lawes and proceedings subiect to the controlment of their Synodes and Consistorie. For whatsoeuer they in their propheticall (as they

The same incountreth with the authoritie of parliament.

terme it) or rather phantasticall iudgement shall thinke contrarie to the lawes of their discipline, that they presumptuouslie take vpon them to censure and disanull.

The same is preiudicial to the liberties of her subiects.

Most proudelie the same marcheth vpon the liberties and priuiledges of her maiesties subiectes, and with one worde vndoeth that, which with so much labour and blood hath bene purchased. by the lawes of *Magna Carta*, no subiect ought to loose life, member, libertie, landes, or goodes, but by iudgement of his peeres, and according to the lawes of the realme: but he that is excommunicate by the consistorie, is in danger to loose his countrie, his lands, his goods, & libertie; yea, is not allowed common succour of appellation to the prince, & no way to recouer ẏ same, but by throwing himself downe, & submitting himselfe to their censures, & susteining what shame & vilenie they shall impose vpon him. to the prince they giue no appeale, nay, they make him their seruant & Minister to apprehend and punish those that wil not obey. they allow an appeale to the synode, but the same doth seldome meete, & the partie shal still stand excommunicate, & some of the same that did excommunicate them, shall be their iudges in the second instance. lawes they haue none to direct them: but are ruled as they pretend, by their collectiõs out of *S. Pauls* Epistles, which some expound one way, some another way, some diuers wayes. by this meanes they haue made kinges & princes stoupe where they rule, & against poore men do what they list. for that *Iohn Morelly*, disputed in a certeine treatise, that the wordes *tell the Church* belonged not to the Consistorie, &c. his booke was burnt, & the man excommunicate. two Ministers at *Geneua*, were deposed & banished for speaking against vsurie allowed in that state. another was glad to flie, for speaking against vnleauened bread. and it is said that *Th. Cart.* at *Middleburg*, would haue excõmunicated a certaine marchant, that dealt sharpelie with his prentise a brother, that had defrauded him of great summes. excommunications flie out vpon euerie light grudge, among them. compare the Ecclesiastical proceedings of this realme with them, you shal see nothing more reasonable. for no man may be condemned or excommunicate, but where the lawe sayeth, he shalbe condemned or excommunicate. nothing more papall & vnreasonable, then their consistorial iudgements, for if they say, that anie man offendeth against discipline or conscience, it is sufficient, although there be no lawe. Wherefore, if lawe be a king (as the heathen poet saith) & wil a tyrant; & if that gouernement be best that leaueth least to mens discretion: then let all those that esteeme their libertie, looke how

Ordonances of Geneua doe imprison, and after banish him that will not stand to the Consistories order. *Art.91.*

Pindar.

Arist. Rhetor.

how they refuse a quiet gouernement, to submit their necks vnder the tyrannical yoke of the lordings of the Consistory, that rule all by wil.

If this Consistoriall gouernement be receiued; with our liberties, we loose also a great part of our lawes, and those not of least moment, but euen the fundamental lawes whereon our state standeth. the vnion of the three estates of parliament is first dissolued: her maiesties supreme power in Ecclesiasticall gouernement remoued: the liberties of *Magna Carta* empayred: away goeth a great part of the statutes & lawes concerning her maiesties reuenues, concerning the custodie of Bishops lands & temporalities & eschetes during the vacation, concerning presentations by lapse, nominations to bishopricks, *Conge des lire*, concerning premunire against Ecclesiasticall persons that encroch vpon her iurisdiction, concerning dispensations, conuocations, and synodes, heresie, and matter of Religion, the statute concerning articles of Religion & subscription, and the age of the Ministers, shall be abolished. for they meane to make vs a new forme of Religion, & to adde a parte of the gospel, which they call their discipline, & deny and exclaime against subscription, saue to their discipline, whereunto they will haue men, both to subscribe *and sweare*. the statute of fish dayes must depart: for it is contrarie to the platformers dyet, that are no Friday men, & hold more of flesh then fish. the statute of first fruits & tenths, & all statutes concerning subsidies of the clergie, haue their congé: for the propheticall sentence of the disciplinarians hath determined these to be vnlawful exactions. all statutes & lawes concerning assurances, & limitations of leases of landes of bishops, & cathedrall Churches, and Ecclesiasticall persons, shall haue no great vse: for the Deacons & Elders make a vante, that they will discharge all those matters themselues. all statutes & lawes concerning the dissolution of Abbeies, nunries, chantries, colledges, & concerning obites, lampes, lightes, likewise concerning the fruites of spirituall liuings during the vacation, shall cease; for that the lordes of the Consistorie haue otherwise determined of these matters. the statutes for collections to be made for reliefe of the poore, and the offices of iustices of peace in that behalfe are to expire; for that they hold this to be a part of the Deacons office, which (they say) is profaned in these mens hands. all statutes & lawes concerning benefices, aduousons, tythes, vnions, & appropriations, preaching and administring the Sacramẽts, and vniformitie of common prayer, likewise of excommunication for fighting in Church & Church-yarde, and other causes, for *non residencie*, purgation, mortuaries, probates of willes, executors, admini-

The fundamentall lawes of the land dissolued by the entrance of the Consistorie, and diuers other lawes withall.

Ordon. de Ge. Art. 14.

strations, mariages, sequestrations, dilapidations, citations, appeales, bastardie, incontinencie, vsurie, must be repealed, or rather annihilated: likewise all statutes and lawes concerning ordinaries or incumbents, or *quare impedit*, or *quod non permittat*, and generallie whatsoeuer concerneth Ecclesiasticall iurisdiction, or anie Ecclesiasticall matter or proceeding, must cease: for they meane to assume all these thinges into their holie handes, and purpose partlie for the ease of students to make a short booke of statutes, and for ease of the Queenes courtes, to decide these matters by the worde of God.

The common lawes abbridged by the platformers, and repealed.

Neither may the common lawes thinke to goe free in this general reformation. all writs to the Bishop, as that of *quare impedit, quare non admisit*, of Bastardie, and marriage in an action of dower, of right of aduouson: all writs of prohibition & consultation and the rest, must giue place and depart, together with Bishops themselues. the writ *de comburendo hæreticum*, must henceforth come out of the fierie and zelous Consistorie. to make a summe of all, so much in all other writs as concerneth either the persons, lands, or liberties, and all pleas, answers, replies, reioynders, which are proper and vsuall in these cases, the platformers (to remedie he tediousnes of the studie of lawes) dash out with their penne. so that as *Gnato* sayde to *Parmeno*, they may say to the common lawyers, *Ego te otiosum hoc triduo reddam*: for thirtie yeeres after wee will prouide, that the common lawyers may goe play. the students of lawe that knowe the rules of this newe discipline, can tel what other laws & statutes by the same are shaken, and dissolued. these came to view at the first search, in the bookes of assises, and termes, there is no leafe, but it susteineth some losse, neither is their priuiledge anie warrant for them. if then that bee true which is said comonly: κακὸν εὖ κείμενον μὴ κινεῖν, that is, stirre not euerie matter that is once setled for euerie inconuenience: what reason haue the Iudges and gouernors of this land, to suffer so lightlie those that would take away the good lawes of this land, being men that vnderstand neither gouernement, lawe, nor scarse common reason? They purpose (hauing dissolued most of the lawes of the land) to concurre with the Queenes courts of Kings bench, & Common pleas Chancherie needeth not, for they erect a Chancerie in euerie parish. all matters of treason, felony, & trespasse (wherin there is breach of Gods lawe) they meane to examine likewise before their consistorie: yea if the Iudge do not right, he must answere before them. of which, who doth not see a world of cōtention, confusion, & slander, that wil arise?

The Queenes courtes of iustice dissolued or crossed by the presbyteries.

Presbyteriall plats preiudi-

Where they teach, that a Doctor ought to be placed in euery parish to informe the youth, and others that are to succeede in the Ministerie, they goe about to make an vniuersitie of euerie parish: but their deuise is like that mans fancie, that imagined he could drinke vp the sea. for where are rewards for so manie doctors? where are so manie learned men to be found? beside that, it is impossible to doe it in all, it is vnprofitable to attempt it in some, & direct against the priuiledges of the vniuersitie, which permitteth not artes to be read in the countrie. and good reason. for by studying in corners, manie melancholike modelmakers, and church-coblers may be made, but not one sound diuine: for schollers profite by mutuall conference, disputation, exercise, mutuall emulation & example, as much as by hearing and reading. but those helpes they lose that teach in corners. There is but small hope, that they would make learned men, or semblant that they meane any such matter, whẽ taking away the liuings of the clergie, and hope of rewarde from the leraned, they turne men vp to liue vpon pensions, and to stand to the courtesie of vnlittered Elders & Deacons; that thinke crusts too good for learned men. then which no greater heartburning can be to men of learning, & qualitie. what man that considereth this course, will send his sonnes to the vniuersitie, where hauing spent their patrimonie in learning, they shall returne home to liue vpon a thinne pension vnder the lordlie dominion of marchants, clounes, and artisans, and so continue a beggerlie life, vntil hunger hooke them out of the world, where they shall leaue a poore wife, and manie poore orphans, to begge for their liuing? I do not a little maruel, that anie that are learned should fauour this gouernement: but I see there are alwayes some malcontents that hope to rise vpon the ruines of others: and when they are out of hope to attaine that they iudge themselues worthie of, would take all away from other that be in deede worthie. This gouernement, it is also, and will be the decay of the Ministerie. we see it alreadie in the Churches that be about vs: those that hope for the spoyle will not see it. learned men are prouoked by reward, by honor, by priuiledges. if the Ministers haue rewarde taken away, & liue in contempt, and be made the abiects of the people: few men of learning or qualitie, will enter that function. God worketh not now as in the Apostles times: he taketh not men from their nets & toll table, to teach in the Church. neither is it his will that they should gnaw their fingers, but liue vpon the altar: nor that they should liue in contempt, but in reputation. they that thinke otherwise, let them for euer bee drudges of their consistoriall Elders: but wise men, let them take heede that they driue not the wise and learned out of the Ministerie, and let those that be in the Ministerie take heede, they be not beaten with their owne roddes.

ciall to learning, and the Vniuersities.

The cõsistories ouerthrow the Ministerie in diminishing the rewardes of learning.

The trouble and innouation that is like to follow of the receiuing of the platformes.

Neither is this deuise the wracke of the Ministerie onelie, but a faire passage to further trouble, and innouation. for if the Ministers of the worde (which are a calling most lawfull and necessarie, and haue warrant for their maintenance out of the word of God, against whose spoyles the prophet speaketh *Mal.3.*) cannot keepe their landes and liuings, but they must be made a spoyle of seditious and factious Martinists, which hauing spent their owne, vnder pretence of Religion, gape for the spoyles of others: let noble men and gentlemen, that haue farre greater possessions & honors consider, how they can keepe their estate & liuings, from these greedie gulfes. there are manie texts in scriptures against such as ioyne house to house, land to land, and manie strong proofes against oppression, couetousnes, and pride, and such like faultes sometimes reigning in great men, which must come vnder the censures of the consistorie. *Cartw.* teacheth, that wee ought to haue the same communitie that was in the Apostles times, at least so farre forth, that no man want. so that if the spoyle of the Church now, will not satisfie their Elders and Deacons, and the poore, that is, such as are of the factious brethren: they that haue possessions, must either come to further reckoning, or out must excommunications flie. the poore must be prouided for, much more the Elders & Deacons; which (saith *Cartw.*) were commanded to be maintained, notwithstanding the great pouertie of the first Churches. these textes which the platformers vse against the titles and liuings of Ministers, the *Anabaptists* vsed against their temporal Lords. admit they were vnaptlie applied, so are the same against the Ministers: but yet those wrought dangerous effectes in the heads of the multitude, and so they will againe, if the Consistorie (whose sentence they take to be the oracle of the holie ghost) doe but so expound them; the common sorte (as appeareth by the seditious actions of *Saturninus* and the *Gracchi*) are easilie moued to embrace a new diuision of lands. if the Consistorie doe but misconstrue these places, downe must the nobilitie goe, vnlesse their sworde serue them better, then the worde hath serued the Ministerie.

The oppression of the commons likelie to follow the enterteinement of the new Consistories.

They of the common sort that yane after the spoyle of the Church, doe not consider the small gaine that shall redounde to them by it. they may see among their neighbours, but that they looke not so farre abrode. if they complaine of charge now, when the Church beareth a great parte; they would cry oh my backe, if they were put to beare the whole. and yet no remedie: for the countrie must bee defended against the enemie, although all their liuing went to it.

The mule that would not relieue his felowe (that fainted) of parte

of

of his burden (as the Apologue telleth vs) was driuen to cary the whole, and his fellowes skinne too, in the end. they that haue knowledge can applie it.

They that haue lands or leases of bishops or cathedrall churches, if they change lords, they shall perceiue what difference there is betwixt them and their newe lordings, whose consciences will digest yron, if once they be well inflamed.

What confusion will insue in mens euidences and titles, when the Consistorie shall haue made a new diuision of parishes, and what difficulties will arise about the boundes of mens lands, and in the limits of the commons, it is easie to iudge: when as nowe that parishes are exactly deuided, there ariseth vsually about such matters, no small contention. But it is no marueile if they that haue passed the ancient boundes of scriptures and fathers, and care for no termes nor orders, but their owne fancie, litle esteeme the bounds of lands and right of mens inheritance. yet wise men that knowe what belongeth to gouernment, will haue care of it.

Confusion likely to ensue in mens titles and euidences where this gouernment is embraced.

To conclude, what are we to looke for in this newe gouernment which is not directed nor restreined, put forward nor backeward by lawes, but a meere confusion? the gouernors of the church & men of learning, are most shamefully railed at, & trode vnder foot: the cõmon sort abandoning their trades, intrude into the gouernment, & from the butchers stall or tailers shop-board ascend to the highest tribunal in the church: & from the tribunall of Excõmunication, returne to the mattocke, the spade, or their thatching ladder. Children in yeres entituled doctors, pastors & elders, shal dispose matters of religion & state. Sixe or seuen clownes or artisans shall be iudges of faith. for *T.C.* taketh them to be the church. will shall rule, & not law. men shalbe driuen from their countrie by the malice of wicked men: & euery thing shalbe ordered by fauour and pluralitie of voyces, without regard of vertue, iustice or merits. all which disorders notwithstanding, yet they threaten, & that not with small words, that they will haue their consistorie, or els it shal come in by a meanes that wil make al our hearts to ake, which I confesse if any such matter should euer come to passe, to be in part true. For what Christian heart would not ake, and whom would it not grieue, to see religion, iustice, lawes, and mens liberties trode vnder foote and ouerthrowen by these Consistoriall deuices? but wise men will foresee the seditious attempts of mal-contents, and godly gouernors will mainteine the cause of religion and the state, which vnder the pretence of religion, is vndermined.

Confusion of state wrought by this newe gouernment.

 Of

Of the Consistories and their vsurpation.

CHAP. 7. SECT. 6.

Wherein the imperfections of their platformes about their Consistories, are declared: First, in that they are not resolued vpon the partes, nor the president, nor his authoritie: and Secondly haue not set downe the age nor qualities of Consistoriall gouernours, nor the proceedings of the Consistorie, nor incountred finally with many inconueniences, which may prooue the ruine of their discipline, and hinderance of the Gospell.

The strange imperfections of their deuices concerning the Consistorie.

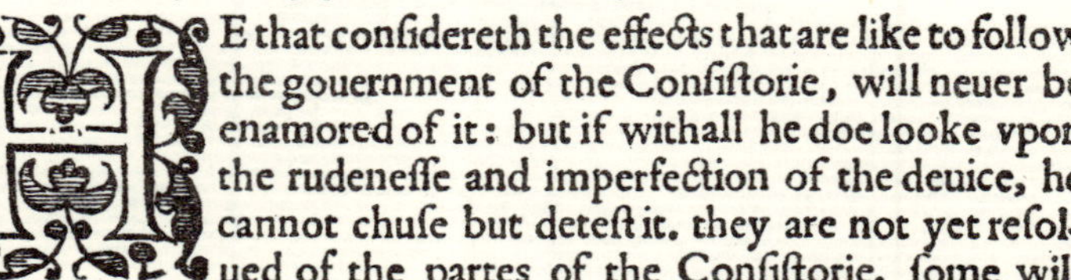

HE that considereth the effects that are like to follow the gouernment of the Consistorie, will neuer be enamored of it: but if withall he doe looke vpon the rudenesse and imperfection of the deuice, he cannot chuse but detest it. they are not yet resolued of the partes of the Consistorie. some will haue deacons, some will not haue deacons: some will haue doctors, others thinke them an ornament or rather conuenient for their Consistorie, but yet esteeme them not necessary. Concerning the president of the Consistorie, there is no small difference amongst them. some will haue the pastor of the parish to be president, for that pastors are called προϊστάμενοι: others will haue any chosen by the companie to moderate. *Caluin* alloweth a magistrate to be president. some will haue him chosen but for one action, others for a certaine terme. How a Constorie that is to be chosen by the voyces, at least by consent of the multitude, may be established, where most of the companie is suspect for religion, or vnwilling to haue it among them, they cannot shewe. what title a pastor that dwelleth in another parish hath to meddle in other Churches, as to ordeine with the elders a pastor, vnlesse they make him either an archbishop, or an euangelist, or an intruder, they know not. How a lord that is chosen of the Consistorie together with his tenants, may be restrained, that he ouerrule them not at his pleasure, it is a hard matter to set downe. Likewise to restraine the tenants that they excōmunicate not their lord if he take excessiue fines or rentes, or iniuriously put them from their fermes.

Sum. cap. disc. Gen. inter epist. Cal.

These questions following are not yet resolued: of what yeeres he must be that is called an elder, for to make a yong man of 18. or 19. yeeres an elder, hath some repugnance in nature and Grammer. likewise whether there be any precedence in the same order, or betwixt diuers orders, as betwixt pastor and elder, or doctor and pastor, or elder or deacon: and whether the president refusing to propound a matter, another may do it: or whether they may displace the president without cause, or with cause. we are in some paine to learne, whether the

the Consistorie may proceede contrary to the lawes of England, if they deeme them repugnant to their discipline. & whether a prohibition being serued vpon their elderships, they meane to proceede that notwithstanding. and (because it were good that things were done orderly) whether those that dissent only, or all the eldership is to be attached when they refuse to obey the prohibition: whether they may not censure the Iudges of England, if they prohibite the Consistorie to proceede in a lawfull cause. and whether they allowe the Iudges to determine matters concerning Church landes or goods, or whether they meane to trie these causes in the Consistorie.

It is likewise a matter of doubt: the consistorie determining against Gods word or iustice, whether their sentence may be called the sentence of Christ or the holy Ghost: or by what reason an appeale may be admitted to the Synode, seeing there is no appeale from Christ. and howe they can condemne the pride of popes, seeing they challenge to themselues this papall power, as if they were Christes vicars, and vndoubtedly possessed of Gods spirite, as directour of all their Consistoriall actions.

It were a matter worthy their consideration to shewe whether the Consistorie may punish one of another parish that offendeth with one of their parish, or censure the next Consistorie not doing their duetie: and to tell vs whether they may compell a man that sueth at the common law too rigorously to surcease his suites, and excommunicate him if he refuse. In what cases of mariages, testaments, pensions, and how farre the Consistorie may deale, they shewe not. they as yet haue set downe no rules how they meane to deale in censuring treasons, felonies, trespasses. for in all these cases they require publike satisfaction, yea notwithstanding the Queenes pardon.

Their rules concerning excommunication are yet vnperfect. they doe not tel vs what faultes are to be punished with excõmunication, what not. If drunkennesse, gluttonie, couetousnesse and such like (as some say) yet they doe not declare what is drunkennesse, nor what gluttonie, nor what couetousnesse. they declare not for what causes, nor in what sort they may excommunicate the Q. and Councell, nor whether the consistory consisting of 13. 7. may excõmunicat 6. they doe not declare in what sort they wil haue the magistrate to execute their sentence, whether vpon the parties body or goods, or both: what time ÿ party that is excõmunicat hath to reconcile himselfe before he incurre any losse, they declare not: what be the effects of excõmunication they sparely tel vs. whether it be exclusion *ab omni actu licito*, that is, a debarring from lawfull acts, or what, they dare not ſpeake out.

Concerning the maner and time of appeales interpoſed from the Conſiſtorie to the Synode, and the charges and the keeping of recordes, their diſcipline is yet in their heads. where they make the people acquainted with their excommunication, they doe not tell vs whether the people or greater part of them may reuerſe it, or what they may doe.

If they would perfect that which hath no forme, I woulde deſire them to declare what officers they meane to haue to publiſh their excommunication, in caſe it needeth publication. likewiſe who ſhall cite offenders to the Conſiſtorie (for it is nothing ſeemely that the elders ſhould be ſummoners alſo) againe to declare the forme of their aſſemblies, trials, proceedings, ſentences, and execution of ſentences: and laſtly, who ſhall write their actes, and ſuch like. which matters if they be not reſolued, will breede many quarrels.

All which particulars being not yet reſolued, nor ſcarce mentioned either of our platformers or the ordonances of *Geneua*, or the articles of *French* diſcipline: I ſay their diſcipline is *tanquam ſtatua in ligno* (as Logicians call it) that is, a worke perfect in conceite. Further, ſeeing they cannot reſolue theſe things out of the word of God: I conclude that their diſcipline both is borowed, and muſt be borowed other where then out of the word of God, and yet all imperfect too.

Wherefore conſidering that the Conſiſtorie is an office deuiſed by man without inſtitution, commendation, or precedent of Chriſt or his Apoſtles, not practiſed nor knowen of antiquitie, and that it diſſolueth ẏ orders left by Chriſt, & bringeth in a new forme of gouernment, preiudiciall to her Maieſties lawfull authoritie, the reuenues of the crowne, the eſtates of parliament, the liberties of the commons, the lawes of the realme, the courts of ciuill iuſtice, the priuiledges of the Vniuerſities, and vtterly ouerthroweth the Eccleſiaſticall ſtate, which hath lawfull authoritie from God, and without which the Church would come to confuſion: and further, ſeeing their plats and deuices concerning the ſame are ſo imperfect, that if all their braines were put together, they could not ſupply the wantes of it: although I ſay nothing, euery one may gather this concluſion, that the ſame with the autors of it is to be reiected & repelled. which may ſerue to all platformers, deformers, admonitours, libellours, and mal-content Church modellours, and diſcipline forgers for a full anſwere; to all moderate Chriſtians and ſubiectes for a ſufficient ſatisfaction in this controuerſie.

Of

Of Conferences, and the nouelties of them.

Chap. 8.

Wherein the causes, why conferences are to be refused, are set downe: First, for that there is no rule, nor Scripture for their institution. Secondly, no practise of them in the apostles time. Thirdly, no vse of them in the ancient Church. Fourthly, for that they inuade the iurisdiction belonging vnto the magistrate and ministers of the word. Fifily, for that the same is a confused gouernment. And lastly, contrary to their plats and rules. The same reasons that make against the consistories, make also against the conferences, and their imperfect platformes in that behalfe.

FOr that Synods do not often meete, and diuers causes require present helpe; therefore haue the disciplinarians deuised these conferences to supply the want of synods, and to take order for matters, that in consistories can not be determined. Whence the same hath his originall, by what authority the same commeth in, by what lawes the same is moderated, it is no maruell if we know not, seeing the authours of these deuises are ignorant of the same themselues: whereof few mention conferences, and those that mention them, are able to say litle of them.

The same we haue iust causes to refuse: and if they beleeue their 1
owne rules, themselues will not long vrge them. First, for that the Of the conferences, no institution of *Christ*:
same hath no originall from *Christ* or his apostles. They themselues say that those offices which *Christ* hath appoynted for the gouernment of his Church, are mentioned, *Ephes.4.* and *1.Cor. 12.28.* but there is no inkling nor signe of any conference. The pastours office will not serue to hide consistories, conferences, and synods. The apostles committed the charge of the church to their successours, the godly bishops: and so they appointed *Timothy* at *Ephesus*, *Titus* in *Crete*, *Epaphros* at *Colosse*, *Marke* at *Alexandria*, *Linus* at *Rome*, not so much as mentioning any conference.

Secondly, the practise of the apostles, which is reported in the 2
holy story of their acts, and to be gathered dispersedly out of their e- Nor practise of the apostles:
pistles, doth not allow, nor mention any such conferences. the whole story doth mention other gouernours.

Thirdly, there is no steppe of conferences found in antiquity. nay, 3
the same doth allow archbishops and bishops generally; which be- Nor of antiquity.
cause the disciplinarians will not seeme to need, they haue deuised these absurd conferences: absurd I iustly call them, that (of those that will seeme to frame all according to Scriptures) are deuised contrary to the institution of our Sauiour, his apostles, and all antiquity.

4 Fourthly, the ſame taketh away the lawfull authority, which the godly magiſtrate, and vnder him paſtours and biſhops, haue in the church of God, being the apoſtles ſucceſſours; and without authority vſurpeth power to chuſe paſtours, to depoſe them, and to compoſe matters, hauing no authority, nor preſident out of the word of God, or ancient hiſtories.

The authority of conferences ouerthroweth the paſtors & churches iuriſdiction.

The ſame bringeth in a confuſed popularity, odious to thoſe that
5 know the experience of it, ſuſpect to all thoſe that conſider it. for how is it poſſible that they ſhould agree, that know not what to do, nor how to doe it, nor by what authority they may doe it? and how can they atchieue, and compoſe matters, that by law haue no iuriſdiction, nor can ſhew any originall or preſident of their doings?

Conferences bring in confuſion.

They that deny archbiſhops power out of one pariſh, how can they allow inferior paſtours iuriſdiction in diuers pariſhes? how can they deny that which all antiquity affirmeth, and affirme that which all antiquity denieth, if they had reſpect what to affirme, and what to deny?

6 Laſtly, this conference doth ouerthrow moſt of their models and platformes: for if the conſiſtory hath power to chuſe their paſtour, and to determine all matters, or els the ſynode; then is the conference ſuperfluous, & hath no authority. If the conference be an officer, then is their rehearſall of offices imperfect; then is it lawfull for man to erect new officers; then hath not the conſiſtory and ſynode that iuriſdiction, which they giue vnto them, and ſay that *Chriſt* hath indowed them with the ſame.

Conferences can not ſtand with their own platformes.

All thoſe reaſons that are alleged againſt the conſiſtory, for the moſt part may be alleged againſt conferences. they are new. they inuade the iuriſdiction of other paſtours, and breake the limits of pariſhes. they bring in ſchiſme and diuiſion, when no man hath any certaine gouernor to controll him. they bring in confuſion, for no officer knoweth what to do. The parts of the body (to vſe their owne ſimilitude againſt them) do not keepe their office and ſtation. the conference leapeth into the ſeat of the ſynode, as if the ſhoulders ſhould aduance themſelues aboue the head. the ſame inuadeth the place of the conſiſtories, as if the elbowes ſhould ſettle themſelues about the heart. and euery part runneth out of ſquare.

The reaſons that haue bin alleged againſt the cōſiſtory, make againſt conferences.

Finally, their deuiſes concerning conferences, are imperfect. the parts are not preſcribed, nor the limits, nor the authority, nor the formes of their proceeding, and (which is moſt abſurd) theſe conferences, they are like a diſmembred body, without a head, and by conſequent,

consequent, without wit: and therfore we returne them to their first deuisours, to set downe order concerning their conferences; least while they thinke to set order, they bring all matters into disorder. These conferences are not much spoken of by our platformers, till of late, in their newest platforme; but I haue added them out of the *French* gouernment, that you may see when their discipline hath all her parts and members, that it is not as they make her, a faire woman seemely girt, but a misshapen body without forme or beauty, or any bond of wisdome or gouernment, to gird her or adorne her. *Cartw. L. Tom.*

Of their Synods, and their nouelties.

Chap. 9.

The forme of their new Synode is declared to be neither apostolicall nor ancient, and therefore to be reiected, especially being preiudiciall to the prince, to the people, to courts of iustice no lesse then their consistories: lastly, the proceeding is prooued to be contrary to their platformes, yea, most ridiculous, very imperfect, and defectiue.

He beginning of Synods, we confesse is ancient, & the vse necessary, that consent and vnity throughout prouinces and nations, may be preserued and maintained. and we mislike nothing more, then that diuers of the disciplinarians haue them not, as they of *Geneua:* and others haue but lately taken them vp. for the *Admonition* and *Th. Cartw.* (their champion) required them not at first. now he and certaine of his followers vpon better aduisement mention them, and seeme to allow them. and which deserueth most reproofe, in stead of a forme of ancient synods vsed in time past, they haue brought in a new deuice of their owne, which hath nothing of ancient synods, but the name and shadow: so that hoping to finde a great treasure, we haue encountered with nothing but a few char-coale.

This synode deserueth no credit: First, for that it hath no testimony of apostolicall times. The synode assembled at *Ierusalem*, consisted of apostles and elders, that were ministers of the word. These discussed and tried matters of faith: these met (as *S. Luke* saith) ἰδεῖν περὶ τούτου, that is, to consider of these matters. Deacons, and the people intromitted not, but submitted themselues. Now (as matters goe) our lay elders, doctours, and deacons, will haue deliberatiue and decisiue voyces, and will be two to one pastour in the Synodes. The people challengeth a consent, and these ouerule all. Bishops which succeede in lieu of the apostles, they haue not. This meeting *The new synods vnlike to apostolicall synods.*

 of

of the apostles was extraordinary, vpon occasion. these will make their synods, at least the prouinciall, to be ordinary and set courts.

Vnlike to ancient synods.

Secondly, the same is of a forme diuers from all ancient synods, and councels. The synodes of ancient time consisted of godly bishops, assembled by the princes commandement, and gouerned by the prince or his lieutenant. whose acts were confirmed and ratified also by godly princes. which is confirmed both by the councels of *Nice, Ephesus, Constantinople, Calcedon*, & diuers other, both generall and prouinciall councels. These late synods consist of certaine ministers, and merchants, and men of occupation: as for example, knitters of cappes, heelers of hose, and coblers of shooes, as if religion were to be patched and pieced together. who, if most voyces may cary away matters, will not sticke to sell away religion for a *sous*. These come together without princes commandement: they desire no ratification of king nor prince: they chuse a moderatour, such as themselues like: and talke not onely of ecclesiasticall, but politicall affayres, yea, take vpon them to rule kings and princes.

For he hath no authority, say they, in the church.

In Northhampton shire, a moderatour was chosen by the play, called *Primus, Secundus*.

New synods preiudiciall to the prince and state.

Thirdly, it is a matter preiudiciall to the prince and state, and contrary to the lawes of this realme. It is dangerous that multitudes should meet without the princes knowledge. and in this land no synode ought to be called without the princes writ. how dangerous it is our neighbors feele, and if God had not preuented some attempts of the disciplinarians, this church might haue rued. and how can it be but dangerous, when the synode may make lawes, and excommunicate princes, as they holde?

Preiudiciall to courts of iustice, and to the commons.

Fourthly, these new synods incroch vpon courts of iustice, with whom in all matters, wherein they pretend breach of Gods law or conscience, they meane to concurre. The same treadeth downe the liberties of subiects, who are bound to answere both before ciuill iudges, and before consistories and synods, and may not appeale to the prince. The same will be very chargeable for poore ministers, and troublesome: for twise a yeere they will haue prouinciall synods. so that those that speake against *non residence* so bitterly now, are content their pastours should be *non resident* twice in the yeere, perhaps three moneths together, and all litle enough, if all appeales from consistories and conferences be to be made to synods.

Fiftly, the proceeding of synods is most slow and tedious: for if an appeale lie from the consistory to the synode, from a prouinciall synode to a nationall; if a nationall synode meet but once in twentie yeres, when will the cause come to conclusion? especially when the

causes

causes of ten thousand consistories shall be appealed thither, whereof euery one will giue grieuances enough.

Sixtly, it is absurd to make a college of iudges consisting of so many, as all which can not iudge, and some can not heare. Of iudges painted without hands, I haue heard : but the president of iudges without eares, is but now found in the synods. Some will excuse this by sending deputies to the synods: but what commission they haue to chuse deputies of prouinces, I desire to know.

The iniurious proceeding of synods.

The proceeding of Synods is most iniurious : they that are iudges in the consistory, are iudges likewise in the synode prouinciall. While few acts or depositions are recorded in the consistory, how easily shal poore men be ouerborne by those, that contrary to law, are iudges and parties ? the party that is excommunicate in the consistory, is not absolued in the synode, til the cause receiue end. so that to saue charges, the best course is patiently to beare the first iniury.

Their proceeding in synods woulde be laughed at of the common sort.

How ridiculous will it be in the eyes of the common sort, for the highest iudges of the church to creepe out of some smoky alehouse, in that towne where the synode is assembled, and from thence to go on his feet, faire and softly home ? Is it not absurd that they that take vpon them to dismount princes, haue not allowance to maintaine one poore palfrey, on which they may mount themselues, when they go to synods ? How ridiculous is it for merchants that sell a farthing woorth of mustard, and tailers, & laborers that worke for sixe pence a day, to pronounce the highest sentence in the Church, and from the seat of iustice to steppe behinde their banke, and sell mustard and oatmeale ? Would it not be a parti-coloured religion, thinke you, that should be made by men of motly coats ? For this cause, the *French* discipline, better framed then our platformes, saith that the Church-aldermen may not giue deciding voyces in matters of religion.

Their rules concerning their synods are contrary to the rest of their platformes.

The same is contrary to their owne rules of discipline. for if the sentence of the consistory be the sentence of the Holy ghost, what hath the synode to do to reforme it ? If euery pastour be to rule within his parish, why do the synods crosse his gouernment ? If all church gouernours are to attend their owne flocke, what haue the synods to do with other mens flocks ? and if no man may haue rule of the ministers of a prouince, what hath the moderatour to do to put men to silence, and propound what and when he listeth in synods ? Thus while they refuse a setled gouernment, they fall from one absurdity into another, and euery day change opinions ; neuer resting vntill ſuch time as they returne to their wits, and in effect, returne to the orders of our church, and onely change names and termes, becauſe they would ſeeme to be the wiſeſt men of their liuery. Some there be that would borow their ſynods from the *Iewiſh* church; but that is the ruine of the ſynode. for of the eccleſiaſticall presbyteries of the *Iewes* we do not finde that any one general aſſembly was compounded as they haue framed of their conſiſtories, one ſynode. the high prieſt was alwayes chiefe miniſter, vnto whom they haue nothing anſwerable in their ſynods.

The ſynode not borowed frō the *Iewes.*

The gouernment of the ſynode, not being limited nor diſtinguiſhed from that which the conſiſtories & conferences chalenge, muſt needs prooue confuſed.

The ſynodical gouernment confuſed and imperfect.

To conclude, there are ſo many things in this gouernment not determined, that if nothing els were, yet it would be put backe for the manifolde wants and imperfections of it. If a moderatour of a ſynode may be choſen for a yeere, they can not ſhew why the office of archbiſhop is not lawfull, ſeeing there is no difference in the ſynode, but that the one is for the life; the other for one time, or a yere: and things ſimply vnlawfull, are not for an houre lawfull, vnleſſe they will allow a man to be leud for a ſpirt, ſo he be honeſt afterward.

They are not yet reſolued of the parts of their ſynode. ſome will haue deacons: ſome content themſelues with paſtours and elders: ſome will haue elders to ſpeake: others (as they in *France*) when matters come to deciſion, place the elders for cyphres in the ſynode, and will not haue them ſpeake, but heare what the paſtours will ſay.

How many ought to meet in euery ſynode, and at what times, and places, they haue not yet determined: neither doe we heare as yet, whether the multitude of euery pariſh (which ſome make a part of the ſynode, and will haue their conſent) may ſend deputies, or muſt go thither themſelues.

Lern. diſc. and all thoſe that will haue the conſent of the multitude.

Whether the acts of the ſynode be good, which are not confirmed by the people, and of what pariſh this people muſt be, and whether the people of one pariſh may confirme the acts made concerning other pariſhes, *Th. Cartw.* I truſt, will tell vs in his next new platforme: at what time it may pleaſe him to ſhew vs by what authority, and in what ſort they meane to alter the limits of pariſhes, and what limitation and diuiſion he will make of ſynods, and what ſynode it is that hath authority to proceed againſt the QVEENE and Councell, and other officers of her houſholde. for I truſt they will

will not make her subiect to the iurisdiction of euery consistory and synode prouinciall, as *W.T.* in his *Eccle. discipline* seemeth to meane.

They haue not yet declared vnto vs, the maner of proceeding of their synods, whether by citation, or arrest; nor whether they may excommunicate the whole consistory, or a whole towne or corporation, or whether they meane to examine witnesses, or to proceed only vpon confession, or in cases notorious. or who shall write & keepe the acts of the synode, and what the title of his office shall be. they shew not what expedition they meane to make of appeales: for if from the consistory to the conference, from that to the synode prouinciall an appeale may be made, and thence to a nationall; their causes will be spunne forth to a faire length. they can not shew by what law he that sate iudge in the first instance, should be iudge againe in the synode.

They do not set downe any rules, whereby those that are wronged in synods, may hope to haue redresse. Generally, they determine not by what lawes they meane to proceed; which is a great presumption against their synods. for if men be gouerned by lawes, beasts by their appetite; it will prooue a brutish proceeding, if there be no lawes prescribed.

Let them therefore set downe a forme, that we may know whether the synode may impose taxes for the mainteinance of their pastours, doctours, elders, deacons, or other necessities of the church; and whether it may reuerse the sentence of ciuill iudges, pronounced against good conscience, and whether they may compell the prince and her officers to execute their sentences and decrees, and by what writ.

Neither do they shew by what law a man may be imprisoned for speaking his minde in the synode: nor for what causes a man deserueth to be shut out of synods: which matters, by their silence, we deeme to be hard, and almost inextricable.

Wherfore, as we allow godly synods, of bishops and ministers of the word, assembled by the authority of the prince, and directed by lawes long approued: so we protest against, or rather detest their synods assembled without authority, and consisting of merchants, and men of occupation, which presumptuously take vpon them to patch and botch vp discipline. and we deny that any such is to be admitted, as wanting confirmation of Scripture and antiquity, and being preiudiciall to her Maiesties royall authority, and to the liberties of the people, and a deuice confused and imperfect.

Repetition of the argumēts against the new synods.

Of the Confirmation, consent, and authority of the people in matters of the Church.

CHAP. 10.

Whereas the platformers are still talking of the confirmation, consent, and authority of the people in Church causes, the same is heere prooued to be contrary to the word of God, the practise of the Iewes, *the vse of the Apostolike churches, their owne platformes, and all good gouernment. finally, combersome, chargeable, and imperfectly described.*

Ere it, thinke you, any maistery, to driue the disciplinarians into straits, that of themselues, when no man pursueth them, runne into so many absurdities and contradictions? it should seeme no, by their new conceits concerning the people. for although they had no cause to mention the people, making them no officers in their new Common-wealth; yet, as wanting memory and iudgement, they cast out words, which if they mainteine, the same is like to prooue, not onely a braue officer, but also the supreme gouernour in their new church discipline. and good reason they haue, that depend vpon the peoples applause and willes, some way or other to winne the peoples fauour.

Lern. disc. One of them saith, that a chiefe point for moderation of the elders authority, in such sort that their sentence may be the sentence of the church, is this, that when the consistory hath trauelled in examining of causes pertaining to ecclesiasticall discipline, and agreed what iudgement ought to passe vpon the matters, they propound it to the whole multitude, that it may be confirmed. and at *Geneua*, being a popular state, the people was made acquainted with their ordonances. *Ordon. de Geneu.*

Now if the last allowance and confirmation of sentences & iudgements, without which they are void, (as it should seeme) be a high point of of souereignty; and if he that confirmeth the sentence, hath authority aboue those that onely examine and giue counsell: then is the peoples iurisdiction and authority aboue the consistory, as the prince that confirmeth is aboue his councell that aduiseth what is to be confirmed. *Th. Cartw.* goeth one point of the compasse further, and saith that the people by *Christes* purchase and grant, hath right to giue voyce in the election of ministers (as hath bene before declared) which is another point of soueraignty consisting in the election of the chiefe officers of the Church. Others minse at the matter, and say the people must be present, and dare go no further for very shame. *Beza* in excommunication, thinketh it sufficient, if it be inflicted *Conscia multitudine*, the people knowing of it. yet in

Aduer. Erast.

in most matters at *Geneua*, the people knowe iust nothing, but in wonderment beholde the diuine sentences of the holy Consistorie. these therefore are but colours cast to shadow the deformitie of popular gouernment established by ỹ former opinions. for if the peoples presence at actes be required, and yet the same hath no power to allowe or disallow, but must perforce consent; then were it a bondage: if their presence be required to no purpose, then were it a mockerie. If they be required that their actes may receiue strength, then hath the people supreme authoritie. and so that saying taketh place, that wise men debate matters, and simple people determine. for hee that seeketh for iudgement, wisdome, discretion, constancie in the multitude, he rather imagineth what ought to be, then then what is like to bee. and therefore seeing beyond all reach of reason and authoritie, they would make not onely the assemblie of the learned, but her Maiestie and the states subiect to the controlment of the rude multitude in the gouernment of the Church: the autors are to be reputed witlesse, their platforme sencelesse.

λέγουσι μὲν σοφοὶ, κρίνουσι δ' ἀμαθεῖς

It is contrary to the word of God, that giueth the gouernment of the Church to the prince, & to godly bishops & pastors. the people is euery where commaunded to be obedient and subiect to the prince, *Rom.13. & Tit.3.* to their pastors and gouernors. *1.Pet.5.* the people though present in Synode *Act.15.* yet had no authoritie to confirme or giue voyce, but was there to receiue direction from their gouernours. otherwise that example had bene contrary to the former rule. The Apostle prescribeth orders to the *Corinthians* which were not receiued because of the peoples allowance, but by reason of his Apostolicall authoritie. the same giuing commaundements to *Timothie* and *Titus*, yet no where required either presence of the people or their allowance, or that *Timothie* or *Titus* shoulde doe things by the aduice or consent of the people: which if it had bene required, then would neither the Gospel nor order haue bene receiued.

The peoples supreme confirmation or consent in Church causes, is contrary to the word.

This proceeding is diuers from the practise of the people of God, and their gouernment. God gaue lawes by the ministerie of *Moses* for the gouernment of the Church established by his power, not receiued by popular suffrages. The Princes and Iudges appoynted officers. *Moses* consecrated *Aaron* and *Eleazar*, *Samuel* made his sonnes iudges. *Dauid* chose out of the most sufficient of the *Leuites* and made them Iudges and gouernours beyond *Iorden*: which example *Iehosaphat* tracing, appoynted iudges and officers throughout all *Iudah*. where the people confirmed the actes of princes, they

Contrary to practise of the *Iewes.*

 cannot

cannot shew.yet was the gouernment of that people somtime aristocraticall, and in the times of the *Maccabees* almost popular, and therefore not in all things to be followed.

Ioseph.

The confirmation or consent of the people not required in ancient Synods.

Thirdly it is direct against the orders of the primitiue Church.the Emperours confirmed & caused the acts of Synodes to be receiued: let the disciplinarians shewe where the actes of the *Nicene, Ephesine* or other Councell were confirmed by the people, nay where they were propounded to any such purpose. In the time of persecution, the bishops gouerned the Church as long as good order was obserued: if the people preuailed,it was by tumult and sedition.

The same contrarieth their rules of discipline.

Fourthly,the soueraigne power of popular confirmation of Ecclesiasticall acts, is contrary to their rules of discipline,which giueth soueraigne cognition & decision to the Synode,of which the people is no part: and placeth gouernment in the officers of the church,among which they spare the people no place.much standeth it them vpon to looke that the people encroch not too farre. if the people be vnderstood by the church,*Mat.18*.then is there no place for ye Consistorie, and *per consequens* away must doctors & elders go,*tanquam milites expuncti ex centuria*,as souldiers or rather as officers wiped out of ye rolle.

Confirmation of Ecclesiasticall matters is absurdly giuen to the multitude.

Fiftly,it is most absurd,and contrary to all good gouernment holy and prophane,olde & new, to giue the hearing of causes & last confirmation,or resort of iudgement,to the confused multitude. neither was it euer practised in the confused popular state of *Athens,Thebes, Megara*, or other common wealth. onely I reade that the people of *Gaunt* called forth *Iaques Dartuel*,and would haue the hearing of his accompts, & that the people of *London* would haue a reckoning of the *Stapeletons* in the dayes of *Edw*.the 2.but the same was a seditious & disorderly proceeding, & cost ye accomptants their liues.of which I doe not thinke that the disciplinarians will borowe any precedent.

The same is cumbersome.

6 The deuice is very cumbersome & inconuenient,if not impossible. for although the people of a Citie may assemble, yet hard it were to gather all the multitude of a shire: and were they assembled, they would not easilie agree,and peruersely would they iudge. if the deputies of parishes might serue, then is not the multitude required: if a part of the people were sufficient to confirme actes, then might one parish decide matters belonging to another,one countrie to another, as if we in *England* should decide matters perteining to the church of *France* or *Scotland*. of which it would followe,that pastors would be thrust vpon parishes without their consent,although *T.Cartw*. thinke contrary.

7 Howe

7

Popular confirmation chargeable.

Howe chargeable it would be we neede not caſt, ſith ſuch things cannot be: but if any ſuch thing ſhould be attempted, it would be chargeable for the countrey. For howe ſhould poore men liue, that forſaking their trades are ranging to Synods? how ſhould the ground be tilled, and domeſticall buſineſſe diſpatched? muſt both houſe and common wealth be diſſolued, that theſe new fancies may take place?

The ſame is dangerous.

It would further be dangerous. for ſuch a huge multitude as is required being aſſembled, is more likely to doe any thing then to reforme the Church. but ſure it would be very ridiculous, if the baſe ſort of the people leauing the ſhuttle, the plough & ſpade, and ſhopboard, ſhould buſie their heads in diſcuſſing of matters of religion, and gouernment. for I do not thinke but they muſt haue leaue to talke of ſuch matters as the diſciplinarians will haue them to confirme. the matter is ſo intricate, that the wiſeſt platformer cannot finde the endes of theſe knots. That which deceiueth them, is that they do not diſtinguiſh betwixt the chiefe of the people and the common ſort, that they eſteeme that the common ſort of our people, which is ſo rude and ignorant, is able to do that the people did in the firſt Churches, when for building of the Church, extraordinarie giftes were powred out vpon the people: and finally, for that they endeuour to bring our Church gouernment to that of *Geneua*, which is a popular ſtate, and popularly gouerned.

The imperfection of their plats concerning the autoritie that they giue to the people.

As yet the timber of this part of the platforme is very rough hewen, and not ſquared: they haue not ſet downe what number of people, & of what pariſhes wil ſerue to confirme the acts of a Synode. they haue not yet declared vnto vs whether the people can ſet order without the Synode or conſiſtorie. they haue not preſcribed by what rule the people aſſembling together ſhalbe gouerned: they will percaſe ſet that downe in ſpace. they cannot ſhew howe the people aſſembling in Synodes twiſe euery yeere, and weekely at Conſiſtories, their poore wiues & children ſhalbe maintained, while they are brabbling about idle queſtions, which they vnderſtand not. they are vncertaine whether moſt voyces, or the beſt ſhall ouerrule matters, *tanquam in centuriatis cõmitijs*. whether ſuch acts be voyd as be not confirmed by the people, they affirme nothing. they tell vs not to what purpoſe this aſſemblie or confirmation is made, if the acts be good otherwiſe: nor if any ſedition ariſe, who ſhall appeaſe it. for excommunication is no defence againſt drawen ſwordes. Infinite matters there are, which though not nowe thought vpon, yet will proue infinitely troubleſome, if they ſhonld come to execution. the more you consider the matters,more euidently you may see the confusion of their broken conceites. which notwithstanding, if they can not haue; they speake very bigge,and threaten broken pates. but for any consent that I can conceiue will be in the multitude, or any agreement that is in their platforms:I thinke they are more likely to breake one anothers pates.

When either thou hast more leasure to heare, or I to report the storie of their platforme, thou shalt heare more. in the meane while this is sufficient to giue thee a taste of the confusion and disorder, which they would worke by their new discipline.now let vs procede to speake of that wrong which they offer the Christian magistrate.

Of the godly magistrate, and his office in the gouernment of the Church.

Chap. II.

Wherein is declared what wrong the disciplinarians offer to the Christian magistrate, whom they shut out from all office of gouernment in the Church, and place last of all in their platformes, and behinde all their officers, whereas the highest gouernment of the Church is prooued to belong vnto him: First, for that to him it belongeth to set orders and Ecclesiasticall lawes: Secondly, for that he alwayes commanded and gaue speciall directions in those causes. Thirdly, for that he appoynted commissioners and officers for Church gouernment. Fourthly, for that he had the soueraigne iudgement and last appeale in Ecclesiasticall controuersies. Fiftly, for that he had right to dispose of Church goods. Sixtly, for that no Eldership did euer practise this, vnlesse it were by the kings commission, or were chiefe magistrates, as the Sanedrin *at* Ierusalem. *All this is prooued by the word of God, the histories of the* Iewes, *and practise of the ancient Church. Lastly, the reasons to the contrary are answered, and the generall discourse concluded.*

Hus you see the building and braue worke of discipline finished, and, as the disciplinarians conceiue, brought to perfection. their groundworke is layde vpon their fiue diuers officers the description and delineation of euery mans function and duetie doth answere, as it were to walles, sollars, and roofe. the people like a soueraigne commaunder, is placed in the toppe and ridge of this worke to ouerrule all, neere to the chimney, that they may be perfumed with some autoritie. The Christian magistrate,as a thing vnnecessarie, is scarce named & mentioned, and that after the distribution of all offices & bestowing of their blessings, & finishing of the worke. some leaue him out of their platformes:others place him for no great purpose, and lesse honour: for what honour can be in seruice? the charge they giue vnto him in their building, is no better

First newe Communion Booke.

better then the place of a common laborer, that beareth morter and stones to serue the Masons. they make him the executioner of their sentences and decrees, and place him as it were sentinell, to keepe watch without the Church, while the lordes of the Consistorie are within either discussing of matters, or sitting idle at the helme. a bare name of authoritie they giue vnto him, *viz.* to compell the Consistorie or synode to doe their dueties: but neither doe they giue him power to iudge, nor allowe him to intermeddle, so long as they say or thinke they doe their dueties. which power the papistes call *Potestatem facti*, or rather, seruice without power.

They say the Church was perfect in all her members, before there was anie Christian magistrate. others say, the Church florished most without him. so that after all their plats ended, they put the magistrates authoritie, as it were in the bottom of the leafe, conteining their last will for Ecclesiasticall gouernement. Which how soeuer other things hang together, doeth verie well agree with the rest of their deuise. for if the magistrate haue soueraigne iurisdiction in Ecclesiasticall causes: then hath not the Consistorie, nor Synode, nor people such prerogatiues as are pretended, and contrariwise. for nature admitteth neither two heads, nor two beginnings. Of the Consistoriall encrochments we haue heretofore discoursed. now we are to proue, that the soueraigne externall gouernement of the Church, doeth belong to the Christian magistrate, whome the disciplinarians most iniuriouslie wrong, and disloyallie impugne, when they giue it to their Consistories, Synodes, and to the people.

Ler.disc.

In ima cera.

The soueraigntie or chiefe gouernement in the Church, as it is here on earth, and externallie considered eyther wholie, or especiallie, doeth consist in making of lawes, and disanulling them; in commanding, and not being subiect to the commandement of others; in appointing the principall officers or gouernors, and in supreme iudgement. but these matters, as they belong to the prince: so they belong to no others, as appeareth both by the practise of the kings, and princes of the people of God, and by the histories of godlie Emperors.

*The lawes concerning the gouernement of the Church, were deliuered vnto the people of God by *Moses*. when the same was for certaine matters to be altered, king *Dauid* gaue orders and directions. the same authoritie was practised by *Salomon*. all thinges concerning the tabernacle, were appointed by the Ministerie of *Moses*.

*Ecclesiastic? lawes and orders alwayes were appointed by godlie princes and such as had authoritie vnder them.

 all

all orders concerning the temple, by *Salomon*. When the brasen serpent grewe offensiue, the same was broken downe by *Hezekiah*. there came no direction to priestes, much lesse to anie supposed consistories or Elderships.

If they say this power was extraordinarie; let them shewe against what order and what lawe or custome the same was vsed, and how that can be called extraordinarie, that God commaunded and allowed fromtime to time. let them shewe to whome the same belonged by order, or custome, and shew where the same is to be found.

The Christian Emperors both had, and exercised the same authoritie. *Constantine* gaue strength to the canons of the *Nicene councell*, concerning externall order. writing to the Bishops and people, he declareth, that the doctrine of *Arrius* is vtterlie to be remoued; and in an Epistle to ỹ Churches, decreeth that Easter is to be celebrated, according to the decree of the counsell. *Eusebius* doeth report of him, that by his labour, orders were obserued, and Ecclesiasticall matters compounded. the Emperors *Gratian*, *Valentinian*, and *Theodosius* made a lawe of the worship of the holie Trinitie, and of the Christian faith.

Socr.l.1.c.6.

Cod.de sum.tr. & fid.cath.l.1.

Iustinian propoundeth a forme of faith, which euerie one was to embrace: those that otherwise beleeued, he condemned for heretikes. diuers lawes of Emperors concerning faith & Sacraments, and the Ministerie, are set downe: *Cod.de sacros.Eccl. & Episcopal. audient.* the same power did *Charles* the great, & *Lewes* challenge & vse. neither before the tyrannie of Popes grew intollerable, did either Synodes meete, or publish their decrees without the Emperors authoritie, and confirmation. as for the new Consistories, and new Synodes, they were not then extant, and therefore no wisdome to enquire what they did.

Ansigisus.

Directions in causes Ecclesiasticall proceeded from princes. *Ios.3. & 4.*

Speciall directions and commandements concerning Church causes, proceeded from the soueraigne magistrate. *Moses* prescribed *Aaron* what he was to do, not contrarie. he prescribeth him his whole office. *Iosua* directed the priestes what they should doe, when they should moue the arke, and when they were to circumcise the children of *Israel*. when the *Reubenites*, and *Gadites* were to returne, he gaue commandement and instructions concerning the lawe. *Dauid* gathered the princes of *Israel* together, to take counsell for the bringing backe of the Arke. Both he and *Salomon* gaue commandement, and ordred, what the priestes were to doe in the seruice of the lord.

2.Sam.6.

Ezekiah

Ezekiah and *Iosiah*, restored things to their ancient order: and they commanded the priestes, and were not commanded by the priestes. *Iehosaphat* proclaimed a fast, and so did *Ezra*, who also at his returne, directed all things, both in the temple, and in the seruice of God. to say that this power was not ordinarie, is asmuch to say, as God doth things against his order, and that these kings did cõtrarie to Gods lawe. *2.Chron.20.*

The same authoritie was exercised by Christian Emperors: they appointed whẽ Bishops should meete, how they should proceede. *Constantine* gaue order for the building of churches, & copying out of Bibles. he gaue order to *Athanasius* & *Alexander*, for receiuing *Arrius* vpon his repentance. concerning Churches, Ministers, Sacraments, & faith, such orders as were deemed cõuenient, the Emperors apointed from time to time: as appeareth by the lawes of the Emperors, by the lawes of *Charles* the great, and *Lewes*, and diuers other godlie Emperors. wherein as it is euident, that godlie Emperors and princes commanded not Consistories (for there were none) but Bishops and priestes: so there is no apparance, where the Consistories commaunded Emperors and princes. the fact of *Ambrose* and of him that did excommunicate *Philip* the Emperor, cannot be applyed to Consistories. neither was that excommunication of theirs, anie iudiciall proceeding or iurisdiction; but denying the Sacraments to Emperors, which anie poore Minister might then doe, if there were notorious causes; nor doeth it appertaine to this question of iurisdiction. the same may be answered to the fact of *Azarias*. and this further. that it was a violent course, not to be practised by Consistories. sure it was no iudicial power, nor superior iurisdictiõ, which he exercised against the king, for it was done suddenlie, but such as anie priest might haue vsed, who is bound to declare to princes their duties, out of the word of God, although he haue no superior iurisdiction by the worde of God. but I trust the disciplinarians will not vrge these places anie longer for their Consistorie, which haue bene so often answered, being with more probabilitie alledged for the Pope, and yet proper for neither. That kings did command, and prescribe orders, & were not commanded by priestes or Elderships, these reasons beside the discourse of stories may assure vs.

Socr. lib. 1.

Co. de sum. tr.

Cod de sacr. &c. & Episc. audien.

Godlie kings prescribed Ecclesiasticall orders, and commanded, not being counter-manded.

First, for that the obseruation of the lawe of God was enioyned principallie to the magistrate. *Deut. 17. & Ios. 1.* and those lawes which concerne orders, and formes to be obserued, are committed and belong to him especiallie.

Secondlie, if the magistrate did not see it done, he was punished, as was euident in the example of *Heli* and *Saul*, and the idolatrous kings.

Thirdlie, if Religion and lawes florished, princes especiallie were blessed of God, and praysed of men: Ecclesiasticall Consistories we finde none. and priestes were not further charged to see the people walke in Gods lawes, then the teaching of it. where they were punished for the peoples transgressions, if they taught lawe, or were commended for the good order of the Church and common-wealth, wee see not.

Fourthlie, The prophets of God were not sent to the priestes, that they should see princes and people obserue Gods commandements: but they were sent to princes, that had power ouer priests and others. neither did that power cease vpon the publication of the Gospell. for Christ Iesus came not to dissolue the law, nor to abrogate the authoritie of princes. he sayeth, that what is due to *Cæsar*, is to be giuen to
Tit.3. him; and the Apostle willeth all men to be subiect to higher powers, and to honor the king. and the king is Gods minister, for the main-
Is.49. tenance of the Church. *Isai* doeth prophesie, that kings shalbe the foster fathers, and Queens the nursing mothers of the Church. which is not in executing the commandements of others, but in prescribing
August. de correct. Donatist. cap.13. what is conuenient. yea, although in the Apostles times, when the Emperors were heathen, the Apostles did gouerne the Church: yet had they no power to command princes, nor did they throw out their excommunications against them, but taught others to be subiect, and shewed it by their owne example.

Godlie princes appointed officers for gouernement of the Church.

Further, as princes themselues did gouerne; so they appointed vnder them gouernors for the direction of Ecclesiasticall causes, and remoued those that euill demeaned themselues in their gouernement.
1.Sam.8. *Samuel* apointed his sonnes iudges. *Dauid* of the *Leuits*, chose out fit
1.Chron.26. men for gouernement, & placed thẽ in the countrie beyond *Iordan*. *Iehosaphat* of the priests & Leuites, and chiefe of the families, consti-
Ezr.7. tuted a colledge of iudges at *Ierusalem*. *Ezra* by commission of the king of *Persia*, receiued power to appoint Iudges and officers according to his discretion, which was also likewise done of Christian Emperors in their times.

Euseb. de vit. Constant. *Constantine* appointed Iudges in the cause of *Cecilian*: likewise in the cause of *Athanasius*. and by their authoritie, Synodes were apointed,

ted, which iudged all matters of faith and Religion. where the presbyteries appointed Iudges or gouernors, they (God wot) can not shew: nay, the priestes had not that authoritie vnder the law. Godlie Bishops ordeined priestes in the Christian Church. but that is the ouerthrowe of the Consistoriall election, and concerneth not this question, which is concerning that part of gouernement that consisteth in electing and deposing gouernors, which I haue shewed to belong to Christian princes. *Salomon* displaced *Abiathar*, placed *Zadok*. *Theodosius* and *Valentinian* made a decree, that those that sauored of the impietie of *Nestorius*, should be deposed. and *Constantine* threatneth to depose those bishops that should neglect his commandement. *Si quis &c, recuset ad concilium aduentare, hinc à nobis aliquis mittetur, qui eum regio mandato de dignitate sua deijciat*. If anie &c. doe refuse to come to the councell, wee will send one, that shall depose him from his dignitie by our royal commaunpement. he writeth to the Bishops that were to assemble at *Tyre*. *Iustinian* is commended, for that hee deposed *Syluerius* and *Vigilius*. but where anie Consistorie deposed, or did chuse anie gouernor of the Church, the place is not yet founde. what boldnes then is it, to take from princes that power which they haue alwayes had, and to giue it to those, of which we haue heard but late newes, and are assured they neuer had that authoritie in ancient time?

Cod. de sum. tr. & fid. cath.

Theodoret. lib. 1. c. 29. Eccle. hist.

Mart. Polon.

Resteth now the supreme iudgement in Ecclesiasticall controuersies. wherein, as princes haue iudged of Bishops, and priestes: so it cannot bee shewed, that princes were iudged and deposed by them. *Salomon* iudged of *Abiathar*. the cause of *Ieremie* was heard of the princes. difficult causes were reserued to *Moses*, and consequentlie, to all princes that succeeded him. he that appointeth the hiest iudge, hath power aboue him, as did *Iehosaphat*. *2. Chron. 29.*

Princes iudges in Ecclesiasticall causes.

Ierem. 26.

Exod. 18.

Giue iudgement to the king.

Cecilian and *Athanasius* being wronged, appealed to *Constantine*. and therefore most lawfull is that authoritie of soueraigne iurisdiction, which is vnited to the crowne, and disloyallie and absurdlie translated to these new Elders, that of late are sprong vp in ẏ Church, and haue inuaded the princes authoritie. that which they alledge of the soueraigne iudgement of the priest, *Deut. 17.* maketh nothing for the new Eldershippe, nor against the prince. for that authoritie was subordinate vnder the prince, as appeareth in that *Iehosaphat* appointed the Priest to iudge, and gaue him directions; and in that the keeping of the lawe was inioyned to the prince, not to the

2. Chron. 19.

1. King. 2.

the high priest. and lastlie, for that some princes haue deposed, and iudged the high Priest; but no priest euer iudged the prince.

Disposing of Church goods to whome it belongeth.

The disposing of Church goodes, and nominations to bishopricks depend vpon the princes authoritie, in prescribing orders & nominating officers of the Church: and therefore is lawfull, if the other bee. howsoeuer it is, they cannot say so much for their consistories, and therefore fewe wordes are best, where no reason nor authoritie helpeth their cause.

Answere to their obiections against the princes authoritie in causes Ecclesiasticall.

They obiect against the prince, that hee is an humane ordinance. as if the Ministerie, as Ministers are chosen by men, are not likewise humane: and as if the prince, as his authoritie is of God, were not deuine: and so much surpassing the Consistorie, for that it is no diuine constitution, nor long since inuented by man.

They saye further, that magistrates are not named among the officers in the Church, which is not true: for both in gouernances *1.Cor. 12.* and in the honour due to the king, and in the subiection which euerie one is commanded to yeelde vnto princes, the same is set forth. neither may we thinke, that Christ dissolued the gouernement of states. Finallie, seeing the scriptures giue him publike iurisdiction and authoritie, and commandement in the Church, and they themselues giue him power ouer all causes: by what title hath he the same, if he be no officer of the Church? For eyther hee must be an officer, or an vsurper.

Tit.3.

1.Pet.2.

Rom. 13.

Yet *Saul* say they, is reprehended for sacrificing, and *Vzziah* for burning incense: as if there were no difference betwixt gouernement, and the priests office, which no man might vndertake, but they that were of the stocke of *Leui.* but gouernement was common to princes, and necessarilie enioyned them.

Seeing therefore they impugne the princes authoritie, let them henceforth make no bragges of their loyaltie, and true seruice. it cannot stand with the ouerthrowe of the princes Ecclesiasticall authoritie. and seeing their contention for their Consistoriall iurisdiction, is such an absurd and strange deuise; let them giue it no more such extrauagant titles. as there cannot be too sunnes, the one shining at noone, the other at midnight, nor two heads of one bodie: so there cannot bee two supreme iurisdictions in one state, the one not depending of another. For if the one commaunde, the other forbid; whome should we obey, if both be equall?

The Consisto-

This gouernement as hath bene shewed, ouerthroweth the princes

ces supremacie in Ecclesiasticall causes, and leaueth little in ciuill causes. for who dare obey the prince that is giuen to Satan, vnlesse hee feare not that hee shall be deliuered vp to Satan for companie? It is most absurd, that the prince should be cited, appeare, and be examined, and in the ende condemned by a sorte of clownes or marchants: his garde in the meane while had neede to be bound to the peace.

riall gouernement aboue the prince absurde.

Wherefore, considering as it were at one view, the nouelties, absurdities, contradictions, inconueniences, imperfections, & impossibilities of their deuises: it may seeme strange, that they durst obtrude the same, not to the multitude onelie, who may easilie bee abused, but to her maiestie & counsel also, who looketh more deepelie into matters. but seeing they haue intitled ye same the lords discipline, a marke of the Church, a part of the Gospel, the eternall counsell of God, & haue forced and racked the scriptures to serue their purpose: I wonder the lesse that they haue abused men, that haue so shamefullie abused the holy worde of God. the papists they commend vnto vs certeine traditions as the word of God, yet ingenuouslie and plainelie, they tell vs they are not written: their traditions of discipline these men would haue vs beleeue that they are written in the worde, and yet neither can they proue them, nor we finde them.

T.C.

These things I haue, as you may see, layd open before you, not to stirre, but I hope to end contention: for what is he, that can contend against the trueth, if once he see it? my onelie desire and prayer to God is, that it will please him to open the eyes of the blinde, and to remoue all preiudicate opinions, that seeing the trueth, we may embrace it: and considering the preiudice that mutual contentions haue wrought, we may detest them, and with one onsent and minde, glorifie God the author of peace, and trueth, and all felicitie; whose name eternallie be praysed, Amen.

Of the contrarietie of their *discipline.*

CHAP. 12.

Wherein is declared, that their owne generall rules drawen from the kingdome and faithfulnes of Christ, from the perfection of scripture, authoritie of the calling of the Ministerie: and that their assertions, wherein they compare their discipline to the tabernacle and temple of God, and make the same a marke of the Church, and parte of the Gospel, and prescribed in the worde of God, vtterlie ouerthrow their doctors, their Elders, profane deacons, or rather col-

lectors, their widowes, their Consistories, conferences, and synodes, the authoritie of the people, their confusion of pastors, and their whole discipline: for that the same to the worldes end can neuer be proued to be drawen out of Gods worde, or to answere those rules.

Ere not the nature of man verie desirous of nouelties; and beside the common affection of all, were not some singularly (as *Thucydides* sayeth) δοῦλοι ἀτόπων, ὑπερόπται ἀληθινῶν. that is, seruilely addicted to strange opinions, and proudelie disdeining trueth commonlie knowen: it could not be, that so many refusing a gouernement so agreeable to the worde of God, so approued of antiquitie, so conformable to the lawes of the realme, should like of new platformes contrariant to the worde, neuer knowen of antiquitie, and moreouer, which dissolue the gouernement and lawes of this land, and hazard the state of the Gospell, and are onelie supported by faction, and blowen vp with a windie stile of vaine wordes of fantasticall persons: as I haue shewed in all the particulars of the same, by reasons vndoubtedlie true. will it please you to consider now, how their owne rules doe ouerthrowe their owne deuises.

Their reasons drawen from Christes kingdome make against themselues.

They haue told vs, that in respect Christ is called a king, and is said to bee more faithfull in his house, then was *Moses*: that he hath prescribed a certaine forme of lawes for the gouernment of the Church, which none is to change nor to alter, nor to forsake or refuse. this engin they bend against the forme of our gouernement. the same maketh against their platformes ẏ were neuer deuised by Christ, nor haue testimonie of the word. their officers and offices are all new, as hath bin shewed. if they thinke otherwise, let thẽ in schooles or writing defend or prooue their distinction and office of Doctors, their confused equalitie of pastors, their Elders, and their commission to make lawes, to chuse officers, to iudge of faith and manners, to vse the censures: let them shewe their Consistories, conferences, Synodes, and their iurisdiction out of Gods worde, or answere my reasons, directlie shewing the contrarie. To winne credit vnto their discipline, they discourse vnto vs full soberlie, and demurelie, that Christ Iesus concerning the outward policie of the Church, is a lawe giuer, as was *Moses*, and that wee ought in externall matters of the Church to bee ruled by no other lawes, then such as he hath appointed. a matter (as I saide before) strange, and which confoundeth

Christes

Christes offices,and destroyeth the nature of faith, and taketh away Christian libertie. but of that we shall haue more occasion to speake particularly in another place. here it shall suffice to shewe howe this position ouerthroweth all their platformes, their Synodicall decrees, their freewill sentences giuen without lawe by most voyces: for that themselues confesse in part, and I doubt not but to prooue throughout, that they are none of Christes lawes, nor came from him nor sauour of Christs wisdome and very sawcie they should be if Christ were the lawgiuer,for all matters of externall Church policie, to take vpon them to adde,to diminish, and to alter his lawes, and to arrogate to the Consistorie and Synode power to make other newe lawes.

They tell vs that the scriptures doe teach vs euery good way. the same maketh against their discipline. for not being found in scriptures by their owne confession, it will be proued no good way : and being no good way, how can it be found in scriptures?

They make the common sort beleeue, that no discipline is to be receiued into the Church, but the word of God. the same doctrine ouerthroweth the Canons of *Geneua*,the articles of discipline of the *French* Churches, their owne models, which may not without great boldnesse be matched with the word,or affirmed to haue bene found in the word. I would make him blush that durst in Schooles defend it. Let *Tho,Cartw.* as he hath boldly affirmed it,proue it if he can, or defend it publikely if he dare.

Against the Archbishop they alledge that no officer or office is to be receiued or tollerated in the Church, but such as Christ hath instituted.the which as it maketh nothing against him,which as archbishop hath no authoritie but to moderate Synodes and to receiue appeales made to him from inferiour courtes within his prouince : so the same ouerthroweth the commission and office of doctors, the president of Consistories,Elders,Consistories,Conferences, & their forme of Synode.

To call in question the iurisdiction of Archbishops, they affirme that no man is to take vpon him an office but hee that is called,as was *Aaron*:but they are not aware,that the same position shreddeth away the wilde autoritie of doctors,elders,consistorie,conferences,& their absurd and irregular Synodes, which (as enemies in an assault enter the breach) would steale into the Church through the ruines thereof.

They abuse the similitude of the temple, and tabernacle, to prooue that euery thing ought to bee done in the Church according to the prescript of Gods word: yet in their platformes performe nothing lesse. for they are more like the confusion of *Babylon*, then the temple of God. This I haue shewed throughout this discourse.

T.C.and T.Bez. They boast that the discipline of the Church, is as wel conmanded in the word, as the doctrine, and that it is the eternall councell of God: but this their discipline is no where commanded nor conteined, nor inferred out of the word of God, and is no part of Gods counsel; and therefore likely by their owne positions, to proue some base and peruerse discipline, and not the true discipline of the Lord, as they gloriously vaunt, coldly prooue, peruersly beleeue.

T. C. They say further, that discipline is a part of the Gospel, and to be beleeued as the articles of our Creed: but this discipline of theirs is no where to be found, neither in nor out of the Gospel, nor any where beleeued, nor to be beleeued: and therefore this forme which they prescribe vnto vs, not true discipline, but some fond deuice & dreame, fondly matched with the Gospel, and the word of God.

They tell vs, that no man dealt in the ministration of Sacrifices, nor in the Temple, but such as had a lawfull calling: but these put the keyes of excommunication in the handes of their prophane aldermen, nay of the multitude to whom they giue power of confirmation of matters, and make men deuoyd of iudgement and learning, Iudges, Controllers, Censurers, electors, and deposers, and gouernours of the Church, which haue neither calling nor authoritie thereunto: and therefore rashly violate the boundes of their calling.

In the limitation of their offices, they make very faire and large discourses, yet doe they not distinguish the office of Elders from the Consistorie: nor the office of Consistorie from the Conference: nor the Conference from Synodes: and absurdly inuest these with the office of the pastor, and make a gallimaufrey of offices. which albeit might be tollerated in the base sort of the clamorous disciplinarians: yet me thinke *Thom. Cartw.* that maketh such a shewe of learning, should haue reformed.

They say that the substance of discipline (which consisteth, if we beleeue them in officers and offices) is not to be changed. yet in some Churches there is but one Consistorie: in some no doctors, in others no deacons, and none haue widowes. Some haue no Conferences nor Synodes. and the iurisdiction is diuersly giuen and deuided. some denie gouernment to deacons, some to doctors: others giue the same iurisdiction to Consistories, Conferences, Synodes, which marreth all their discipline. some make Christes lawes part

of

of discipline: others omit the same, and admit none, vnlesse it be the Church Canons of *Geneua.*

To prooue their officers, they alledge *Ephe.4.* and *1.Cor.12.* yet neither doe we finde Elders nor Deacons, nor widowes, nor Consistories, nor Conferences, nor Synodes: in any of those places: nor hath the people any supremacy giuen vnto it in those places or otherwhere.

It were infinite to prosecute all those rules which they alledge, yet are direct against them by these you may esteeme the rest, and easily iudge what cause they defend, that is beaten downe with their owne weapons. but for that some of their principles require larger discourse: I haue thought it not amisse to examine some of their chiefe groundes particularly. and first this, whether the gouernment of Christes Church be alwayes one and the same.

Of the alteration of Church gouernment.

Chap. 13.

Wherein is proued that there is not alwayes one forme of gouernment of the Church to be obserued. First, for that the officers and gouernours of the Church are often changed: Secondly, for that the lawes of the Church receiue addition, diminution and alteration. Thirdly, for that the examples and customes of the Apostles times and gouernment, doe not binde vs. The first is shewed by the diuerse times of the Church, which sometimes is in prosperitie, sometime in affliction: Secondly, by the ceasing of Apostles and Prophets. Thirdly, for that widowes are ceased. Fourthly, for that the Sanedrin *and policie of the* Iewes *is long since abandoned of the first Church. Fiftly, for that the giftes of miracles, healing, tongues, and such like which were in the chiefe gouernours of the Church in the Apostles time, are nowe no where found. Lastly, for that the disciplinarians themselues haue not all the same gouernours. The second is declared by enumeration of diuers lawes vsed in the Churches of the Apostles foundation, and the* Iewish *Synagogue, which nowe are abrogated. and Secondly by diuers absurdities following, if the lawes of the Church should alwayes continue and binde the conscience. The third poynt is declared by diuers customes and fashions obserued of the Apostles, which nowe are out of vse.*

GReat paines and labour haue the disciplinarians taken to prooue that the gouernement of the church is perpetually one and the same. which, notwithstanding that it were graunted, woulde helpe them nothing. for so farre are they from proouing that euer that forme of discipline which they desire was either in the Church of the *Iewes* or first Christians, that they haue not yet iustified any one materiall poynt in controuersie betwixt them and vs, or declared that euer it was vſed.

Their Synodes,Conferences, Conſiſtories,Doctors,Elders,Deacons, Widowes, and all their ſalt conceites concerning their offices, are but of yeſterday: that they were neuer before of late, wee haue brought proofe not to be anſwered. If therfore they had exchanged ſome of their zeale with a ſcruple of iudgement or diſcretion, they would haue fled from this poſition as Mariners flye from Rockes and Sands. for thereon the miſerable and deſperate caſe of their peruerſe diſcipline is pitifully wracked. But that you may perceiue that not only their reaſons are faultie, but their premiſſes falſe: you ſhall ſee (if the diſciplinarians be not peruerſe, they will alſo confeſſe) that their ground is falſe, and that the ſame forme of externall diſcipline of the Church is not alwayes the ſame.

Cic.de legib.2. The forme of gouernment taketh his name eſpecially from the chiefe gouernours,yet the ſame ſtandeth partly in lawes and orders, and cuſtomes: which if they be changed in the Church, the fourme of Church gouernment may be ſaid to be changed. ſo that if I ſhew that the Church hath had at diuers times diuers gouernours,and that it admitteth change of lawes;they cannot denie,but that the fourme of Church gouernment is altered. but foraſmuch as they vnderſtand no language but their owne *barraguin*; and for that I woulde not haue them cauill; I will (God willing) ſhewe that the officers of the Church haue bene at diuers times, diuers: whereof ſome haue bene added,ſome ceaſed. Secondly,I will prooue that the orders and lawes of Church gouernment conteyning their functions haue bene altered.and laſtly,that the examples and practiſe of Apoſtolike times are not nowe to be obſerued.

1 The firſt is apparant, for that the Church ſometime liueth vnder the croſſe, ſometime in peace; ſometime hath the magiſtrate fauourable, ſometime contrary; and is ſometime gouerned by godly princes,as in the dayes of *Moſes, Ioſhua, David, Salomon, Conſtantine, Theodoſius,Valentinian, Martian*, and others; ſometime is diſperſed and gouerned by other gouernours and paſtours, as in the captiuitie of *Babylon*, and firſt perſecutions of Chriſtians. ſo that either they muſt denie that diuerſitie of chiefe gouernours doth alter the ſtate: or els that the prince hath any gouernment in the Church. but in that poynt they haue all that knowe what gouernment meaneth for parties: in this they haue ſcriptures and their owne friendes aduerſaries. for by ſcriptures I haue ſhewed, that the prince is chiefe officer and

Confeſ.c.5. gouernour of the Church in externall matters: and *Beza* confeſſeth,

that

that he is a member or officer of the Church, and hath *potestatem* ἀρχιτεκτονικὴν, that is, the power of a chiefe commander; and necessarily must they yeeld the same, vnlesse they will either deny that he hath power in the church, or say that he hath it by vsurpation without office or title. Considering therefore the diuers face of the church in persecution, and in peace, he must haue a strange sight that can see no diuersity in gouernment.

But be it they lust to quarrell against the gouernment of princes, 2
vpon which stone they are still stumbling; yet can they not take any exception against the ceasing of apostles, euangelists, and prophets, which were the chiefe gouernours of the first churches. Apostles, prophets, and euangelists, were appointed by *Christ*, which of elders, consistories, and the rest of the fabulous discipline, can not be said: but those are ceased. and although apostolicall iurisdiction continue: yet no man is now ordeined an apostle. that which they say of extraordinary & ordinary, is the ouerthrow of their cause. for if these offices be extraordinary; and all offices that are reckoned vp *Eph. 4*, be not ordinary, then the gouernors of the church ceasing, the forme of Church gouernment must needs be altered. for it is absurd to call that forme of gouernment the same, which hath diuers chiefe gouernours.

And not onely apostles are ceased, but diuers other officers then vsed in the church of *Christ*. In the church of *Antioch* there were prophets and teachers. that they were not in all churches, nor alwayes continued, the words of *S. Luke* doe shew: ἦσαν δέ τινες ἐν Ἀντιοχείᾳ κατὰ τὴν οὖσαν *Act.13.*
ἐκκλησίαν προφῆται, καὶ διδάσκαλοι, that is, (if you interpret the words) there were certaine prophets and teachers at *Antioch*, according to that forme of gouernment that then was. if any say otherwise, let him shew how these words can otherwise be expounded. Likewise, in the church of *Corinth* there were certaine prophets, or interpretours of Scripture: which though imitated at *Geneua* once, and once here, yet are for causes, left off in both places.

The widowes which are reputed so necessary officers, of some of 3
the platformers, are (notwithstanding) no where found. in *Geneua* they rather vse in their hospitall, the seruice of poore men then poore women. in *France*, and other churches, they haue no shadow of widowes remaining. where is then the substance of discipline, that standeth partly in this officer? and where is the same gouernment, the gouernors, or (that I may speake more fitly) the officers pretended, being changed? What should I speake of the alteration and change

 of

Hebr.7.8.9. of the prieſthood, and the Leuiticall order, which by *Chriſts* eternall prieſthood is abrogated? is that alſo remaining? and if not remaining, where is this ſelfe ſame forme that they would haue to be in all churches? where was it before the law, when there was no ſuch diſtinction of prieſthood, but that the chiefe of the families, were prieſts alſo? To holde that all this was one forme of gouernment, is to make things differing, and things continuing, with things ceaſing; and things done diſtinctly, with things confuſed, all one.

4 Beſide the office of prieſthood, the ſanedrin and great councell at *Ieruſalem* is no where extant. Here I thinke that the diſciplinarians will anſwere, that their conſiſtories are but a tranſumpt and counterpane of that office. ordinarily they make a long diſcourſe of the tranſlation of that office into the Church, powring out ληρὸν πολλὸν καὶ φλυαρίαν, that is, much dotage and vanity in lieu of Diuinity: and painting out *nebulas in pariete*, that is, a cloudy conſiſtory neuer found, *Auſon.* but of late, vnleſſe it were on a painted wall. This deuiſe haue I, in this & other diſcourſes, refuted. vnleſſe they can bring other reaſons, they ſhall not onely looſe a conſiſtory, but acknowledge that the Church is diuerſly gouerned. eſpecially, ſeeing the ſame was ſometime monarchicall in the externall forme, to wit, when *Chriſt* was heere vpon earth: ſometime ariſtocraticall, as in the times following: and ſometime popular, as at *Geneua*, where the people hath power, by the lawes of that city, not onely to quaſſe any order, but alſo to quaſſe the conſiſtory in pieces, as is euident in the diſcourſe of that ſtate.

5 And great reaſon there is, that the officers and gouernment of the church ſhould oft times change, ſeeing the graces of propheſying, healing, tongues, miracles, and other gifts, which are neceſſary for execution of ſome offices, ſometimes ceaſe, ſometimes floriſh, ſometime are giuen meanly, according to Gods diuine wiſdome. Seeing then, the extraordinary gifts do ceaſe, and ordinary gifts are diuerſly beſtowed; the extraordinary offices of gouernment muſt needs ceaſe, and others receiue alteration.

That the ſame forme of gouernors is not alwaies, nor euery where the ſame, it is euident, for that at *Geneua* there is but one conſiſtory for diuers pariſhes, no doctours of Diuinity diſtinct from paſtours, none but profane deacons, no widowes. in *F[illegible]nce* onely paſtors and elders are thought neceſſary. in *Flanders*, ſ[illegible] farre are they from perfection, that they want paſtours in diuers c[illegible]rches for want of maintenance, fooliſhly ſpoiled by the default [illegible] the patrons of diſcipline.

will

will our platformers condemne them for maimed Churches, where their discipline is but newe creeping out of the ground? it is hard to say what they will doe: but let them not be too bold, least for one reproofe they receiue three.

Nowe that I haue shewed, that the same forme of Church gouernment is not perpetually to be obserued, by reasons drawen from the gouernours; the same is likewise to be confirmed by reasons drawen from the diuersity and ceasing of orders and lawes sometime vsed in the church. not that I acknowledge that the lawes of the new platformes haue testimony from Scripture (for this whole discourse hath shewed the contrary) but that you may see they builde on false grounds, as well as they worke with misshapen arguments.

Our Sauiour *Christ* instituted a ceremony of washing of feet, which 1
he inioyned his disciples to obserue. the same was long continued in *Iohn* 13.
the church of *Christ*, as is euident in a certaine discourse attributed to *Cyprian de ablutione pedum.*
Cyprian of that argument, yet is the same now ceased.

The apostles decreed that all should abstaine from bloud, & from 2
things strangled; which is now discontinued. *Th. Cartw.* saith, the same is to be obserued in his case: but the same was neuer so enacted by the apostles, that in any case then it might be broken. and therefore he is not a litle wide from the apostles meaning. If this law cease now, which was then obserued of all; then is the law ceased, and he saith nothing to purpose.

The apostle willeth the *Romans* to greet one another with an holy 3
kisse. which rule, although some of the disciplinarians obserue with lesse then holy deuotion; yet, I thinke, they will not haue this commandement obserued literally, nor yet mystically, as do the papists in their *pax* kissing. This custome, it had course onely in those times.

The rules of the apostle, whereby he inioyneth *Timothie* to drinke 4
wine, and yoong women to marry; are not so in vse, but weake stomacks may refuse, and women containe without offence. and leudly doth *Th. Cartw.* apply the charge of the apostle, inioyning *Timothie* to obserue this order without preferring one before another, (which is meant of doctrine, and of iudgement, as πρόκριμα & πρόκλισις sheweth, and the apostles vehemencie declareth) to a ceremony not necessary: and where the apostle speaketh of proceeding in iudgement, to turne it to the rules of church gouernment. in which offence those are partakers with him, which wrest the commandements *1.Cor.11*, meant of doctrine of the Gospell, to their discipline, contrary to the Scriptures, and to the apostles meaning.

1.Cor.11.

5 Euery man praying or propheſying with his head coucred, diſhonoureth his head (ſaith the apoſtle:) which rule, if the diſciplinarians obſerued, or thought all orders then in vſe, now to be obſerued; they would not preach in their hats, or flat-caps, nor pray in their night-cappes.

1.Cor.11.

6 Like wiſe, the apoſtle giueth order, that women ſhould not diſcouer their heads; which neither the maidens of *France* nor *Piemont*, that go with their heads vncouered, and are attired onely in their haire, do eſteeme as a perpetuall law. wherfore, if (notwithſtanding) the apoſtles commendation of the *Corinthians*, for obſeruing his orders, theſe rules are vaniſhed, & *Chriſtians* left to their liberty; wherfore ſhould men be tied in other matters, which they are neither commanded to keepe, nor commended for keeping of them?

1.Pet.3.

7 The wearing of golde is forbidden to women; yet who more gorgious then the ſiſters of the fraternity of diſciplinarians? nay, which is more (as if it were a matter indifferent, to neglect the apoſtles order) the paſtourall order, among them, ſaith nothing, nor reprehendeth it.

1.Cor.11.33. Yet was the ſame continned vntill *Iuſtins* time.

8 What ſhould I ſpeake of the apoſtles orders concerning loue
feaſts? συνερχόμενοι εἰς τὸ φαγεῖν, ἀλλήλους ἐκδέχεσθε (ſaith the apoſtle) that is, when
ye come together to eate, ſtay one for another. which cuſtome of
loue feaſts, and all the apoſtles orders concerning the ſame, are now
expired: and all thoſe rules that concerned the iudges, *1.Cor.6*, the
9 order of propheſying, *1.Cor.11*, the widowes, *1.Tim.6*, their mutuall
ſalutations, and their waſhings, are not in obſeruance.

If then not ſo much as the lawes preſcribed by the apoſtles, are to be obſerued; what is to be thought of the diſciplinarians fancies, which (except men affected like to themſelues) no man euer conceiued to be commanded by the apoſtles? and if this ſubſtance (as they call it) receiueth ſuch change; what may we thinke of their circumſtances, which all are changeable, as *Engliſh* mens faſhions?

10 That the lawes of church gouernment are not perdurable, the abrogation of the whole ceremoniall and iudiciall policy of the *Iewes* doth declare. ſo that obſeruing the morall law of God, and whatſoeuer hath dependance of that which is the true rule of diſcipline of maners: the rules of their Church gouernment deſerue no credit, being nothing but counterfet diſcipline, and hauing neither atteſtation of the morall, nor other law of God, and being no where to be found in his word, or other where.

This diſcourſe (as I ſaid) I make againſt the diſciplinarians, not as ſuch

such as haue their rules of discipline prescribed in the word (for their whole frame of discipline I haue prooued to be drawen from their owne inuention) neither as if I disputed against such as much esteemed apostolicall rules (for no man neglecteth them more in their attire, dict, greetings, brauling feasts rather then loue feasts, and the whole platforme of their discipline) but to shew, if all this were granted, that we are not tied to all rules prescribed by the apostles, which they to no purpose vrge.

Finally, if all the apostles rules & formes of proceeding in the gouernment of the church were to be obserued; then were it sinne not to haue widowes, and sinne for weake stomacks not to drinke wine, and not to haue loue feasts: and then the morall law should not be perfect, and *Christ* and his apostles should not be ministers and teachers of the gospell, but second law giuers: and then should all churches in the world be maimed, & deformed; and the platformes halting and deformed platformes. all which would they grant, yet I trust they will not be so venterous, as to defend.

That we are neither bound to the gouernours nor lawes of the apostles times, we haue sufficiently declared. now we are to shew that we are not tied to their examples, practise, or proceedings, which is farre more easie to be prooued. for if lawes are not to be followed, when the common rule inioyneth vs to follow lawes, rather then examples; sure examples can not binde vs, which rest not vpon law. *Legibus non exemplis viuendũ.*

The apostolike church had a custome of loue feasts, somewhere 1
moderated by rules, in most places obserued by example, as is euident by the sixt of the *Acts*, where the apostles for the trouble of them, gaue ouer the ministration of tables: & *Iudes* epistle where the blots of their loue feasts are noted: and *1.Cor.11*, where their gluttenie and gormandise is touched. the same order continued in the time of *Iustin Martyr*, and so vntill the age of *Cyprian*; yet for the manifolde abuses generally abandoned. which, albeit some of the disciplinarians, as prety louing pigeons, would recall: yet the maister workemen will not (I thinke) deny to be well left. *Apol.2. ad Anton.*

In the first propagation of religion, those that had lands, solde thẽ, 2
and brought the price, and laid it downe at the apostles feete, and the *Christians* then had all things common: which none but anabaptists striue to put in practise. *Th. Cartw.* sometimes he held that the community vsed in the apostles time, should now be practised, and that the vse should be common, the possession priuate. but seeing he refuseth to put the same in practise in his owne lands, and bringeth

nothing to his godly pastours feet, nor yet fingers; and rather purchaseth others liuing, then selleth any thing of his owne: we neede to argue no longer against him, which hath yeelded in this matter long since. and I know none but holdeth that the community in the apostles times vsed, if it were now recalled, were anabaptisticall: for the anabaptists desire no other. If any do hatch any such opinion, it is some hungry deacon or elder, that hath morgaged or spent his owne, and now would banquet and feast at others charge. whose nailes, vnlesse they be pared with the knife of reformation, they will marre all the platforme with their greedinesse.

3 The church of the *Corinthians* did receiue the Lords supper together with their owne supper. the same had a custome, to meet for mutuall consolation & interpretation of Scriptures. among them there was a custome, that such controuersies as did arise in ciuill causes, should be composed by iudges of their owne. Women vsed to prophesie amongst them, as is apparant by the words of the apostle: where he saith, *A woman praying or prophesying with her head vncouered, dishonoureth her head.* which customes are now abolished. and albeit among the disciplinarians, the women (as those which *Tertullian* speaketh of) are *nimis procaces*, that is, too saucy, and full of prattle; yet the sober sort alloweth (I thinke) no such order.

1.Cor.11.
1.Cor.6.
1.Cor.11.5.
De præscrip.

4 In the election of *Matthias*, the people presented; in the choise of deacons, the people first considered of the matter: among the disciplinarians, the aldermen be the belweathers of the flocke, the people foloweth in silence & deuotion; and among them, *qui tacet consentit*, he that holdeth his peace consenteth, contrary to the rule, *qui tacet non consentit, verum tamen est eum non dissentire.* that is, he that holdeth his peace, consenteth not, although it be true that he dissenteth not.

5 The custome of washing of feet is ceased. that which our Sauiour would not permit, that they of *Geneua* command, to wit, that ministers should not only bury their father and frends, but attend the bodies of others, and follow them to the graue. they thinke it not vnlawfull to compose the different of frends that are at variance, albeit our Sauiour refused it. generally, the example of our Sauiour and the apostles, that receiued the Communion at night, is reiected. ministers now liue vpon lands or tithes, & among the disciplinarians vpon pensions; they wander not abroad, as did the apostles of our sauior *Christ*.

6 Those therfore that apishly striue when they speake *English*, to vse the apostles phrase, and speake so as the common multitude rather woondreth then vnderstandeth, & in other things leaue the apostles

example

example and practise; let them not brag that in their discipline they follow the apostles, or that, wherein they follow them (vnlesse they do as we do) they deserue any commendation. but we must beare with them: for albeit they haue not the thing, yet it is some comfort, that they haue the glorious phrase, and stile of discipline.

Lastly, seeing in their life and proceedings, the apostles vsed not alwayes one course: as they taught vs that these things which these fellowes would haue firme, are indifferent; so they teach vs that their examples can not alwaies be imitated, seeing they did things diuersly. Sometime in their elections they cast lots, sometime they permitted matters to the people, sometime they did all themselues, sometimes the apostles in common consulted, sometimes one apostle prescribed what order he thought conuenient. sometime the apostles, sometime bishops heard causes, and ordeined ministers. sometime women prophesied, sometime they kept silence, sometime all prophesied by the apostles permission, sometime one apostle did vse correction, as where *S. Paul* threatneth that he will come with a rod: sometime, as may be coniectured, more of the apostles ioyned together. In some places they appointed deacons first, in some place bishops. sometime elders or priests liued together in society vnder a bishop, sometime one elder or pastor had the cure of one church. and infinit other varieties there are, which no man obseruing one continuall course, can vse in all his proceedings.

Epistles to *Tim.* and *Tit.*

1. Cor. 4.

Act. 6.

Act. 14. & 20

Wherfore, seeing neither the same gouernors, nor lawes, nor practise, which was in the apostles time, hath course now; it is a fond assertion that we ought to haue the same externall gouernment that was vsuall in the apostles time, and so *Sadeel* their frend holdeth: and had we, yet should the disciplinarians receiue no profit by it, for that in their gouernors, lawes, & customes, they haue digressed, not onely from the apostles times, but from all sober practise of gouernment.

Ad repetit. Turr. sophism.

Of certeine common distinctions, vsed by the disciplinarians. CHAP. 14.

The distinctions of ordinary and extraordinary, substance and circumstances, and thirdly of officers and offices, which they holde out as bucklers to receiue our arguments, are extorted out of the disciplinarians hands, as neither grounded on Scripture, fathers, nor reason, nor greatly fitting their owne fantasies.

AS souldiours beaten from their ground, defend themselues vnder their palissades & trenches; so the disciplinarians, as distressed in opē field, do retire behind certain distinctions. when we shew that the same discipline is not permanent, nor perpetuall for all times, nor all gouernments: they yeeld in circumstances, they make head in the substance (as they call it) of discipline. when we vrge them to declare what substance is perpetuall, they tell vs that their officers, and their functions are perpetuall, howsoeuer some lawes are changeable, which may seeme to be matters of substance. when we shew them that the functions are not so perfectly obserued in Scriptures, and that the magistrate is gouernour of the church, and that ministers oft times are chosen ciuill iudges; they would winde out by the distinction of ordinary and extraordinary. out of which holes, now (God willing) I purpose to driue them, beginning with the distinction of ordinary and extraordinary.

What is ordinary, what extraordinary.

Ordinary is taken diuersly, according to the word whereunto it is applied, and so likewise is extraordinary. In nature that is called ordinary, that is according to the course of nature; as that is called in nature extraordinary, that is miraculous or against the common course of nature. In law that is called ordinary, sometimes that is by common course of law, as *Iudex ordinarius*, that hath his authority by law; or *Pœna ordinaria*, that is inflicted by law. and likewise extraordinary is called, that is done either by speciall grant, or speciall power, by the princes authority, either confirmed by law, or repugnant to law. and sometimes ordinary or extraordinary is vsed for accustomed, or not vsed. and this is the vse of the word ordinary among those that speake *Latine*, and correct *English*. Of late I confesse, that ordinary hath beene taken of diuerse, for that which hath continuance: and so we take ordinary succession for continuall succession, and account that ordinary (as I said) which is continuall, and commonly vsed.

This vnderstood, we say that their distinction of ordinary and extraordinary is disordered and absurd. for our question in this dispute concerning discipline, being what is lawfull, what vnlawfull: when we shew that princes haue gouerned the Church, and haue appointed and executed diuers orders and lawes; their saying, that the same is extraordinary, is to no purpose. for were it not vsed by continuall discent; yet not being contrary to the law, the same must be ordinarie, according to the question in controuersie. therfore, vnlesse they shew that the same is contrary to order and law, they say nothing. likewise, when they allege that the intermedling of priests and prophets is extraordinary, they consider not what the word doth meane; and say nothing, vnlesse they can shew that by law priests & Leuites ought not to deale in ciuill matters.

When

When to proue that miniſters haue iuriſdiction one ouer another, we produce the autority that the Apoſtles had ouer inferiour degrees of the miniſterie; they alledge that the ſame was extraordinarie: yet they know that it was lawfull, and vſe the word extraordinarie to ſignifie that which hath not continuall ſucceſſion. but they cannot ſhew why being lawfull, the ſame ſhould not haue continuance. for being autoriſed by Chriſt, practiſed by the Apoſtles, receiued in the Apoſtolike Churches, and confirmed by decourſe of yeeres: it is abſurd to call that autoritie vnlawfull: which may alſo be ſaid of the power of princes which they haue in the Church.

As for that iuriſdiction that prophane elders and their conſiſtories, conferences, and Synodes claime in the church, the ſame may well be called extraordinarie, being againſt lawes & orders, and vſe, & hauing no ſucceſſion from antiquitie. and not only that, but irregular, abſurd and confuſed alſo, as hath bene ſhewed. This doubt cleared, let vs diſcourſe of that which followeth of ſubſtance and circumſtance.

Subſtance in termes of Logike is συμβεβηκότων ὑποκείμενον, or the ſubiect of accidents, & very improperly is called in our language the ſumme or chiefe grounds of any buſineſſe or matters: which phraſe the diſciplinarians as it ſhould ſeeme would rather vſe, then the common ſtile of the learned. This therefore I reprehend: firſt, that dealing in a controuerſie of ſuch weight, & ſo much debated among the learned, they haue moſt ignorantly and leudly placed ſubſtance in externall matters. which is as much as if they would confound things of diuers kindes, & miſtake accidents that are external, for the ſubſtance that is external. for although accidents haue a certaine being, yet they muſt remember that their nature is in *inhæring or being in other things*, and that they cannot be called ſubſtance, no more then beautie, proportion, & whiteneſſe can be called a man. If they had but the iudgement to auoyde a blocke where others haue ſtumbled before, they would not haue fallen headlong into that errour which *Sadeel* their friende reprehendeth in *Turrian* that woulde haue ſubſtance or an eſſentiall forme to be in the externall forme of the Church.

Accidentis eſſe eſt ineſſe.

Adu. Tur. Sophiſ.

Secondly they fault, for that ſpeaking as the vulgar vſe made them, contrary to the learned, they neuer declared their meaning, nor ſet downe in plaine termes what it is that they call circumſtance, what ſubſtance, but runne away in a cloud of wordes, as if they meant rather to ſteale away their cauſe or winne it by faction, then to iuſtifie it and defend it in diſputation.

A third errour there is, that they haue not contrediuided ſubſtance

 and

and accidents, but substance and circumstance: as if there were nothing in that which they call circumstances, but matters of time, place and person, which properly are termed circumstances, and as if all that is not circumstance were with them substance.

But most grossely do they erre in that they themselues doe not obserue their owne distinction. for taking substance for that which is not changeable, and circumstance for the rest, it hath alreadie & shall be proued, that they themselues change matters of substance, & stand vpon circumstances, as if they could not be changed.

Substance of discipline sometime changed by the disciplinians.

Substance some place in officers & offices: but both these euen by their owne practise receiue change. At *Geneua* and other Churches they haue but one Consistorie in diuers parishes: they giue the office of doctor to the pastor. they haue no deacons, but prophane proctors of the hospitall: widowes they haue none at all. Fewe Churches in *France* or *Scotland* haue doctors, none widowes: the office of the Consistory is communicated sometime to Conferences, sometime to Synodes.

Tit. du Consist. art. 10. *Eccl. dis. & discip. de Fr. Tit. des anciens. Art.* 2.

The office of elders as it was at first forged by thē, so is daily changed & altered and new forged. some make them Iudges of religion. the articles of *French* discipline ashamed of their absurd dealing, doth by expresse articles barre them. some make them promoters, some informers, some cannot tell what to make them. some make doctors gouernours, some take away that part of his office. but what should I speake of one or two things, seeing both about their officers and offices, and euery of them, they set downe nothing certaine, vnlesse it be somewhat which they borowe of our gouernment, and make it worse?

Circumstances likewise which is the changeable part of their discipline, as themselues giue out, (for they make it like *Diana* whome Poets feyne to be in heauen a goddesse, and in earth mortall, and so giue her diuers names) notwithstanding are with them vnchangeable. for, that the doctor should teach, and pastor exhort, is a circumstance. for they will haue the same executed by those two persons, which is a circumstance, or els they cry out shame and confusion of officers. that the magistrate should meddle in making ecclesiasticall lawes, they will not suffer. they meane not to haue the persons altered. the deacons they will not haue called proctors of the Hospitall, nor masters of the Hospitall, nor collectors for the poore, but plaine deacons. they will not haue the president of Synodes called archbishop: so curious they are not only about circumstances, but words

words allo which they will not haue changed. so that although they talke much of the varietie of circumstances, and change their discipline like the Moone, yet these things they will not haue changed.

The fift. fault of this distinction is, that it doth not comprehend halfe of that discipline, which is requisite in the gouernment of the Church. therein is left out the orders for the maintenance of the Church, and the officers and the lawes of discipline, and the Christian magistrate, and their formes of proceeding.

Sixtly, seeing substance is subiect to generation & corruption, and is in continuall motion, and that actions cannot be without circumstances; they absurdly take the name of substance, for that which can not be changed; and the name of circumstance, for that which is subiect to alteration. for which, without circumstances they must be tolde, that their deuices be a packe of fond nouelties, without ground or substance.

Neither doth the distinction of officers & offices helpe the matter. for it is as much as if a man should distinguish a Iustice frō his Iusticeship: and a christian man from the duetie of a christian man. which may well beseeme the disciples of *Ramus* that vnderstood Logike in his time as much as *Raclet* did *Aristotles Metaphysickes*. but seeing we can haue no better, let vs examine it such as it is. the substance of discipline they deuide into officers & offices. a strange partition (me thinke) that offices and dueties should now become substances: and stranger in this, that the qualities and dueties of men shoulde be deuided from the officers, as if the life shoulde be deuided from the soule.

A third errour is this, that the offices of Christians being varied ac- 3
cording to diuers respects and circumstances (for one thing is required of olde men, another of yong, one thing of the same men as they are fathers, another as they are masters, another as they are friendes) they make their officers men of one respect, alwayes like marble men looking one way, and say that their offices are not changeable.

Adde hereunto that they themselues doe not obserue this di- 4
stinction. for they attribute diuers offices to the same man: as to the pastour, who sometime is chosen president of the Synode, sometime not: sometime visitour, sometime not: and is not such a *Stoike*, but hee changeth faces and countenance, and taketh on him the office of a Counsellour, of a subiect, and of an officer. and my lordes of the newe Consistorie, gentlemen of fiftie yeeres standing almost, are sometime lordes, sometime magistrates: and

they of the baser sort, are sometime elders, & presently thatchers, mustard makers, and candle sellers, which is a mightie change of offices.

5 Now whosoeuer denyeth that officers & offices are to be altered, let them looke ẏ ecclesiastical orders of *Geneua*, & compare them with the articles of *French* churches: and then with *Caluin* & *Beza*, and *Daneau* the fountaines of discipline, and the late holy articles of discipline with former platformes: and then he shall see their harmonie, how little melodious it is. some make more offices, some fewer: some giue that, which another taketh away, and yet we must beleeue that nothing in officers or offices is to be stirred. for my part although the disciplinarians beleeue all the rest, I cannot beleeue one line of their discipline more then is maintained in this Church of *England* already. and therfore if they will maintaine their discipline, they must finde vs out better reasons, and forge vs newe distinctions. for these which hitherto haue bene vsed, (you see) are all in pieces.

Chap. 15.

Wherein is declared, that it is an impious vntrueth to affirme the Consistoriall discipline to be a part of the Gospell, or a marke of the Church, by diuers reasons drawen from the nature, antiquitie, certaintie, authoritie, effectes and qualities of the Gospel, and markes of the Church, which without great boldnesse the disciplinarians, cannot applie to their discipline. Many inconueniences are likewise declared to followe that assertion, which they cannot well admit.

Lthough they cannot winne matters with reasons; yet some of the disciplinarians haue good hope to preuaile with the simple, by great crakes: and therefore do not sticke to call their discipline the temple of God, the mount *Zion*, the tabernacle of the Lord, the eternall counsell of God, the scepter of *Iudah*: and to winne all, *T. Cartw.* saith, that the discipline he contendeth for concerning the eldership, and that gouernment, is a part of the Gospel, and a marke of the Church.

Which opinion, although it be rather to bee corrected with certaine *Homericall* stripes then refuted with wordes: yet for that it hath taken some roote in the mindes of the weake, and is both the mother and nurse of a goodly race of *Brownists* and *Barowites*; and for that I would leaue vnto the disciplinarians neither defence of reason, nor shew of words; shalbe here razed and refuted. and the rather, for that by profession of Christianitie, I am bound not to suffer the intemperate fancies of mens braines to be matched with the eternall, and most holy word of God.

I say

I say therefore, that whosoeuer mainteineth that the discipline which the platformers striue for, is a part of the Gospel, and a marke of the Church; holdeth opinions very impious, and slandrous against diuers Churches professing the Gospell, and vtterlie vntrue.

It is an impious assertion that maketh their discipline a part of the Gospell.

1 The effect and summe of the Gospel, is conteined in the writings of the prophets, and by them foretolde, as the Apostle witnesseth, where he sayeth: εὐαγγέλιον Θεοῦ, ὃ προεπηγγείλατο διὰ τῶν προφητῶν αὐτοῦ ἐν γραφαῖς ἁγίαις. but this their discipline was neither fore-tolde, nor fore-knowen, nor mentioned by the prophets. if they can shew it, or anie part of it out of the prophets, why doe they proceede so slowlie? why are the prophets mentioned, and cited so rarelie? of Christes eternall kingdome there is mention made in the prophets: but we speake of the externall gouernement of the Church (a matter of another sorte and nature) and talke of a new forme of discipline.

Rom.1.

2 No parte of the Gospell is knowen by nature: but some parte of discipline, as that which concerneth order and comelines, and certeine rules deriued frō the moral law, is knowen by nature, *Ergo.&c.*

3 Againe, no part of the lawe is parte of the Gospell: but discipline conteineth the speciall parts of the lawe, as namelie such as concerne decencie, and comelines, and equitie.

4 The Gospel is receiued by beleeuing, and he that beleeueth the Gospell truelie, doeth that which Christ Iesus requireth: but discipline is not receiued by beliefe: neither doth he satisfie that which discipline requireth, that beleeueth, but he that doeth it. and therefore vnlesse they meane to confound faith and workes; let them not mainteine this opinion of discipline.

5 Christ Iesus himselfe in his owne person deliuered and taught all the Gospell: but he taught not this discipline. if they holde the contrarie, let them shew out their officers and offices of the Gospell: nay let them shewe it them out of anie part of scripture, and it shall suffice. if not, let former follies warne thē hereafter to be more wise, then to make their deuises Christes Gospell.

6 The Gospel hath authoritie from Christ, was preached by the Apostles, receaued by antiquitie, deriued by succession to vs: but this their discipline conteining a rolle of officers, and a description of their functions, hath neither authoritie from Christ, nor was preached nor taught by the Apostles, nor hath testimonie of antiquitie, as I haue in the seuerall parts of their discipline confirmed. let them therefore cause *Th.Cartw.* to recall his vntrue assertions.

7 The description of the Gospell is most repugnant to their dis-

cipline. the Gospell is the glad tidings of saluation: the subiect of it is Christ Iesus: it is apprehended by faith: it is the power of God to saluation, and is in expresse wordes comprised in the writings of the prophets and Apostles, and hath continued, and bene preached since the fall of Adam. it worketh life, and is not the Ministerie of death; and conteineth ioye and comfort, and not lawes of punishment and correction: but this their discipline is a message of contention, and brawling, and hath wrought great discomfort in the heartes of the godlie. it hath destroyed manie soules, which haue departed from the Church vpon offence taken by it. the same saueth none. the subiect of it is the external gouernement of the Church, whose vse is in practise, not in beliefe. for litle doeth it helpe the disciplinarians to beleeue it: their onelie griefe ariseth vpon the refusall of it. if they beleeue to be saued by their discipline, their faith is built on sand: in respect of the disorders of it, it is a rope of sand. the same was latelie deuised, and neuer heard of in ancient time. it is the Ministerie of death, when men are cut off by excommunications, and the whole force and sinewes of it consist in censures, and punishments: and therefore, neither is it a part of the Gospell, nor like the Gospell.

8 Further, it were a matter altogether incredible, if a part of the Gospel should neyther be found in the new Testament nor olde, nor yet mentioned of so manie godlie Bishops, and fathers of the Church, and onelie be reuealed to *G.W. W.T. I.P.* and *T.C.* of late time.

9 And being a parte of the Gospell, it were a verie bolde part for them of *France* and *Geneua*, not onelie to make new Canons, but also to abrogate their Canons, and to alter them and transforme them: which in the Gospell or anie part of the Gospell, is not lawfull, nor sufferable. moreouer, seeing *Th. Cartw.* giueth out, that it is a part of the Gospell; he may content himselfe, seeing he will not denie I thinke, but that this Church embraceth all the Gospell.

10 Finallie, if their discipline be a part of the Gospell; then are not they the true Church of Christ, that refuse the same: then haue the *Barrowists* iust cause to depart, and separate themselues from vs: then is *Th.Cartw.* defence against *Harr.* a most weake and childish defence. I maruell with what face he durst take vpon him the defence of our cause, handling the same so weakelie and vnfaithfullie. it was an error vntollerable, to make discipline a part of the Gospell: but hauing layde downe that for a position, it was more absurd and senceles to defend our Church that refuseth his discipline. therefore, if he will heare good counsell, let him laye hand off our

cauſe, which we are by Gods grace able to defend, as well againſt him, as againſt the *Barowiſtes*; both which conſent together alike, in defacing the Church of England. wherein his fault is ſingular, for that his erroneous poſitions gaue occaſion of fall to others of weake iudgement. for this cannot be denyed, if the diſcipline which they ſtriue for, be a part of the Goſpel; then is not the Church of England the true Church refuſing it: and *Th. Cartw.* ſtriueth both with his aduerſarie and himſelſe, moſt ridiculouſlie.

To excuſe himſelfe, he will ſaye as he hath heretofore, that his diſcipline may be concluded out of the word of God. but both his allegation is falſe, as hath bin ſhewed in this whole diſcourſe: and were it granted, yet his excuſe and defence is moſt ſimple, and weake. for there is alwayes as great differēce betwixt the text & the concluſions, as betweene the premiſſes of a demonſtration and the concluſion. they are πρῶτα ϗ ἄμεσα: that is, ſuch as are true of themſelues and neede no proofe: theſe neede proofe. the arguments of law, though eſteemed where there is no lawe to the contrarie: yet are farre inferior to the allegation of the text. out of one text diuers concluſions are drawen, diuers one from another. *Beza* thinketh that hee hath well concluded in his annotations and interpretations: yet is he not generallie receiued. nay, wee receiue not the fathers without ſcripture, much leſſe *Th. Cartw.* who renounceth diuers of his concluſions, and may be aſhamed of the reſt, if hee ſaw their deformitie and bad ſequele. to helpe the matter he ſayeth, he meaneth not all that is concluded out of the Goſpell, is Goſpell: but that which is well concluded: which is the bane of his diſcipline, then which, neuer argument was more peruerſelie concluded. beſide that, it is not true altogether. for it may be concluded out of the Goſpel, that *Th. Cart.* beleeuing the Goſpell ſhalbe ſaued, yet is not that ſpeciall propoſition anie parte of the Goſpell. the aſſertion is ſo deformed, that it hath no colour to couer it. the onelie colour and couer is a ſponge, wherewith it ought to be wiped out, that the *Barrowiſtes* do no longer triumph ouer *Th. Cartw.* their firſt patriarke and top of their kinred.

The ſame courſe is to be taken with the other opinion of his: *That diſcipline is an vnſeparable marke of the Church*. for if this be graunted, then is not the Church of England the true Church of God. and by conſequent, is is not without cauſe, that the *Barrowiſtes* haue departed out of the Church. for the Church cannot bee without her proper markes, no more then the ſunne without light, or faith without good workes. but that it is no marke, these reasons may shewe.

1 The Church of the Iewes was the true Church of God in the times of *Dauid* and *Salomon* and the kings: yet had they no such discipline as this, which is commended for true discipline.

2 Neither had the Church anie such discipline in the Apostles time, nor in the times folowing, not after that the Emperors became Christians, as hath bene shewed in this treatise.

3 Nay, they of *Geneua* and *France*, differ much in their gouernement from those orders which the disciplinarians seeke for, as also hath bene shewed.

4 Finallie, they themselues must needes bee out of the Church, for that they haue not their discipline but in conceite: and that so broken, as nothing can be deuised more peruerse, nor defectiue.

The generall conclusion.

Wherefore, seeing (my deare countriemen) that the disciplinarians haue neither reason to vphold their platformes, nor colour to make so great bragges: be no longer abused with vaine wordes of men that either speake for that they would haue, or commend that which they would still reteine: but search out the groundes of trueth, embrace godlie peace, refuse fond nouelties. and so the God of all trueth after this lamentable contention about order, shall blesse vs both with knowledge of trueth, and with perfect peace. which God graunt vnto vs for Christ his sake, which is the onelie author of trueth, and worker of our peace.

FINIS.

These errors following correct thus.

As oft as you finde *Brownists*, put the worde out, for the head of that companie hath reformed himselfe.

In the Epistle dedic. pag.1.l.9. for *and the other*. reade, *or the other*.

Fol.153. the wordes *in the counsell of Nice*. l.1. should make the end of the sentence going next before.

Fol.218.l:24. for 1.*Tim.6*. reade 1.*Tim*.5. the figures and notes by reason of the euill writing of the copie, are somewhere euill set, somewhere mistaken. Other light faultes that you shall espie, amend with your pen.

Imprinted at London by *George Bishop*, and *Ralph Newberie*.
1591.